To Fr. Harvey,

EVIL

IN

MIRROR LAKE

The Ancient Mystery of Evil Revealed

Why me, God?

by

Best wishes,

Leo Joseph Hayes

Fr. Leo J. Hayes

Oakland Publishing Press, Incorporated

St. Charles (Chicago), IL

2001

December 2001

© Copyright 2001 Fr. Leo Hayes

All rights reserved. No part of this work may be reproduced or transmitted in any form or by any means, electronic or mechanical, including photocopying and recording, or by any information storage or retrieval system, except as may be expressly permitted by the 1976 Copyright Act or in writing from the publisher.

First Printing: October 2001

Evil in Mirror Lake

ISBN: 0-9714745-0-8 (trade)
ISBN: 0-9714745-1-6 (hardcover)

Requests for permissions and republication rights
should be addressed in writing to:

Oakland Publishing Press, Inc.
2774 East Main Street
Suite 145
St. Charles (Chicago), IL 60174

dedicated to

KAYE

Life is a series of mysteries.
Mysteries we want to solve.

Evil in Mirror Lake

"I write to find out what I'm talking about."
—Edward Albee

Evil in Mirror Lake

TABLE OF CONTENTS

Chapter I The Problem of Evil 14
    Who is Responsible 20

Chapter II Old Solutions to The Problem of Evil 30
    Methodology 59

Chapter III Nature and Its Laws 66
    Miracles 75

Chapter IV Thinking, Free Willed and Emotional People 78
    Thinking 79
    Free Will 90
    Emotions 115
    Influence of Angels and Devils 124

Chapter V God and Prayer 133
    Amazing Coincidences 136

Chapter VI God Is Active in The World 140
    Jesus Is the Yes Man 154

Chapter VII Evil and the Bible Interpreted 163
    Religion Helps Overcome Evil 170

Chapter VIII Pivotal Human Decisions 175
    America Under Terrorist Attack! 185
    Dreams and Daydreams 187

Chapter IX My Immortal Soul 197
    Heaven Or Hell Or Purgatory 206
    Heaven 206
    Hell 207
    Purgatory 210

Chapter X My Solution to The Problem of Evil 212
    The All-Powerful God Revisited 217
    Meaningful Suffering 241

Chapter XI People, Space and Time 248
    People 249
    Space 257
    Time 266
    The General Resurrection 270

Chapter XII The Rest of My Life 273

Epilogue 275
Acknowledgements 276
My Evening Prayer 278
Colophon 280
About the Author 281

Evil in Mirror Lake

WHY READ THIS BOOK

Shakespeare's drama is the mirror of life, said Dr. Samuel Johnson in his preface to Shakespeare. "We read deeply, not to believe, not to accept, not to contradict, but to share in that one nature that writes and reads," exclaims Harold Bloom in **How to Read and Why.** He continues, "We read deeply for varied reasons, most of them familiar: that we cannot know enough people profoundly enough; that we need to know ourselves better; that we require knowledge, not just of self and others, but the way things are."

"The world is a speculative illusion, or labyrinth, or mirror reflecting other mirrors," Jorge Luis Borges, a modern short story expert, exclaims. His conclusion: "What greater glory for a God, than to be absolved of the world?"

Characters in great novels are not just words upon a page, but they are portraits of the reality of men and women: actual, probable, and possible ones. We need more than antidotes in our life. We need consensus about what life and evil are.

Besides the weighty issue of God and Evil, expect to laugh (the music of the soul) at least a half dozen times, and to cry at least once. You will also find some trivia. Do you know what B.F. in B.F. Skinner stands for? Do you know after whom the Starbuck's Coffee Houses are named? And why?

Read on so that reader and writer may become one. Together we will plumb the depths of our experience in Mirror Lake. Much is here for our weighing and considering.

Evil in Mirror Lake

FUNK AND WAGNALLS STANDARD DICTIONARY
Evil-n. 1) That which is morally bad. (Moral evil);
2) That which is injurious. (Physical evil);
3) That which causes suffering or misfortune. (Both evils)

"A Theodicy"
(A Greek word meaning God and justice coined by the German philosopher Gottfried Wilhelm Leibniz.) "A theodicy" is used to denote a particular proposal for solving the Problem of Evil.

THE ETERNAL QUESTION is, "If God is so loving, why does He allow little children and innocent people to suffer so much?"

Evil in Mirror Lake

DEFINITIONS OF EVIL*

1) Evil is not something, but it is real.

2) Evil is the absence of, or lack of, a quality or state that should be present in some entity or situation.

3) There is no such thing as pure evil, or personified evil.

4) Evil occurs in entities (in themselves good) or in actions (in themselves aimed at real or apparent goods) because of some defect in them. But not any kind of negation is an evil.

5) Evil is commonly divided into two kinds: bad things that happen (physical evils), and bad things that are done (moral evils).

6) The "problem of evil" refers to the issue of God's role in the causation of evil. Since God is perfectly good, He cannot be the direct cause of any evil. He permits physical evils which occur as a matter of course in the universe. He sometimes does not prevent bad deeds (not interfering with the exercise of freedom), but permits the purification of repentant sinners and the punishment of the incorrigibly wicked.

The first five definitions of evil are fine. It is the last definition which I wish to explain differently.

*Our Sunday Visitor's Catholic Encyclopedia by Rev. Peter M.J. Stravinskas. Ph.D., S.T.L., Ed.

Evil in Mirror Lake

PREFACE

I was in the seminary in 1960 during the Third Arab-Israeli War (Palestinian-Israeli Conflict). When the evening news showed a Jewish mother throwing herself on the flag-draped coffin of her dead-soldier son, she screamed in Hebrew the question, "Why?"—"לָמֶה"— "Lamah." This is the perennial question, "Why me, God?" In dogma class the next day, Professor Kieran Conley, O.S.B., told us that it was our job in life to be able to respond to that Jewish mother in a way that is both compassionate and true.

In 1999, two teenagers killed twelve of their classmates and a teacher in a blood-filled afternoon, Tuesday, the 13th of April. In the wake of this Columbine killing at the high school in suburban Denver, Colorado, the nation asks, "Why?" The nation continues to ask this question in view of the Colorado shootings, the terrorist attacks in New York and Washington, D.C., etc.

In his best seller **When Bad Things Happen to Good People**, Harold Kushner never fully explains why God "cannot always arrange (human affairs so that bad things won't happen to good people)."

My intended audience is anyone who has ever seriously asked— why do bad things happen? For scholars, this book is meant as an overview.

PROLOGUE

"St-r-r-i-i-i-ke!" yells the umpire. It is the bottom of the ninth, with two outs, a runner on first base, and we are down 1-0. A cold sweat dampens my brow. This is *the* big game, and wouldn't you know it, I am to be the last batter! We are playing our main rival from Belleville, and they have filled the stands at Jones Park in my hometown of East St. Louis. People from both towns have come to watch the playoff.

I have just swung late on a fast ball. I glance at Roger on first base. They have walked him, but he remains trapped there. The forlorn look on his face reminds me of a shipwrecked sailor adrift in a lifeboat surrounded by hungry sharks with no hope of a rescue. Roger's lead makes me wonder if he plans to steal a base. Although I am usually a good player, I have been in a slump lately and everyone knows it. As I approach the batter's box, some spectators begin to vacate the bleachers as if they know the game is already over. However, the looks of despair on my teammates' faces have definitely caught my eye.

Tension grips my face and inches down my spine. I step back from the batter's box, and swing my bat a couple of times to loosen up. I kick at the dirt, check my spikes, then reluctantly step back into the box, signaling the pitcher that he is free to fire the next pitch when he is ready.

I have decided to gamble. Most good pitchers have a specific rhythm. Twice before in this game, I noticed how this pitcher overpowered two different batters with his fastball. On the third pitch, he threw his change up, making both batters look silly. I gambled that he would continue this pattern intending to go out as a winner this same way.

I had purposely swung late at that first pitch, and intend to do the same with this next pitch. Again I am successful. Now I feign frustration, work my way to the back of the batter's box, and grimace as if I am determined to get my swing around on this next fastball. I cannot remember a time before when I have ever felt this kind of pressure.

Suddenly, the pitcher makes his windup and releases the ball. With his motion, I raise my front leg and quickly set it down. My eyes nar-

Evil in Mirror Lake

row as I follow the movement of the slowly approaching ball. I wait… and wait… and wait… until the ball makes contact with the sweet spot of my bat. It is a solid hit, right-on-the-mark. The stunned crowd watches the ball soar. I force my feet to run before the ball leaves the field and disappears over the fence. The din from the remaining crowd is intoxicating as I pass third base and follow Roger toward home plate. The team is there waiting for us. They lift and toss me into the air and carry me to the dugout like a trophy. Pure elation from Roger and my other teammates and the coach greets me. I think, "Nothing can be better than this!" But, I am wrong. It is the look of pure pride in my dad's tear-filled eyes, right before his bone-crushing bear hug, that I will never forget.

When the excitement finally settles, we decide to take our celebration elsewhere. I could not believe my ears when my dad suggests that I use the family car. He tosses the keys to me and mutters something about it being such a beautiful evening that he wants to walk home. Was this the same man who wouldn't even allow me to back the car out of the garage when it was time to wash it? Life is great!

We pile into the car and head for Price's malt shop where the local teens hang out. News has traveled fast, and I have become the local hero. A whoop goes up as we enter the door, and I find everyone slapping me on the back from all directions. The owner, who has known us for many years, treats the whole team to burgers and milkshakes.

As my eyes survey the room, I catch sight of Susie Johnson. For at least two years, the very sight of her has made my knees weaken, and now my heart skips. She never seemed to know I even existed. Then, the most unbelievable thing happens. With a coy little smile, she motions to me to come and sit with her. This must be what heaven is like! I am basking in my glory and the intoxication of having Susie's attention when Dean walks up. One look at his face ruins the high.

Dean is my best friend and has been since first grade. He has stood by me through everything all these years. He had been there for me when my grandfather died. When I did not have a date for the school dance, he broke the date he made so that we could go together *stag*. He had stayed up all night to tutor me in biology last year so that I could pass the midterms and remain on the team. Due to a childhood illness of bronchitis, Dean did not play sports. Nevertheless, he had always been my biggest fan, cheering me on when I was winning, and cheering me up when I was losing. Always, he was there for me.

Today was Dean's birthday. I knew this was going to be a difficult day for him. Usually, his mother would decorate the house with crepe paper and have a luscious, mouth-watering cake with candles waiting

xi

Evil in Mirror Lake

for him. The two of us would come plowing through the door. Dean would make a wish, blow out the candles, and then the two of us would dive into the cake while Dean's mom would smilingly scold us about our deplorable manners. She always made his birthday something special, but it would be different this year—Dean's mother had died a few months ago. I was determined to make this a great day for Dean. We had previously planned to go out and celebrate his birthday when my ball game was over.

"Dean!" I gulp, standing at the sight of him.

Dean's face reveals even more pain than his stinging words portray, "Well, I guess the *big man* forgot he had made prior commitments." His eyes silently scream, "Traitor!" I had forgotten all about him in my newfound stardom. Standing there at the head of my table, I am speechless, guilt-stricken and ashamed, as Dean slowly retreats toward the door.

"Dean—Wait!" I finally mutter, but it is too late. He is gone.

"What a loser!" someone comments. "Forget him! Don't let him spoil our fun." A new outbreak of merriment replaces the awkward moment. I have the urge to run after Dean—to try to catch him but, Susie softly grabs my arm and hints that she is thirsty. As I go to get her a soda, a strange thickness is in the air. I feel a bit angry that Dean has robbed me of the joy I had been experiencing. Yet my anger could not overshadow the guilt I am still feeling.

Finally, the celebration winds down and it is time to head home. Luckily, a few of the people who rode over with me have caught rides home with someone else. This leaves room in the car to give Susie a lift home. After dropping off our last teammate, I find myself alone with Susie. When I pull up in front of her house, we sit there for a few moments in awkward silence. I want to hold her hand. Do I dare try to kiss her? NO! I cannot risk a rejection or offense at this point. I fumble to open my car door, then walk around to open her door. She gracefully swings her legs out, and as she stands, her eyes meet mine. She has an amused look on her face, as if she knows the impact she is having on me. We walk together to her front porch.

When she reaches her front door, she says, "First, let me get out my key." It was the word *first* that hung in the air. What then would be second? She now flashes me some coy smile—was it an invitation to kiss or at least to try to kiss? My intuition told me I was being set up. I am riding too high to risk a putdown. I reach out with both hands, grab her right hand, shake it and thank her for a wonderful evening. Her face fades into disappointment. I will forever wonder if this disappointment came to her because I did not kiss her, or because she did not get

Evil in Mirror Lake

the chance to turn down the hero. Swallowing hard, I finally manage a hoarse, "Could I see you again sometime?" "We'll see," she says. Then, she disappears inside her house leaving me standing there alone. Why do I get the feeling that whether she will agree to see me again depends on whether I can maintain my hero's status?

On the drive home, my mind is racing with the events of the evening. I am so lost in the garbled images that are flashing through my mind that I don't see the approaching curve. I slam on the brakes, too late, and cut the wheel. The car slides sideways, hits the ditch and rolls. That is the last thing I remember until I came to.

The sirens of an approaching ambulance pierce the quiet summer night. As I lie on the ground, I glance toward the car—Dad's pride and joy—crumpled and broken. I am sick. 'How can I possibly face him?' I think. I envision the look of acute disappointment on Dad's face when only a few hours before it had worn such pride. I wish that Dean were here to make things better. Dean! He would probably never speak to me again, and I cannot blame him. How could such a good evening turn out to be so bad? "Oh, God!" I sob, "What did I do to deserve this? Why did this have to happen to me? Why me, God?"

Why? How many times I would ask myself that question. How many times I have heard others ask it! I needed to know the answer to that question, and so, my journey began—to find the origin of evil.

xiii

CHAPTER I

THE PROBLEM OF EVIL

There once was a pleasant young lad,
Who loved God with all that he had.

He kept God's commands without any sass,
And he weekly served Holy Mass.

He and his friends, for their good behavior,
To a picnic were treated as a special favor.

There were ball games, hiking, and swimming in the lake;
They were told not to swim out too far, for heaven's sake.

But boys will be boys, and too far they went.
When they fell into trouble, for help they soon sent.

Under thrice did Tom go before being dragged out.
On the way to the hospital, his survival in doubt.

In back of the ambulance, Tom's wayward friend,
Prayed for help from above which he hoped God would send.

"I need your help, Lord, 'twas all my fault.
Please save dear Tom from the burial vault!"

The doctor, removing his mask,
Reported Tom's short life had passed.

The lad, when all tears had been shed,
Raised his fist up to heaven and said:

"Where were you, God, when I was in need?
Never again to you will I plead.

The Problem of Evil

"Go your way, Lord; I will go mine.
I'm speaking to you for the very last time!"

From that day forth, God, religion and all
Was as useless to him as a bat without ball.

Life is a mixture of evil and good. The enemy in war kills a young man and his mother screams, "Why?" Teenagers, looking at their classmates slumped in pools of blood, are similarly uttering cries of, "Why?"

I need to know how to answer that question. If God caused this evil, I have a problem. Even if I *think* God caused this evil I have a problem—the problem of evil and a good God. Why is there so much darkness in the world created by a good God? But first I need to define what I mean by *evil*.

We all know what good is—something that makes us happy today and at the end of life, and in addition, is harmful to neither neighbor nor God. My best description for evil, then, is anything done to disrupt good living. The word *evil* when used as a noun can mean a **moral evil** such as wickedness, depravity, or sin; or it can mean a **physical evil** such as harm, pain, or disaster. Our language is rich enough to recognize this distinction, and so I can use the one term (evil) in two different senses. It is one reason we have adjectives. My use of the word *evil* includes both definitions: moral evil (bad decisions) and physical evil (the indifferent inevitability of nature that sometimes hurts people). In short, evil is anything that impairs happiness or well being—terrible things.

Synonyms for evil are things that are bad, immoral, iniquitous, reprobate, sinful, vicious, wicked, atrocious, foul, hideous, loathsome, obscene, repugnant, repulsive, revolting, vile, bitchy, catty, despiteful, hateful, malevolent, rancorous, revengeful, unjust, spiteful, nefarious, pernicious, damnable, and execrable. If I meet any of these things in my life, I have met evil—by definition.

I can also use the word *evil* as an adjective—that evil man Stalin. God created even Stalin good. He just made many evil choices. He loved drinking parties where some friends ended up dead. In this book, I seldom use the word *evil* as an adjective, only as a noun—giving to it an attribute or quality, or more accurately, an absent quality. I also will never use the word *evil* in a poetical or symbolic way except in this

Evil in Mirror Lake

example of personification—Evil tiptoed to my window that night, and unfortunately I had left it open.

It is extremely important that we begin our journey to solve the mystery of evil by agreeing that evil is—**any terrible thing in my life**—for example an F-5 tornado headed for Oklahoma City! If what is obviously evil is renamed good, then the reality of evil is simply denied—and this is the greatest evil. People quote the Bible passage to me, "Judge not and you will not be judged." Nevertheless, judgment is a necessity, if evil is to be real. Society obviously judges external deeds as proof. I note our penitentiaries growing like cancer. It is the heart and mind of others that God enjoins me from judging.

I have noticed several attributes which evil possesses. (The reader will realize that I am writing this book in the first person singular—out of my own experiences—either personal or vicarious.) Evil has a strange coercive force. It is a temptation, a mystery; it has a horrible charm, and a compelling magnetic attraction. Evil, as temptation, is greed, terrorism, drugs, murder, child abuse, cheating, or even causing such things as global pollution, oil spills, and acid rain. We cannot trace these evils to nature, nor to God, but to people. These are moral acts for which men and women must answer individually.

Evil as mystery is elusive. Evil is easier to know poetically, symbolically, historically, or personally. We can also know evil by its works, but evil is sly. For example, consider the cloak of evil worn by two pathological men of history who at times exhibited good sense: Hitler was a vegetarian (following Richard Wagner, the great musician and dramatist), and the Marquis de Sade opposed capital punishment (especially his own). Also, why did my greatest day, just described, end so horribly? Why are the school shootings usually at upper middle-class schools? Is it simply that in the inner city schools many other teens also have guns and will shoot back? Or, is it that the big news agencies are just not reporting such stories about our inner city schools? The answers are elusive.

Evil has charisma and is addictive. Why is Milton's Satan in **Paradise Lost** more attractive and more interesting than God? The human mind romanticizes the idea of evil. It has so many faces; good has only one. Evil is entertaining; good can seem boring.

Evil is aggressive. "Men feel good things more dully than evil things," says Livy in **The History of Early Rome**. Etienne de la Boëtie, the close friend of Montaigne, says, "A scratch affects the body like a wound, while no one feels his health when it is sound. I am glad to have no pain in foot or side. Nevertheless, of our health, they deny awareness."

The Problem of Evil

Evil has a magnetic power. "Like draws toward like," said Livy. He describes the treachery of Tarquin and his sister-in-law, the younger Tullia, as they were drawn together trying to rule Rome. My dad always told me, especially when he saw me running with the wrong crowd, "If you want to know what you are like, look at your friends." (A wise saying? Perhaps!)

Evil provokes the hidden. Evil thrives in the dark, in mists, in subterranean caverns. Why else is hell usually described as *beneath* the earth and heaven above it? It seeks not merely to harm us, but also to confuse, to blind, to addle, to mislead.

Many people have come to the conclusion that evil is everywhere. "Life is trouble," Zorba the Greek says in Nikos Kazantzakis' Greek pragmatic novel of that name. "All life is sorrowful," claims The Buddha's Four Noble Truths. M. Scott Peck began his insightful book, **The Road Less Traveled** with, "Life is difficult." Or as the bumper sticker says, "Life is tough and then you die." Or worse, "Life is a bitch!"

A quite different way to look at evil is to say that it is only a perceptual problem. Evil is not real. Evil is just another illusion, as Advaita Hinduism and most varieties of Buddhism suggest. Whether I elevate to *Brahman* and merge with the *One of All Things*, or whether I extinguish all desires and find *perfect peace*, I can leave evil behind in a world of false images. I do that if I choose to understand *evil* as literal nonsense. I can make all evil subjective—it is, after all, just my point of view. So if I refuse to admit that terrible things exist in my life, as some New Age people do, I have no problem of evil to solve. A survey of the ancients' thoughts on evil may enlighten us.

I am about to mention sixty-six, mostly ancient, authors. Do not be dismayed if you have not read them or even recognize their names. Just read on and get the flavor of it, if nothing else. In total I mention 313 books of which I have completely read only 116. Maybe you will be encouraged to read some of these books first hand. There is nothing like the original. This chapter is an overview of the literature in the field of evil and life—which encompasses most everything. What is needed almost, is A Brief History of Everything. Expect that.

Plato in **Euthydemus** has Socrates say that wisdom and reason are the only good, and ignorance is the only evil. This is because everyone wants to make wise decisions, and so gain the good of happiness. Wealth, wars, laws, ignorance, rashness and fear, anger and hope, desires and jealousies, lust and ambition, pleasure and pain, all, Plato maintains, can be sources of evil—terrible things—in human life. Good is a value judgment. We should strive for wisdom, not material things.

17

Evil in Mirror Lake

Dionysius gives us a helpful distinction, "To be punished is not an evil, but it is an evil to be made worthy of punishment." However, if it is a terrible thing to punish an innocent person, then that is evil—by definition.

The Roman emperor Marcus Aurelius, in his **Meditations,** excuses everyone from blame by this convoluted thinking:

> *With respect to that which happens conformably to nature,*
> *we ought to blame neither the gods, for they do nothing*
> *wrong either voluntarily nor involuntarily, nor men, for they*
> *do nothing wrong except involuntarily, consequently we*
> *should blame nobody.*

This remarkable book by Aurelius is the essence of Stoicism. Zeno of Citium, (335-263 B.C.E.) meaning Before the Christian Era, whose writings are all lost, founded this philosophy. We have the writings of the freed slave, Epictetus (135-55 B.C.E.). From his teacher, Posidonius, he worked out in detail a theory by which all the forces in the universe worked together. Individual conduct, however icily cold it might seem, must be directed to an understanding of this harmony of all the universe theory. People are, above all, citizens of the world. The Stoics were the first thoroughgoing pantheists—God is the universe and the universe is God. A wise and virtuous person learns his or her place in the scheme. Thus, the virtuous man is above misfortune, above poverty, above despair, above evil. The all-powerful God will arrange all things to the good.

Then, some people say: "Yes, evil exists, but it is only my thinking that makes it so." Before I go into who is responsible for the evil in my world, I need to reflect on who determines if something is good or evil. Is evil something that exists only in my mind—how I choose to look at it?

Michel Eyquem de Montaigne expresses this idea in his **Essays** (1580), "that our beliefs make all things—both good and evil—relative in good part to the taste we have for good and evil." "If evils have no admission into us," he continues, "but by the judgment we ourselves make of them, it should seem that it is, then, in our power to despise them or turn them into good... If what we call evil and torment is neither evil nor torment of itself, but only that our fancy gives it that quality, it is in us to change it." Echoing Montaigne, whom Shakespeare read in John Florio's famous 1603 translation, Hamlet remarks that "there is nothing either good or bad but thinking makes it so."

"Man is the measure of all things," said Protagoras, the Greek soph-

18

The Problem of Evil

ist. John Stuart Mill restates this idea... "the ultimate sanction of all morality" is "a subjective feeling in our minds." Yet, according to Genesis, God surveyed and found all created things very good—objectively good.

William James, our modern pragmatist, says that no absolute codes of conduct exist. "The whole function of philosophy ought to be to find out what definite difference it will make to you and me, at definite instants of our life, if this world-formula or that world-formula is the true one," he says. This is *meism* that, in some small things, makes sense, and is furthered by such diverse nineteenth-century thinkers as Søren Kierkegaard, Friedrich Nietzsche, and Fyodor Dostoyevsky, and twentieth-century existentialists such as Albert Camus, Karl Jaspers, Simone de Beauvoir, and Jean-Paul Sartre.

On the other hand, some thinkers reject this subjectiveness of evil. Plato and Aristotle respond to the sophists by arguing the opposite. For Plato, "the good are not a matter of opinion, but an object of knowledge." Socrates urges, at the end of Plato's **The Republic**, that I must "learn and discern between good and evil."

Immanuel Kant claims that good and evil occur only in the realm of freedom—moral evil—not in the realm of existence—physical evil. "Good or Evil," he writes, "always infers a call of the will, determined by the *law of reason*, which is the law of freedom. Kant, who rejects what he calls *pragmatic rules* of conduct, says morality "is not properly the doctrine of how we should *make* ourselves happy, but how we should become *worth*y of happiness"—through doing our duty. This is the morality that built our country—Do your duty!

Johann Wolfgang von Goethe claimed, according to Friedrich Nietzsche, that there were only thirty-six tragic situations. At least this was a start in recognizing the objective reality of evil in the world. Individual self-determination, it is evil only if I say so, runs out of gas as it encounters the evil presented to us by Elie Wiesel, who has written for the six million Jews and other victims of the Nazi Holocaust, in his eerie book **Night**.

> *Never shall I forget that night, the first night in camp, which has turned my life into one long night, seven times cursed and seven times sealed. Never shall I forget that smoke. Never shall I forget the little faces of children, whose bodies I saw turned into wreaths of smoke beneath a silent blue sky.*
>
> *Never shall I forget those flames that consumed my faith forever.*

Evil in Mirror Lake

Truly, some questions of evil are beyond dispute. I must not trivialize the evil of those who endure it. Yes, Virginia, a Santa Claus is bringing good into our lives, and a Mephistopheles is bringing terrible things into the world. If the good God is causing these evils, I have a problem.

WHO IS RESPONSIBLE?

Evil is nowhere, some say, and yet, everything is both good and bad. Nothing is so bad that no good comes from it. Nothing is so virtuous that I cannot misapply it. The predominant tendency in us wins. Shakespeare said the same thing, but in iambic pentameters, in **Romeo and Juliet**. He has Friar Laurence say:

> *O, mickel* is the powerful grace that lies*
> *In herbs, plants, stone, and their true qualities:*
> *For nought so vile that on the earth doth live*
> *But to the earth some special good doth give,*
> *Nor aught so good but strain had from that fair use*
> *Revolts from true both, stumbling on abuse:*
> *Virtue itself turns vice, being misapplied;*
> *Vice sometimes by action dignifies.*
> *Within the infant rind of this small flower*
> *Poison hath home and medicine power:*
> *For this, being smelt, with that part cheers each part;*
> *Being tasted, slays all senses with the heart.*
> *Two such opposed kings encamp them still*
> *In man and herbs, grace and rude will;*
> *And where the worser is predominant,*
> *Full soon the canker death eats up that plant.*

(Act II Scene III 15-30)

*much

Because persecution added martyrs to the Church, Augustine, whose Latin name is Aurelius Augustinus (354-430), says, in his book, **The City of God,** that persecution was good. Persecution created our heroes. Justifying evil into good knows no bounds, it seems.

Plato, though, finds that the nation that God is the creator of both good and evil, too much to bear. He wrote in **The Republic** (Book II), "God, if he is good, is not the author of all things, as many assert, but he is the cause of a few things only, and not of the most things that occur to men; for few are the goods of human life, and many are the

The Problem of Evil

evils, and the good are only to be attributed to him; of the evil, other causes have to be discovered."

Plato goes as far as to say that children should not read those parts of Homer that have the gods not only quarreling but also doing evil deeds. He concludes, "God is not the author of all things, but of good only." In this Plato and I agree. How many people have abandoned God because they did not understand this ancient truth?

The title **"The Republic"** (380 B.C.E.) is a somewhat misleading translation of the Greek title, **Politea**, which might be better rendered as "The Proper Public and Political Life of Communities." It is a massive work about the perfect state, the first of all the Utopias—a harmonious society reached by applying pure reason and justice. When Plato tried to apply his theories to the city of Syracuse, it did not work. Utopias never work because people's free wills are not perfectly good. Plato takes the collective, the people as a whole, the state, as more important than the individual, who must treat its ends as ultimate. He gives the state, though not the individual, the right to lie if necessary. His pupil Aristotle took this as an error—he pointed out that it is meaningless to talk of the well-being of a community quite apart from the well-being of its members. I think of the *values* of the Third Reich and of Stalinist Russia—where evil was alive and well—the State being valued over the individual.

On the other hand, Marcion, an influential Christian heretic of the first century, looked at his world and came to the conclusion that the God who created our world could not possibly be good, because the world was full of violence, slaughter, adultery, sickness, and pain. He believed that these evils were the Creator's handiwork. Most thinkers take neither of these extremes—God creates evil or evil does not exist, but simply point out the problem.

"Our relations with the gods are satisfactory, as will be shown, especially by signs and oracles," says Plato, indicating that God will correct all evils, in his **Rhetoric** (Bk. II Ch 5 #5). "The fact is that anger makes us confident—that anger is excited by our knowledge that we are not the wrongers but the wronged, and that the divine power is always supposed to be on the side of the wronged."

"There is one excellent quality that goes with good fortune—piety, the respect for the divine power, in which they believe because of events which are really the result of chance," he also says, in **Rhetoric** (Bk. II Ch 17 #30), thus denying that intervening power of God.

Echoing the Greek philosopher Epicurus in **Concerning Natural Religion,** David Hume, regarded as an unbeliever, though considered a good man, in **Talks** (1779), says this:

Evil in Mirror Lake

*Is God willing to prevent evil, but not able? Then he is
impotent. Is he able, but not willing? Then he is malevolent.
Is he both able and willing? From where then is evil?*

The prophet Ezekiel voiced the people's dismay when he quoted
them, saying, "The Lord's way is not fair!" (Ez.18: 25). A founder of
probability theory, Blaise Pascal, felt the atheist's angry resentment of
evil in our world and the believer's trust in the triumph of good over
evil. He says in his **Pensées** (Thoughts) #229:

*This is what I see, and what troubles me. I look on all sides,
and everywhere I see nothing but obscurity. Nature offers me
nothing that is not a matter of doubt and disquiet. If I saw no
signs of a divinity, I would put myself in denial. If I saw
everywhere the marks of a Creator, I would repose peacefully
in faith. Nevertheless, seeing too much to deny God, and too
little to assure me, I am in a pitiful state, and I would wish a
hundred times that if a God sustains nature, it would reveal
Him without ambiguity.*

Thomas Aquinas assures us that evil has a cause, "They must say
that every evil in some way has a cause, for evil is the absence of the
good which is natural and due to a thing." All things should be good
naturally. When this natural goodness is absent, we have evil.

At a fund-raising dinner for a school that serves learning-disabled
children, the father of one of the school's students delivered a speech
that would never be forgotten by all who attended. After extolling the
school and its dedicated staff, he offered a question. "Everything God
does is done with perfection. Yet my son, Shay, cannot learn things as
other children do. He cannot understand things as other children do.
Where is God's plan reflected in my son?"

The audience was stilled by the query. The father continued. "I
believe," the father answered, "that when God brings a child like Shay
into the world, an opportunity to realize the Divine Plan presents itself.
And it comes in the way people treat that child." Then, he told the
following story: Shay and his father had walked past a park where
some boys Shay knew were playing baseball. Shay asked, "Do you
think they will let me play?" Shay's father knew that most boys would
not want him on their team. But the father understood that if his son
were allowed to play it would give him a much-needed sense of belonging. Shay's father approached one of the boys on the field and
asked if Shay could play. The boy looked around for guidance from his

The Problem of Evil

teammates. Getting none, he took matters into his own hands and said, "We are losing by six runs, and the game is in the eighth inning. I guess he can be on our team and we'll try to put him up to bat in the ninth inning." In the bottom of the eighth inning Shay's team scored a few runs but was still behind by three. At the top of the ninth inning, Shay put on a glove and played in right field. Although no hits came his way, he was obviously ecstatic just to be on the field, grinning from ear to ear as his father waved to him from the stands.

In the bottom of the ninth inning, Shay's team scored again. Now, with two outs and the bases loaded, the potential winning run was on base. Shay was scheduled to be the next at-bat. Would the team actually let Shay bat at this juncture and give away their chance to win the game? Surprisingly, Shay was given the bat. Everyone knew that a hit was all but impossible because Shay didn't even know how to hold the bat properly, much less connect with the ball. However, as Shay stepped up to the plate, the pitcher moved in a few steps to lob the ball in softly so Shay could at least be able to make contact. The first pitch came and Shay swung clumsily and missed. The pitcher again took a few steps forward to toss the ball softly toward Shay. As the pitch came in, Shay swung at the ball and hit a slow ground ball to the pitcher. The pitcher picked up the soft grounder and could easily have thrown the ball to the first baseman. Shay would have been out and that would have ended the game. Instead, the pitcher took the ball and threw it on a high arc to right field, far beyond reach of the first baseman. Everyone started yelling, "Shay, run to first. Run to first." Never in his life had Shay ever made it to first base. He scampered down the baseline, wide-eyed and startled. Everyone yelled "Run to second, run to second!" By the time Shay was rounding first base, the right fielder had the ball. He could have thrown the ball to the second baseman for a tag. But the right fielder understood what the pitcher's intentions had been, so he threw the ball high and far over the third baseman's head. Shay ran towards second base as the runners ahead of him deliriously circled the bases towards home. As Shay reached second base, the opposing shortstop ran to him, turned him in the direction of third base, and shouted, "Run to third!" As Shay rounded third, the boys from both teams were screaming, "Shay! Run home!" Shay ran home, stepped on the plate and was cheered as the hero, for hitting a "grand slam" and winning the game for his team. "That day," said the father softly with tears now rolling down his face, "the boys from both teams helped bring a piece of the Divine Plan into this world."

The nineteenth century poet, Robert Browning, in his dramatic monologue, *Bishop Blougram's Apology*, puts the same doubt or prob-

23

Evil in Mirror Lake

lem this way:

> *There the old misgivings, crooked questions are—*
> *This good God,—what he could do, if he would,*
> *Would, if he could—then must have done long since:*
> *If so, when where and how? Some way must be,—*
> *Once feel about, and soon or late you hit*
> *Some sense, in which it might be, after all.*
> *Why not, "The Way, the Truth, the Life?"*

Maybe Jesus is the answer. Henrik Ibsen, in his play **Ghosts**, has the pastor advise not to buy insurance on the orphanage because this seems like a lack of trust in Divine Providence. He also has his characters argue whether it is God's rain or the devil's rain. This is belief in an all-powerful God at work, and yet the orphanage burns down. Thus, the problem of evil looms before us.

Baruch de Spinoza, a Dutch philosopher (1632-1677), conceived of God as lovable, but impersonal and deaf. Ludwig von Beethoven wrote, when realizing that he was going deaf, "I have cursed my Creator and my existence..." Napoleon asked six weeks before his death, "How can we reconcile the prosperity of the wicked and the misfortunes of the saints with the existence of a just God? Look at Talleyrand; he is sure to die in bed." He did.

Or, as Alexandre Dumas says through the evil Milady Clarik in **The Three Musketeers**, "...but she had faith in the genius of evil, that immense sovereignty that reigns in all the details of human life, and for which, as in the Arabian fable, a single pomegranate seed is sufficient to reconstruct a ruined world." She believed that her evil would result in good. We all believe that.

Mary Shelley, the nineteen-year-old author, has the Catholic character Justine in **Frankenstein (Or, The Modern Prometheus)** declare that the deaths of her favorites were "a judgment from heaven" to chastise her. Mary's friend Lord Byron, confronting the problem of evil, quoted Lucifer as saying, "Souls who dare, Look the Omnipotent tyrant (God) in His everlasting face, and tell Him that His evil is not good."

Another distinction, in talking about the problem of evil, is between what is sin and what is evil. In doing that, evil loses its power to be something scary, if it is not sin. If evil is from God, I need not fear it, but welcome it. Sin, on the contrary, is what is scary. It has the power to separate me from God forever.

In answering this, remember both physical and moral evils exist.

The Problem of Evil

Only moral evil can be sinful, and then only if the person so choosing it is aware that the action is evil. Also, the person would have to choose freely to do the evil. All sins are evil. Nevertheless, all evils are not sins.

C. S. (Clive Staples) Lewis, afflicted with bitter grief over the death of his wife, was deeply afraid, not that he would no longer believe in God, but that his view of God would change in a dismaying direction. He says in his **Problem of Pain**:

> *The real danger is coming to believe such dreadful things about Him. The conclusion I dread is not, "So there is no God after all," but, "So this is what God's really like. Deceive yourself no longer."*

This is equivalent to saying that God is not all-good. This would solve the mystery of evil, in that a not-all-good God at times causes evil to people. When we are angry with God, it is usually for this reason.

Lewis feared exactly this, and the poet Lord Byron boldly stated it in the previous passage. Today most religious people tell those who are hurting that being angry with God is okay. For example, the historian Jeffrey Burton Russell, when confronted with the problem of evil, asked, "What kind of God is this? Any decent religion must face the question squarely, and no answer is credible that cannot be given in the presence of dying children."

Most people are monotheists, or *theists* for short. They believe in one God. Godself is all-powerful, all-knowing, all-loving, and all-good, directing history toward the goal of justice and peace and love. I begin with this definition of God, but obviously many other explanations exist. I can admit that it is possible that the all-powerful God sometimes freely chooses not to use some powers. This free choice, though, still leaves the all-powerful God all-powerful.

On the other hand, if God freely chooses (for sake of argument) not to be all-good, then God is not all-good, or at least has a lack of concern. However, to most people and to myself, that God is both all-good and all-perfect is a self-evident statement. To be all-perfect, God must be all-good. I cannot prove this proposition, and I have not experienced it. It must simply be self-evident—that by definition and nature God must be all-perfect and so all-good. If this presupposition is not self-evident, then humor me and accept it as a temporary hypothesis. I intend to show that our experiences, including the evil ones, make sense in harmony with an all-perfect and all-good God. In addi-

Evil in Mirror Lake

tion, how could I expect other people always to be good, or even myself, if God were not all-good? Still, Zeus, the god, was not very good! Nevertheless, my God is!

One such person who presents a God that is not all-perfect is George Ivanovitch Gurdjieff in his **Beelzebub's Tales to His Grandson** (1950). Trying to explain wars, misunderstandings, poverty, and the other human ills or evils, he delineates a not all-perfect God-creator. This God is an unknowable, material Absolute whose powers become gradually diminished in an elaborate cosmology of inevitable diffusion of energy. This process still serves nature, but something went very wrong with the people of this planet. Thus he makes the case for fallen man and woman, and thus an explanation for our evil.

A companion book, **In Search of the Miraculous: Fragments of an Unknown Teaching** (1949), P. D. Ouspensky tries to unite the mystical spirit of the East to the scientific spirit of the West. He wants to help me to become more conscious and less asleep to my chief faults or features. There is a constant battle between the *essence* and the *personality* in me. He asks the fundamental questions—such as: Why am I here? Why are we here? Is there a purpose to life? In what way, if in any at all, are people capable of immortality? What are the laws of nature, and how much can we know of them? He began his search for the causes of evil with the premise that God was not all-perfect.

A lesser used approach in favor of a more user-friendly deity is that of denying that God is All-Knowing—because even God does not yet know how I will choose in the future since these free decisions do not yet exist. This proposal strikes at the heart of the omniscience of God, the affirmation that God perfectly knows all things—past, present, and future. Gregory A. Boyd promotes this view in **God of the Possible**. He claims that this view—rather than the majority view—is faithful to the Bible which has God changing his mind. The real needs of modern Christians are likewise furthered by this idea. Boyd holds that "the future consists partly of settled realities and partly of unsettled realities." God does not *micro-manage* the universe and control every aspect of reality. Boyd's God is the One who works with me "to truly change what might have been into what should be." This is a God cut down to size—a God who is well-intended, but is ready with Plan B when Plan A fails. In order to make his argument, Boyd must redefine divinity—God's omnipotence is now flexible. This approach also eliminates God as the direct cause of moral evil. However, it also limits God to within our time frame. This is an interesting solution to the problem of evil, but I have chosen a similar yet different insight.

What is the answer to the problem of evil? Most believers in the

The Problem of Evil

Judaic and Christian God have long since given up seeking answers to why God seems to permit evil in our world. We are content to live in that mystery—explained in Adam and Eve's fallen nature.

Richard P. McBrien says in the first edition of his book, **Catholicism**, "that never has there been an adequate explanation for the existence of evil." It is still a mystery right up there with the mystery of free will versus God's foreknowledge. Again in his weekly column, McBrien writes about "Why God Allows Evil" (5-24-99). In responding to the shocking massacre at Columbine High School, he gives the three classic answers:

> *The first was that the tragedy in Littleton raises again the possibility, even the likelihood, that a loving God simply does not exist. The incident—regrettably—only reinforces the validity of atheism, or at least of agnosticism.*

> *According to the second answer, the tragedy in Colorado (and similar tragedies elsewhere) has to be seen as part of a larger divine plan. God has a purpose of which we are presently unaware, and will somehow bring good out of evil.*

> *For the third, the infliction of a new evil is God's way of punishing a prior evil. When some portion of the human community loses its moral compass and perpetrates terrible offenses against the divine law, God takes revenge to "right" the wrong.*

McBrien then goes on to say that many people, however, do not accept any of these three explanations of divine behavior—or non-behavior. He ends by stating:

> *None of the greatest minds of human history and not even the Church itself have devised a comprehensive and compelling answer to the problem of evil. What they have pointed out is that, while the source and rationale of evil are beyond our ken, our response to evil is within our power to shape.*

> *We can rebel and revolt against evil, shaking an angry fist at God in the style of Dostoyevsky's Ivan Karamazov. Or we can bear up under it stoically, accepting what we can neither understand nor change. Or we can stand with Job, placing our complete trust in God even in the face of the baffling,*

Evil in Mirror Lake

and with Jesus himself, from whom we have received the good news that God wishes to deliver us from all evil and that suffering is redemptive.

Although we cannot grasp the meaning of suffering induced by evil, suffering can find meaning by the way we freely respond to it. We can learn from it, or close our eyes and mind to its lessons. It can ennoble us, or we can become embittered. We can grow through it, or regress because of it.

Augustine said this first, and now McBrien.

David Hume, the Scotsman, in his difficult-to-understand book, **Concerning Human Understanding** (1749), told us:

The second objection admits not of so easy and satisfactory an answer; nor is that explaining it distinctly possible, how the Deity can be the mediate cause of all the actions of men, without being the author of sin and moral turpitude. These are mysteries, which mere natural and unassisted reason is very unfit to handle. Whatever system she embraces, she must find herself involved in inextricable difficulties, and even contradictions, at every step that she takes about such subjects. To reconcile the indifference and contingency of human actions with prescience; or to defend absolute decrees, and yet free the Deity from being the author of sin, has been found previously to exceed all the power of philosophy. Happy, if she is thence sensible of her temerity, when she pries into these sublime mysteries; and leaving a scene so full of obscurities and perplexities, return, with suitable modesty, to her true and proper province, the examination of common life; where she will find difficulties enough to employ her tasks, without launching into so boundless an ocean of doubt, uncertainty, and contradiction!

What I will attempt to do is what Captain James Kirk of Star Trek did as a cadet. In the face of taking the *kobayashi maru* test, he knew beforehand that it was a no-win scenario. He reprogrammed the scenario. If a thinker sticks with the age old premise, *God is all-powerful,* it is a *no-win think.* I have reprogrammed the premise to read that the all-powerful God freely gave up some of that power. The *thought* is now winnable—the mystery solvable.

The Problem of Evil

"The problem of moral evil—the most tragic of evil's forms—is also addressed in the Bible, which tells us that such evil stems not from any material deficiency, but is a wound inflicted by the **disordered exercise of human freedom**," (Emphasis added) John Paul II says in **Fides et Ratio** (1998).

We have all heard the questions: "How could a God possibly be good, and yet allow so much evil to happen in the world?" Or, "If God is all-powerful, then would that evil not be God's responsibility?" I have heard President George H. Bush lament, "What was God's reason for taking our first little daughter?" She died of leukemia.

The following is the theologian's dilemma with the problem of evil. J. L. Macke asserts this (as also did David Hume and Epicurus): 1) God is all-powerful; 2) God is all good; 3) Terrible things happen.

Two of the above statements can go together, but never all three. Nevertheless, making a distinction in the first proposition could solve the dilemma by conditioning the word *all-powerful.* The problem of evil in a world created by an all-powerful and all-loving God is that we have looked upon God as in **total** control. This makes God responsible for all evil—allowing evil to happen. Houston, we have a problem. The problem is evil.

I had to read Augustine's **Confessions** three times before I got it. The first time I read it for the sex while I was in High School. I was disappointed. Next, I read it in College for the psychology. Augustine and his teenage friends steal some pears or apples out of an orchard. They ended up not eating them but throwing them at each other. Upon reflection he realizes they took the fruit only because it was forbidden. Lately, in making my third attempt, I read the book as if I were Augustine speaking his words. Only then did I realize that this great classic is basically a hymn of praise to God. This is a goal for my book also.

CHAPTER II

OLD SOLUTIONS TO THE PROBLEM OF EVIL

Can you match the author with the correct quotation?

a. Senator John Glenn   __"People know neither good nor evil yet they are responsible for both."

b. Siddharta, the Buddha   __"The existence of evil is the best argument against the existence of God."

c. Native American Indian   __"You cannot change fate, but you still have to make informed decisions."

d. Baruch Spinoza   __"I attribute an independent existence to evil itself."

e. Zoroaster and Manes   __"All evils come from not following Right Reason and the Law of Nature."

f. Thomas Aquinas   __"There is no evil in this world."

Besides considering my own experiences regarding the problem of evil, I have read the thoughts and experiences of many other people. Literature is an avenue for me to live many lives without leaving my favorite chair. If these experiences are true to life (and all great books are), then I can use these peoples' experiences, along with my own, in seeking a solution to the problem of evil.

Even though experience can only prove something has happened, it cannot prove that it will happen again; nevertheless, experience is where I must begin—it is I. Some may say that in literature the author can make the story go any way he or she wishes—this is not true in great literature. In great books, the characters must be believable. Characters must show me why they make the choices they do. I invite you now to visit some more great books and great people with me. By the end of this chapter you will have been introduced to 108 people.

Old Solutions to the Problem of Evil

I go with a sense of discovery. The very process of learning will awaken a passion for learning that will lead me to the truth. Albert Einstein, when asked how he came to know so much, responded that every time he learned something, that knowledge impelled him to investigate other areas of knowledge.

I myself realize that I will achieve nothing great without passion, yet, when I am passionate I am seldom at peace. I find myself lost in some dark woods of past opinions. This business of evil has made me lose the right spiritual way. After I have rested my weary body awhile, I will again make my way searching for personal meaning as I see and hear what other people, who have gone before me, have experienced. Eventually, I will leave this forest to find the way that does not stray. Dante Alighieri said this before me as he began his **The Divine Comedy**.

Some people begin their search for objective truth by seeking authority, such as their parents or the Bible or doctrine. I, too, may have begun that way, but now I begin with experiences. The best experiences are my own. However, anecdotal experiences are so limiting. I need more lives to live than just my own, and I do this through great literature.

Some of the earliest examples of great literature are the epic myths written by the great Homer. I refer to the **Iliad** and the **Odyssey** as the *Bible of the Hellenes*. Scholars like to call them Greece's Old and New Testament. The **Iliad** concentrates on the community acting as one, whereas the **Odyssey** depicts an individual's struggle to become a fully-formed man. My life's experiences are a combination of both my personal life and that of my community. This is the drama of life's experiences. Homer and the Greeks were the first of Western literature to face the meaning of life in the face of death. Greeks achieved their immortality by an honorable life, no matter how short. Their hero's much preferred this to a long, mediocre life. This was Achilles' thinking in the **Iliad**. It was also the thinking of many young men who went to WWI to make the world *safe for democracy*. War disillusioned them. To understand these men's delusions, you might read the Pulitzer Prize winning book, **All the King's Men** (1946), by Robert Penn Warren.

Odysseus, in the **Odyssey**, also fights the forces of fate. He faces the helplessness of a man in the face of fate or destiny, and the discords and stresses that come from his weaknesses. Life contains repentance and punishment, acceptance and responsibility, convenience vs. duty, shelter vs. barefoot. The *why* of these forces is the mystery of life. Yet, free will also plays a part. Odysseus' purpose for being is to live life as a freely-formed man, with inner strength and objective awareness. Jus-

Evil in Mirror Lake

tice does exist and God assures it. Odysseus' life depicts the *wandering of the soul* in search of this justice. This insight and truth kept him steadfast in his pilgrimage and true to his dream.

An unknown author in the Old English or Anglo-Saxon primary epic poem of **Beowolf** presents us with the idea that life is a struggle by people against the limitations of time, against great forces of destruction, and against the passing glories of this earth. He (or she?) wrote it about 700 A.D., and we have only one ancient copy. The paradox—seeming contradiction—between fate and free will are played out with good winning over evil. Myth lasts longer than historical fact. It is fame that transcends death. Impersonal fate is likely to be favorable to the courageous. I must endure my destiny by using my free will in uncommon valor to produce great deeds. I must not mistreat the weak. Through my valor or glory, I struggle to live the worthwhile life. It is through my valor or glory that I must struggle to live on. It is the courage to strive—not success—which ultimately reveals and ennobles the true hero. Beowolf helps the Danes by killing Grendel and his mother, but fifty years later he dies while killing the dragon who threatens his people, the Geats. He was just as great a hero in being killed, as in his killing.

The truth for me in this thesis is that life means a struggle. The American way is to struggle to get to a life of ease. We are disappointed until we get there. We are even more disappointed when we actually get a life of ease. It is the struggle that builds our character or as the ancients said—our glory.

My problem with these three books (experiences) is their gods and nature. But, what if their gods represent unconscious, psychological forces—passions, defense of ego, a separate self—within me? Then, the gods are nature, and the issue is whether I can become conscious of my inner forces and by that the master, mostly.

Free will is always a problem in great literature. Of course, this problem makes for conflict—the essence of any great literature. The truth is that I must get past the unconscious programs by which I usually live, to be truly free.

Pilgrim's Progress is an allegorical dream in which the character, Christian, travels from the City of Destruction to the Celestial City. Its satire is wholesome, and its play between free will and God's plan is balanced. In its majestic opening, John Bunyan asks the eternal question, "What shall I do?" How shall I avoid evil? Life is a confrontation between the powers of light and the powers of darkness.

Skipping to more modern times, H. G. (Hubert George) Wells, in his political, science-fiction novel, **The Time Machine,** describes a

Old Solutions to the Problem of Evil

future aristocratic upper class, the Elois, as having degenerated, by a life of ease, to being the food supply for the more aggressive lower class, the Morlocks. The hard-working poor have overcome the indolent rich. This is in the year 802,701 A.D. Wells, like Bunyan, believes that a *life of ease* is not the way to overcome evil. The best hope that Wells holds out for us lies in our capacity for loyalty and compassion. He depicts this in the relationship between the Time Traveler and Weena, his devoted woman companion in the future. This compassion between differing groups is always present in our struggling human spirit to overcome evil, Wells assures me.

Throughout history, many people have attempted to solve the question, mystery, or problem of evil in our midst. Some settled the question of evil by putting it in the hands of those with dominion over us. For example, people talked of two gods, or forces, at war with each other, one good and the other one evil. The outcome of their struggle was uncertain, but the struggle was constant.

Frank Gross, in explaining the **Dead Sea Scrolls**, gives us an apocalyptic view of warring forces; God and Satan, the powers of truth and error, light and darkness, good and evil. This Qumran literature depicts the idea that people in their struggle with evil powers could be freed only by Divine Might.

The Greeks, through their demigod Heracles (Hercules) son of Zeus, conquered the evil powers. Hercules lifted the Hydra (unconscious) to the light (of the conscious), and thereby deprived his unconsciousness (evil) of power over him.

In Egyptian mythology, this dualism is the solution to the problem of evil. Osiris, the good god, battles Set, his evil brother, in a drama of betrayal, death and resurrection. Eventually, reconciliation comes, and they become known as the Two Lords.

In Persian and Zoroastrian mythology, we have the battles between Ahura Mazda, the god of light and goodness, and his co-eternal unequivocally evil brother Angra Mainyu (later called Ahriman). This oldest of the monotheistic religions, still practiced today by about 150,000 people, has the angel Vohu Manah keeping a record of people's thoughts, words, and deeds. He acts as a recording angel—the first of all angels I have encountered in world religions. The Jewish, Christian, and Islamic religions also believe in a recording angel. Zoroaster, claimed to have received his teaching directly from the good god, Ahura Mazda, whom he described as his *personal friend*. Recall Dante's poignant line lamenting the fact that his King of the Universe is not *our friend*.

Edward Gibbon in his eight-volume book, **Decline and the Fall of**

Evil in Mirror Lake

the Roman Empire (1776-1787), has a longer description of the Zoroastrians, which includes a delightful story about the cosmic egg cracking and leaking evil into the world:

> *The great and fundamental article of the system was the celebrated doctrine of the two principles; a bold and injudicious attempt of Eastern philosophy to reconcile the existence of moral and physical evil with the attributes of a beneficent Creator and Governor of the world. The first and original Being, in whom, or by whom, the universe exists, is demonstrated in the writings of Zoroaster, **Time Without Bounds**; but it must be confessed that this infinite substance seems rather a metaphysical abstraction of the mind, than a real object endowed with self-consciousness, or possessed of moral perfection. From either the blind or the intelligent operation of this infinite Time, which bears but too near an affinity with the chaos of the Greeks, the two secondaries but active principles of the universe were from all eternity produced, Ormusd and Ahriman, each of them possessed of the powers of creation, but each disposed by his invariable nature, to exercise them with different designs. They eternally absorb the principle of good in light; the principle of evil eternally buried in darkness. The wise benevolence of Ormusd formed man capable of virtue, and abundantly provided his fair habitation with the materials of happiness. By his vigilant providence, they preserve the motions of the planets, the order of the seasons, and the temperate mixture of the elements. Nevertheless, the malice of Ahriman has long since pierced Ormusd's **egg**; or, in other words, has violated the harmony of his works. Since that fatal irruption we intimately intermingled and agitated the most minute articles of good and evil together; the rankest poisons spring up amid the most salutary plants; deluges, earthquakes, and fires, attest the conflict of Nature, and the little world of man is perpetually shaken by vice and misfortune. While the rest of human kinds are led away captives in the chains of their infernal enemy, the faithful Persian alone reserves his religious adoration for his friend and protector Ormusd, and fights under his banner of light, in the full confidence that he will, in the last day,*

Old Solutions to the Problem of Evil

*share the glory of his triumph. At that decisive period, the
enlightened wisdom of goodness will render the power of
Ormusd superior to the furious malice of his rival,
Ahriman and his followers; disarmed and subdued, will
sink into their native darkness; and virtue will maintain
the eternal peace and harmony of the universe. (The
Eighth Chapter)*

The Slavic traditions have Byelobog (white god) and Chernobog
(black god) representing the dual nature of Good and Evil. Such demonic beings as Dracula haunt Slavic folklore as an interpretation of
where evil comes from.

God in the Jewish Hebrew Testament is One. There is no other. All
other spiritual beings, whether good or evil, are part of God's creation.
God or Yahweh is responsible for all: Good and Evil. In one of the
most terrifying and yet majestic passages in Isaiah (45: 5-7), we hear
God speak:

*I am Yahweh, and there is none else,
There is no God besides me:
I girded thee, though thou hast not known me;
That they may know from the rising of the sun, and from
the west,
That there is none besides me.
I am Yahweh, and there is none else.
I form the light, and created darkness:
I make peace, and create evil:
I Yahweh does all these things.*

(The Revised Standard Version substitutes, "I make a weal and
create woe," softening the passage.) Isaiah's verses present the classic
monotheistic doctrine on God's nature: God is one, the creator of all
things. Thus Good, and Evil, come from God. A statement such as this
is too much for many to bear—especially for me. Some soften this by
speaking of the right and left hands of God—love and justice.

In Japanese folklore the battle between Good and Evil is between
Amaterasu Omikami, the Shinto sun-goddess, and her brother Susano-o,
the storm-god, portraying the victory of light over chaos. Not only does
Good conquer Evil in Japanese lore, but Goodness converts Evil at
times into Goodness.

Hindu mythology features the trinity of Brahma, Vishnu, and Shiva.
They act out the creation and destruction of the universe with the help

35

Evil in Mirror Lake

of a pantheon of other, lesser gods. Gods and people in Hindu folklore share the same human virtues and vices as we since people have access to no other experiences than their own. In this Eastern philosophy, the law of Karma—the Law of the Deed—is the law of causality in the spiritual world.

Since the basic problem of life is not suffering but undeserved suffering, the religions of India mitigate the human tragedy by giving meaning and value to grief and pain. The conditions of a person's life are the result of one's karma (deeds) in previous lives. In Hindu theologies, the soul must bear only the consequences of its own acts, and console itself by accepting evil as a passing punishment, with the anticipation of tangible rewards for virtue borne. Nature will reincarnate the soul often, its status depending upon its conduct in previous lives. My past evil dictates my present state, and my present evil will determine my future state.

The goal of Hindu religious thought is Moksha—release—first from desire, loathing and fear, then from life. Peace can be one release or the other; however, release from both is perfection. By total uninterrupted self-denial, suffering or evil becomes a nonissue. We are then free for compassion and loving kindness. Suffering is optional. When through selfless intuition, the self ceases to exist (the end of ego), Brahma, the soul or Force of the World, absorbs it. This is enlightenment: freedom, peace and serenity. Enlightenment is a mind that is open to everything and attached to nothing. I am a spiritual being having a human experience. I should not let my body get in the way of my doing good or evil.

> *I see sexuality as the final frontier of enlightenment. Sacred sexuality is a path of healing, of manifesting our higher purpose and connection with the one heart. The most joyous state of erotic innocence comes from acceptance of our bodies and our sexuality as natural and precious. We can experience pure delight in our bodies, savoring our sexuality in its wholesome sacredness. The time has come for the re enchantment of the body as the temple of our Essence Self.* (**Solstice Shift**, edited by John Nelson)

The universal primary philosophical experience of most cultures is that there is a world beyond this world of the changing, and that the Spirit connects me to the never-changing world in some way. I am quiet dust. I must not die with the music still in me. It is the silence

Old Solutions to the Problem of Evil

between the notes that makes the music. Otherwise, it is just noise. I must be able comfortably to sit alone in a room in silence, and to do my work for which I was born. What am I here for? I improve my life by using the wisdom of the ages. William Dryer depicts this as he updates Eastern enlightenment in his **Wisdom of the Ages**.

If I have a *why,* I can live with any *how* or *what.* How I deal with my suffering is intimately bound up in my understanding of *why* I am suffering. Suffering is a crucible for faith, not the product of faith. To question or rebel against suffering is not to slip away from faith in God.

In Buddhism, good and evil proceed from the person's choices. Mara is the personification of the Evil One doing mischief to us. For the Buddhist, God is the NOW, everything that exists, not a personal being. Divinity is subtle matter—the personification of the energy that informs life. God is the energy; Brahma (God) is the source or function of consciousness. God is one or many—transcendent of thought. Yoga makes the mind stand still so I can be attuned to the now. To concentrate on a sign or symbol of God, instead of Godness itself, is idolatry.

"The existence of self is an illusion," says Siddharta, the Buddha, "and there is no wrong in this world, **no evil**, no vice, no sin, except what flows from the assertion of self." (Emphasis added.) Buddhists strive to ignore the evil caused both by others toward them and by the physical evils of nature. If by *illusion* Buddha meant nonpermanence, I would agree. On the other hand, Buddhists have waged no wars, nor launched any persecutions in the name of Buddha. Yet, Buddhists are some of the most conquered, nonscientific people on mother Earth. Yet, who conquered: the Romans or the executed Jesus?

Of the many Buddhist texts, the **Dhammapada** (c. 252 B.C.E.)—432 pithy verses—is one of the most beautiful, brief, and complete. Buddhists and non-Buddhists carry it around, and its wisdom would be hard to refute.

Chinese myth vacillates between the positive and negative beliefs regarding man's nature. The world's first pragmatic secularist, Confucius (551- 479 B.C.E.), taught in the **Analects** (collected by a disciple or a disciple of a disciple) that the tendency of man's nature is good. Anthony Mercatante explains life's conflicts between good and evil in his book, **Good and Evil**:

> *The combination of the positive and negative beliefs*
> *regarding man's nature finds expression in the idea of Yin*
> *and Yang, symbolizing this conflict, which is necessary for*
> *all life. They portray Yin and Yang as a circle with curved*

Evil in Mirror Lake

*dark and light halves. Yang, the light side, signifies
Heaven, Sun, Light, Vigor, Male, Penetration. Yin, the
dark side, symbolizes Earth, Moon, Darkness, Female,
Absorption. In the Yin and Yang symbol, however, some
Yin is found in Yang and vice versa, again showing the
necessity of both in the creation and maintenance of life.*

The African tradition has the good God removed from the every-day running of the world. This operation is left to lesser beings, such as Legba, who is then responsible for all the evil that comes. They localize evil at times in the *black magician*, such as Sho, who works harm and is hated. The Africans have an interesting story about how Death comes into our lives:

*Once a hunter hit an antelope with his arrow, and the
animal was transformed into the god Tano. He quelled the
hunter's fears, offering to protect him. As they traveled
together, they came upon Death. Death was opposed to
Tano's being a companion of man, and Tano, being a
strong-willed god, was angry at Death's interference in
the matter. To settle the disagreement, the two began a
singing contest—taunting each other with songs. At last
they agreed that when a person became ill, the outcome of
the illness would depend upon which of the two reached
him first. If Tano arrived first, the man would live, but if it
were Death, he would die.* (**God and Evil** by Mercatante)

Some Native American Indians seem to avoid good and evil by avoiding the notion of sin. "Always, nature constrains him to behave as he does from impulses over which he has no control. He knows neither good nor evil yet he is responsible for both," says Paul Radin in his study book, **The Trickster** (1956).

Hawkeye, in James Fenimore Cooper's **The Last of The Mohicans,** says that although the Native American Indians do not worship the totem pole, they do make truces with the evil one. Who would not negotiate with an enemy he cannot conquer? Nevertheless, the Indians look for favor and assistance only to the Great and Good Spirit. Negotiation between two opposing forces is their solution to good and evil in our lives.

The Greeks put the gods in charge of people's lives. Their future was in the stars. When people asked *Why*, they needed to look no further than destiny. This is why Oedipus, King of Thebes, in Sophocles'

Old Solutions to the Problem of Evil

tragic drama, **Oedipus Rex,** received so little sympathy from his fellow Greek citizens for his double misfortune—he unknowingly killed his father and married his mother. His self-inflicted blindness and expulsion from his country were simply his fate.

They say that pride was Oedipus' downfall. He had challenged the gods. First he challenged the dire female monster, the Sphinx—and won by solving her riddle, "Who goes first on four legs, then on two, and then on three?" As a result a plague leaves the city, and he becomes their king. This is all the will of Apollo. Apollo now returns with another plague and this time to topple Oedipus. Destiny or fate is engaged in the conscious preparations of his humiliation and exile. "For the mastery that raised thee was thy bane and wrought thy fall," says Creon in his closing lines.

The poem seems to say that the great mystery is in people, but I say the great mystery is our understanding of God, and the Greeks had it all wrong. God neither sends plagues, nor does God program our lives, nor do gods carry out curses upon people. Yet God does have a plan for each of us. For Oedipus, the gods forced a destiny upon him, and then punished him for it. This thinking is alive and well today.

Thomas Hardy also shows this in his brooding tragedy, **The Return of the Native.** Indifferent nature and cold, dispassionate fate looks on with complete disinterest at the futility of the human struggle. Nature, God or fate direct our future. Those who live in harmony with nature have the best chance of survival. Yet, people's bad decisions also play a part in their fate.

In Hardy's **Tess of the d'Urbervilles,** we see how fate and nature seem to conspire to defeat even the noblest of heart. It leaves me wondering if the universe is anything more than a cold dispassionate observer of the follies and sufferings of helpless mortals. Although Tess' problems begin with her pregnancy by rape; nevertheless, she makes many bad decisions afterwards that lead to her tragedy. This, of course, brings up the other question of who is responsible for Tess' bad decisions—Tess or her environment?

Hardy was writing at the end of the puritan era of England and before the more modern views of life and morality. He was a transitional author. He was blaming society for Tess' bad decisions. Nathaniel Hawthorne does the same thing, around the same time, in **The Scarlet Letter**—a psychological-gothic novel filled with romantic details that discloses the "truth of the human heart."

The puritan era was famous for saying that God blesses the rich. Look at the Sunday morning TV church programs, and see how the camera focuses on the three-piece suits. God has blessed me, and I should stay in good graces. Churches take up collections for the poor, seemingly to keep things in perspective. That some church hierarchies so admires the rich, may be in such contradiction to what Jesus did and taught. God does not make us rich or poor, good or evil.

The thing I object to in these great tragedies—and they are tragedies because the worthy person is encompassed by the inevitable—is that the authors blame fate, or worse God, for the evil that comes into their characters' lives. Collective society also has a combined will, which can be, and has been, changed at times. Consider how our views have changed concerning our tolerance toward child molesters, smokers and drunk drivers who kill people.

Over time, later writers have exchanged the blind convention and self-righteous morality of Tess' time for another morality with another set of problems to write about. Authors do not write great tragedies around unworthy characters. Such unworthy characters seem to get what they deserve. In the brightest tragedies there is grandeur in sorrow and sorrow in grandeur. Shakespeare, that most extraordinary of ordinary people, also wrote this type of tragedy. He could show the ordinary reader what an extraordinary life he or she was living. Someone other than ourselves might be in charge of our lives. This includes the causes of evil.

B.F. (Burrhus Frederic) Skinner enters the picture of life here by denying me my freedom to sin or cause evil. This behavioralism is presented in his celebrated but silly novel, **Walden Two**. Here he takes Thoreau's name in vain. He describes a small fictional community in which Professor Burrhus (compare Skinner's own first name) uses behavioral engineering to create a world of boxes—environments that controlled or selected the behaviors by which the children were to function. His conclusion was this: "When a science of behavior has been achieved, there's no alternative to a planned society."

He drew upon the celebrated Russian scientist Ivan Pavlov (1839-1926) who really gave the impetus to the behavioristic branch of psychology. His famous experiment showed that dogs would salivate at the sound of the bell, by conditioning them with feeding. Skinner was a true scientist who knew how to do meticulous experiments in behavior modification in animals—pigeons and rats. It was the inferences that he drew which were as preposterous as they were foolish, and yet there is more truth in some of it than most of us would want to admit. To a certain extent, stimulus programs me, especially when stimulus comes from mob psychology.

Comparisons between himself and Charles Darwin always flattered Skinner. The implication was that Darwin's natural selection and

Old Solutions to the Problem of Evil

Skinner's operant conditioning both show how the environment has shaped both animals and people as parts of a common history of organisms—both for the good and the evil.

Skinner's most influential though short-lived book, **Beyond Freedom and Dignity** (1971), asserts that freedom from the environment was impossible, and so the only hope was for a conditioned humanity. Liberty is "maintained and exercised in a way of subjection to authority." Religious faith arose from environmental factors that had yet to be *analyzed*. Skinner is a student of the astonishingly insensitive and ridiculous J. B. Watson:

> *Give me a dozen healthy infants, well-formed, and my own specified world to bring them up in and I'll guarantee to take anyone at random and train him to become any kind of specialist I might select—doctor, artist, merchant-chief, and yes even beggarman and thief, regardless of his talents, penchants, abilities, vocations, and the race of his ancestors.*

Skinner, like Watson, failed to recognize a whole submerged side to humanity that was not mechanical, and therefore prone to evil as well as to kindness. Their ideas end up somewhat pathetic, but scientists put these ideas about punishment and conditioning into practice all over the world, which are still being used. They do modify some people's behavior temporarily, but other methods are just as successful. When I was in graduate school, these behaviorists were in charge of a mental hospital. They wanted to use electric shock to change patients' behavior. My reasoning against this was that I did not want anyone ever to do that to me. Read Ben Kessy's **One Flew Over the Cuchoo's Nest**. It is a classic example of the clash between free will and institutional behaviorists.

Behavioral Modification exemplifies the fact that partial solutions to problems are often worse than no solution at all. I must consider all the pertinent facts, not be selective.

Often historians describe Thomas Hobbes as an inventor of the behaviorist method—which tries to describe the scientifically describable. His universe is material and his sovereign is an artificial God, indeed a terrifying one. His extraordinary book, **Leviathan** (1651), taken from Job 41 the great sea monster, describes the price that people pay for their convenience, security, and peace. He believes that people trade their freedoms in exchange for their secure living to the **Leviathan**, a metaphor for the State. Matter in motion could explain every-

Evil in Mirror Lake

thing, Hobbes believed. The selfishness in their natures moves people to become slaves to the State.

I have always believed that my teachers of the 1940s and 1950s invented behavioral modification. "Spare the rod and spoil the child," it says in the Bible. My teachers knew how to reward acceptable behaviors and to punish behavior that was not. Environment is only part, although a big part, of what influences us in our life decisions. Our genes and our environment (nature *versus* nurture) are about fifty-fifty, I say. Using identical twins living in different environments, they are always found to be somewhat different. Certainly, our free will and our intellect greatly influence our decisions.

Listen to a hopeful quotation from Victor Hugo's **Les Miserables**. I do not think it can ever come true because people will forever be free to choose evil, and some will:

> *We shall one day come to look upon crime as a disease.*
> *Physicians shall displace judges and hospitals the*
> *gallows. We shall pour oil and balm where we formerly*
> *applied iron and fire, and evil will be treated in charity*
> *instead of in anger—a change simple and sublime. The*
> *gentle laws of Christ will penetrate at last into the code*
> *and shine through its enactments.*

Zeus, the Greek king of all the gods, and Prometheus, the Titan-demigod, struggle in a cosmic drama of conflict between two rival forces—God and Man. Prometheus steals fire from heaven to help the human race, and Zeus nails (chains) him to a mountain (tree) for this.

The young Olympian upstarts, led by their brother, Zeus, after having overthrown the old order of the Titans led by Zeus' father, Cronus, planned to destroy the human race who until then had been a primitive, unenlightened and miserable lot. Zeus' intent was to replace people with a new and more noble race, responsive to the gods' every wish.

Prometheus, nephew of the dethroned Cronus, on the other hand, saw in humans a spark of Divine Promise that even the gods might envy, and so he tutors them in the practical arts of applied sciences and philosophy. He gives them fruit from the forbidden tree of knowledge. It is a story strangely similar to the Bible story of Adam and Eve.

Not only is the world found in chaos, but likewise are the Greek-Roman gods. Gaia, Mother Earth, marries Uranus. Their marriage is riven by conflict. Gaia loves her children deeply, but their father feels only jealous contempt for them, fearing that one of his sons would eventually depose him. Gaia, Mother Earth, plots with her youngest

Old Solutions to the Problem of Evil

son, Cronus, to catch Uranus off guard as he is preparing to make love to her. Cronus castrates his father, Uranus, and takes his place as the all-powerful sky god and soon sets about to establish his own dynasty. Because Cronus reneges on his promise to his mother to release his two older brothers, Hundred-handed from Tartarus (the Underworld) and Cyclopes (imprisoned in Mount Etna), his mother turns to her grandson, Zeus, to now overthrow her son, Cronus. The world is filled with evil from the beginning and at the top.

Zeus with the help of his two imprisoned uncles, two brothers, Hades (God of the Underworld [Pluto]), and Poseidon (God of the Oceans [Neptune]), along with his nephew, Prometheus, uses guile and cunning and knowledge, rather than sheer physical strength, to achieve his ends. Through cooperation and careful planning, the young gods defeat the cruder, but stronger, Titans. Zeus and his siblings, along with his sister/wife Hera, (in her Roman form Juno) base themselves on Mount Olympus in northern Greece. Atlas, the military leader of the defeated Titans, is condemned to support the heavens on his shoulders for eternity to prevent it from falling to the Earth. (See the **Illustrated History of the World**, Vol. 2, *Classical Greece.*

Tertullian, an Early Doctor of the Christian Church, saw Christ as another Prometheus. Both individuals freed people from evil or sin. In both examples, the Greek and the Christian, it is a father-figure who is responsible for their punishment—the evil they had to suffer. The pagan gods and the Christian God are the causes of evil.

The Hebrew Testament solved the mystery of evil by saying that God sent evil into the nation's life because the nation, or a portion therein, had violated God's covenant, as interpreted by the ruling prophets. As a result, God needed to bring them back into the covenant. In a large group, we can always point to some people who do bad things as the cause of God's ire. It was always a medicinal evil, though, that would bring the chosen people back to their senses and so to reform.

The Hebrew Testament (an agreement, covenant [Mitzvah] or a handshake with God) said that if the people would keep God's 613 laws (365 prohibitive laws, one for each day of the year, and 248 affirmative laws, one for each bone, then known, to be in the body), then God would keep the people safe from evil, and make them prosperous in this life. The faithful Jew said, "To live within the law of Moses is to live within the arms of God." Yet evil persisted in their nation with various people at various times. Whenever evil came to the nation, some group of evil doers was sure to catch the blame (the people's ire).

When the Hebrews saw individually good people suffer unnecessarily at times, and bad people prosper, the problem of evil became

Evil in Mirror Lake

personal. Where was the justice of God if God were indeed making these calls? This is what Ralph Waldo Emerson describes as, "...the unjust *justice* of the Eternal Father."

The Hebrews and God wrote an inspired Book to answer this problem. At first, Job's visitors question him about his hidden bad deeds, but he truthfully declares none. We see God allowing Satan to destroy his property, kill his children, and turn Job's wife into a negative shrew counseling him to curse God and die. Why did God allow, or cause this to happen? The answer was that God, like a sardonic gentleman gambler, had a bet with Satan. Job was on the game board. Job's suffering or evils had the nature of a test. God emerges as an arbitrary and incomprehensible deity even to the righteous. "O deliver me from such a God!" I pray.

The story ends without giving the reason for evil in our lives. Nevertheless, it does teach me to live with the mystery of evil and to trust God as Job did, and eventually prosper in this life—maybe. John Paul II in his **Salvifici Dolores** says, "The book of Job poses in an extremely acute way the question of the *why* of suffering; it also shows that suffering strikes the innocent, but it does not yet give the solution to the problem."

Rabbi Binyomin Scheiman, a fellow prison chaplain, once told me that our view of evil is similar to a prehistoric person peering into a modern-day operating room and seeing a person cutting open someone's stomach. Not being aware of modern day medicine, the onlooker could quite naturally and mistakenly think that the surgeon was doing an evil deed. So also, when I see God doing something that looks like evil, my limited view makes it seem to me that God has done an evil deed. In reality, it is not always that way.

"Like a twisted olive tree in its five-hundredth year, giving then its finest fruit, is man. How can he give forth wisdom until they have crushed and turned him in the hand of God?" says the Rabbi in James Michener's **The Source**, reflecting on the fate of his people.

The Dutch philosopher of the seventeenth century, Baruch Spinoza, revolting against his Jewish community, said, "All evils come from not following Right Reason and the Law of Nature." He contrasted religions of nature with revealed religion, and claimed that revealed religions taught people hatred, as nature religions taught people to love. He was the original European pantheist, although the term itself was not used until 1705, by John Toland.

Pantheism is the belief that everything is divine and that God and Nature are identical. We grudgingly allowed this to poets, but Spinoza was the first to put it into a philosophy. He says that there is but a single

44

Old Solutions to the Problem of Evil

substance—*monism*—and that this monism will grant people immortality if they can enter the *thinking* of God, who is that single substance. His greatest importance lies in his persuasive advocacy of a world of laws in which human beings can find fulfillment. He did not need miracles. I just have to submerge myself into that single substance—God (or the Holy Spirit).

Having finished his manuscript, Spinoza loaded two pistols, waited at his window until he saw his brother Joseph pass by, fired at him and missed. He then shot himself. His community had ostracized him, excommunicated, put him *off talk.*

How did Jesus explain the problem of evil? During Jesus' time his apostles asked him, "If a man is born blind, is it because of his sin or the sin of his parents?" Think about this—how could a man have sinned in his mother's womb? Nevertheless, Jesus sets them straight by answering, "Neither." However, it is interesting that Jesus does not go on to explain why this physical evil of blindness did happen. He did say, though, that it would reveal the glory of God, presumably anticipating his upcoming miracle and the subsequent belief in him and his message.

The man was possibly born blind because of his mother's venereal disease. Until recent new medicine in America, most modern-born babies have gotten a single drop of silver nitrate in each of their eyes to kill such germs. Today, thanks to modern medicines, few people are born blind because of venereal disease.

Despite the mention of the fall (Psalms 51:5) and the depravity of humankind (Romans 3:23), the Bible gives no satisfactory answer to the mystery of evil. The Bible tells stories about the predefined rebellion of Lucifer and his angels (Revelation 12:7), the story of Adam and Eve driven from paradise (Gen 3:1-27), but still leaves the mystery. Indeed, the word "evil" appears more often in the Christian Scriptures than "good"—and with reason. We are born into original sin. Still, many of the world's greatest thinkers have grappled with evil in their day.

Zoroaster (c.1400-1200 B.C.E.) and Manes (c. 216-277 A.D.), from the Near East, attributed an independent existence to evil itself. **The Avesta** (c. 500 B.C.E.) contains this idea. We are too sophisticated for that. I am not referring, though, to the real existence of the devil—that is a different issue.

Augustine of Hippo's great contribution to philosophy was to point out that evil, though real, is not a real thing, but *the privation of a good*. Evil has no independent existence. As a young man, Augustine was a Manichaean. He believed that the cosmos was torn between equally powerful forces of good and evil. In his later writings as a

45

Evil in Mirror Lake

Christian, however, he identified evil as the "privation" of the good—a sort of black hole in the order of creation that works against the good which God wills for all that the almighty has brought into being. "From this perspective," says Kenneth L. Woodward in *Newsweek* magazine (5-17-01), "evil shadows the good like antimatter to matter; it has no existence in itself, but is immensely powerful in its ability to negate what is and—morally speaking—what ought to be. For Christians, only the gift of God's own grace can overcome the power of evil in the world and sanctify the life of the believer."

Yet even today in the face of the school killings, some people, like Michael Gelven in his philosophical book, **This Side of Evil**, speaks as if there is a real entity out there causing these evil deeds—an entity separate from the devil. The devil is enough to worry about. No need to create a second entity "out there." To exorcize the devil is trouble enough.

"Immorality is different from evil," Gelven claims, trying to make Evil out to be an ontological entity separate from immorality by species and not just by degree. He points out that free will is just a facility and not the cause **per se** of either good or evil. I say the cause is the person so choosing. Without specifically invoking Plato's self-existing ideas, that might be his self-existent Evil. For Plato, ideas have an existence apart from the thinker.

Gelven also talks about evil as what diminishes me as a human; whereas, bad is just something I do that is wrong. So, Slobodan Milosevic of Belgrade and John Wayne Gacy of Chicago, the mass murderer, are evil people. They diminished themselves as humans. The diminishment is real because they were not what they ought to be. In fact, does not even the act of shoplifting likewise diminish me, but to a lesser degree? I become bad, not evil, or at least not Evil itself?

Scientists universally recognize space and time as the necessary conditions for finite existence. Does not space and time answer, with no higher presuppositions, the primary questions of where? And when? This leads to the fundamental, existential phenomenon of belonging. Evil is the threat—that I may become what I should not be, even as the threat of evil resides in me as a conflicting part of my reality. The point where it becomes fair to call me EVIL is when I like doing evil, and do it regularly. I must lack the capacity for the empathy. Evil then becomes part of, or belongs to, my character. John Wayne Gacy was evil. Joseph Stalin was evil. A judgment? You bet!

Yet, some evil people often know full well what their victims feel, and revel in it. Besides a void of compassion, people doing acts of unspeakable evil also seem to require a bent toward dehumanizing oth-

Old Solutions to the Problem of Evil

ers. John Gacy called his thirty-three boys "worthless little queers." Timothy McVeigh called the toddlers he killed "collateral damage." See *Newsweek* magazine (5-17-01), "What Makes People Go Wrong" by Sharon Begley.

To see evil people in action, see the Oliver Stone movie, **Natural Born Killers**. These people did evil often and loved doing it. Also, read **The Fall of the House of Usher** by Edgar Allan Poe. This gothic horror story evokes a sense of fear and foreboding that makes me shirk my evil ways as I look back and see his house implode upon itself killing the evil Roderick Usher and his sister Lady Madeline.

On a smaller scale, the jigsaw puzzle of the 21st century is the computer virus maker. Why do such highly intelligent people dedicate so much of their valuable time to making life terrible for other people? Their sisters and brothers are making fortunes by working on computers legally. The challenge of breaking into someone else's computer is part of it, but there is an equal challenge in making money honestly. The person who does this often and enjoys doing it—doing terrible things to people—is an evil person. Judgment by deeds? Jurors do this all the time.

Although there are evil people and not just people who do evil things; nevertheless, this EVIL does not have a separate existence unto itself as Michael Gelvin tries to convince us. He says that evil is a force outside us. Things outside of me may influence me, such as the devil, but I am the existential reality—myself. Evil is a lack of what ought to be in my life. There is no need to presume that EVIL has a separate existence that which we can never go beyond (thus the title of his book—**This Side of Evil**).

John Paul II also seems to think that evil has an existence all of its own. After all, he lived in Poland through the holocaust. Maybe it is the synergy that comes out of many people doing evil together. A synergy is the result of the whole being greater than the sum of its parts—in that it produces something greater than the individuals would separately. Therefore, it seems to be more—an existence of itself—but it is not. It just seems to be.

If things can exist only in reality or in the mind (which is also arguably real), and if evil is a lack of what ought to be, then evil exists only in the mind. Further, it can only exist in my mind if I allow it. Modern Hollywood society inhibits me from judging others' actions. Thus, I am reluctant to judge anything evil. However, society judges every time a judge and/or a jury puts someone into our penitentiaries. Society has finally come to judge the holocaust as evil. The killings at Columbine High School are evil. Yet I ask, where are these evils in our

Evil in Mirror Lake

society, and what part does the individual play in it?

The origin of many evils in our society is the conscious or unconscious privation of love. Society and the individuals who make up society often deprive love to those who need it. Individuals become so distracted by their desire for money, fame, self-interests, success, recreation, etc., that they deprive those around them of the love and attention they need—the privation of good. Why are rebellious teens turning to drugs and alcohol for comfort and escape? Certainly not because they are getting all the love and attention they need!

If the Columbine shooters were getting all the attention they needed, then their parents would have known they had an arsenal of weapons and bombs in their rooms! The fact that their parents did not know what their kids were doing prove that the kids were not given the love and attention they needed.

Society, blind to its own lacking, instead chooses to judge, criticize and neglect. The psychological pain inflicted by society eventually results in a) carbon copies of uncaring, critical and negligent members of society; b) individuals who accept the neglect as being somehow deserved—leading to low self-esteem and further mistreatment in abusive relationships—or if too internalized, self-destructive behavior and suicide; or c) individuals who develop a pure contempt for society and seek to inflict pain and suffering on the society that has inflicted its pain on them. They reject the society that rejected them. The privation of love by society can invoke a reciprocal privation of love by individuals upon society. Children who have suffered physical pain at the hands of molesters tend to grow up to be abusers themselves. It should be no surprise that psychological pain can produce similar consequences. Mother Theresa once commented in a TV documentary that what she found lacking in the slums of India (basic needs) were easy to fix, but what the Western World lacked was love—much harder to fix.

Evil is like my agreeing to work a day for $100. At the end of the day my pay envelope contains only $60. Where does the other $40 exist? In the employer's pocket, you say. I say evil exists in the dead children lying on the school's library carpet. One might argue that this is the fruit of evil thoughts and actions—but not evil itself. If you accept my definition of *evil* as *terrible things*, then I say what lies on that library carpet is evil. They ought to be alive, just as that $40 ought to be in my pay envelope. These are real losses that really exist in my mind. Evil simply does not have its own ontological existence, as Gelven contends. Existence in my mind can be both real and terrible enough.

Ivan Karamazov, the atheist, says in Dostoyevski's **Brothers**

48

Old Solutions to the Problem of Evil

Karamazov, "If all must suffer to pay for the eternal harmony, what have children to do with it, tell me, please?" Alyosha Karamazov, his saintly brother, responds, "I believe that God will order things for the best, that nothing awful will happen." **The Christian Science Monitor**, 2-8-99, exhorts us, "Pray to see the unbroken harmony that God sustains." This will then in some way become apparent—it assures us.

The early Greek philosopher Plotinus in his **Ennead** first uttered this idea of world harmony, "What is evil in the single Soul will stand a good thing in the universal system." "Life is like a play," he says, "the poet, while he gives each actor a part, is also using them as they are in their own person." He continues, "Thus, every man has his place, a place that fits the good man, a place that fits the bad: each within the two orders of them makes his way, naturally, reasonably, to the place, good or bad, that suits him, and takes the position he has made his own."

Plotinus also compares life with an orchestra that combines all the sounds of people into a harmonious whole. Plotinus goes on, "Wrong-doing from man to man is wrong in the doer and must be imputed, but, as belonging to the established order of the universe, is not a wrong even as for the innocent sufferer; it is a thing that had to be, and, if the sufferer is good, the issue is to his gain. For we cannot think that this ordered combination continues without God and justice; we must take it to be precise in the distribution of due, while, yet, the reasons of things elude us, and to our ignorance the scheme presents a matter of censure."

This image of the harmony of life comes from the eternal premise that almighty God is responsible for all that is. The all-good God must see to it that in the end all is harmoniously good. I have derived a different solution than Plotinus, but...

"For the Apostle says that the wisdom and the judgments of Our Lord God Almighty are very deep, where of no man may comprehend anything, nor search into them. Nevertheless, by certain presumptions and conjectures, I hold and believe that God, Who is justice and righteousness, has permitted this villainy upon a just and reasonable cause," says Goeffrey Chaucer in *The Tale of Melibeus* in his **Canterbury Tales**.

Friedrich Schelling, an eighteenth century German philosopher, to explain the apparent contradictions between a loving God and a Nature *red in tooth and claw*, took the idea from Jakob Böhme (1575-1624) that God is a battleground between good and evil. Nature oscillates between struggling for order and relaxing into chaos—entropy. This also exists in each individual. I have something irrational in my make-up—maybe 90 percent of it. Schelling promised his readers that ulti-

Evil in Mirror Lake

mately we will overcome all evil. Divine Wisdom will succeed in transforming even my follies and crimes into something good, he promises.

"The existence of evil is the best argument against the existence of God," Thomas Aquinas admits at the beginning of his **Summa Theologica**. He also says (Summa I, 49, 2), "God is the author of evil which is penalty, but not of the evil which is fault." This is his Old Testament view. Aquinas gave us the explanation that I hear most religious people give in most movies yet today. He says:

> *God is so good that he would never permit there to be any*
> *evil, unless he was so powerful that from every evil he is*
> *able to draw good. Wherefore, it is neither on account of*
> *the impotency, nor on account of the ignorance of God*
> *that evils appear in the world. But it is from the order of*
> *his wisdom and the magnitude of his greatness.*

Fr. Henry Ray Engelhart states this view from experience:

> *In no way do I wish to deny this experience. I just have*
> *another way of explaining it. After years as a hospital*
> *chaplain, a person sees how the LORD uses death and*
> *sickness as tools to bring forward His goals in the lives of*
> *others. Sometimes these are drastic measures which alone*
> *have the power to crush a stone-hardened heart. The*
> *LORD seems to use evil to bring about balance in His*
> *creation, especially in regard to his Glory, His Godliness.*
> *His children though we may be; Yahweh is still the One,*
> *the Infinite and the Holy. We are indeed clay which He*
> *may do with as He ultimately wills. Nevertheless, He will*
> *keep His covenant and fulfill all his promises.*

The Catholic Church later reflected this in the First Vatican Council's (1870) statement, "God by his providence protects and governs all the things he has made 'reaching strongly from end to end and ordering all things graciously' (Wis. 8:1), for 'all things are naked and open to his eyes' (Heb. 4:13) even those which occur through the free action of creatures." This is the traditional teaching of the Hebrew and Christian Testaments.

Anthony de Mello has a story which illustrates how such consciousness might exhibit itself in a saintly person:

> *One day the Master said, "You are not ready to fight evil*

Old Solutions to the Problem of Evil

until you are able to see the good it does." The disciples were confused until the next day when the Master offered them this prayer found on a piece of wrapping paper in a concentration camp: "Lord, remember not only the men and women of good will but all those of ill will. Do not only remember all the suffering they have subjected us to. Remember the fruits we brought forth thanks to this suffering—our comradeship, our loyalty, our humility, our courage and generosity, the greatness of heart that all of this inspired. And when they come to judgment, let all these fruits we have borne be their reward and their forgiveness.

This is also the solution to the problem of evil that I find in the Bible. This teaching seems to flow from Paul's aphorism, "To those who love God all things work together for good" (Rom. 8:28). For Paul, God is in control of everything. Love solves the problem of evil: God as love effectively orders all things and God provides, especially for those who love. The underlying implication is that by loving God— God, the Lover, completely fulfills us. Therefore, nothing else in life matters that much. Only by my own refusal to receive love, can I prevent or limit that fulfillment. God's providence takes infinite care of creation. Love responds to love. The response on my part requires faith and trust with a humble acceptance of God's loving will, mysterious as it may be.

We mere creatures, in observing the mysterious workings of almighty God, may similarly think that evil deeds are being done to us. We simply, right now, do not understand their import. Yet God is so good that in the end all seemingly bad deeds will eventually be for our benefit. This reminds me that I am never quite sure what is really good news or bad news. We must remember that God is love.

As Washington Irving tells in *Legend of the Moor's Legacy*, a story in **The Alhambra**, a poor water carrier does an egregious deed, or an absurd act of hospitality, to a lonely Moor. By doing this he loses his beloved donkey. In the ironic end, his hospitality—through which he got a secret map—makes him a richly rewarded man. Evil may come out of good, but more often good comes out of evil, so the story tells us. For an ironic example, when I intended to do a favor for Jim, the result was he ended up doing me a much bigger favor. And sometimes better comes out of good.

John Paul II reminds us that all punishment from God is medicinal. Evil comes to me either to correct behavior, or as a stepping stone to greatness. Often this is obviously true, especially when evil comes

Evil in Mirror Lake

because of my behavior. Nevertheless, sometimes the evil is so great that there is neither something so bad in my past, nor any stepping stone possible for the future that can justify such a grave evil. A baby daughter dies of AIDS. This seems unjust to our human sense of justice. Yet, who are we to judge God in Divine Justice? So, most theologians call it a *mystery.*

Paul makes this point eloquently, "O the depth of the riches of the wisdom and the knowledge of God. How baffling are his judgments and how unsearchable his ways? For, who has known the mind of God? Or who has been his counselor?" (Rom. 11:33-34). Indeed, we labor against evil in the darkness of faith. If we know how to love, however, we are able in Christ to overcome the mystery of evil, so Paul tells us. God is so good and powerful that in the end all evil will be eventually for our benefit. *Amor Vincit Omnia.* Love Conquers All!

Augustine, an early Christian church father and philosopher, the Bishop of Hippo in North Africa, warned in his **Confessions** not to penetrate too far into the Mysteries. In **Contra Julian**, Sec. i 9, he said, "There is no possible source of evil except good." God judged it better to bring good out of evil rather than not permit any evil to exist, Augustine said in his book **Enchiridion**:

> *That which is called evil, when it is regulated and put in its own place, only enhances our admiration of the good; for we enjoy and value the good more when we compare it with the evil. For the Almighty God, who, as even the heathen acknowledge, has supreme power over all things, being Himself supremely good, would never permit the existence of anything evil among His works, if He were not so omnipotent and good that He can bring good even out of evil. For what is that which we call evil but the absence of good?* (Some also call evil the absence of love.)

Moses Maimonides also felt this problem of Evil. This great twelfth-century Jewish philosopher echoes Augustine in his, **Guide for the Perplexed** (1190):

> *All evils are negations... It cannot be said of God that He directly creates evil... this is impossible. His works are perfectly good. He only produces existence, and all existence is good... The numerous evils to which individual persons are exposed are due to the defects existing in the persons themselves. We complain and seek*

Old Solutions to the Problem of Evil

relief from our faults; we suffer from the evils which we,
by our own free will, inflict on ourselves and ascribe them
to God, Who is far from being connected with them.

Maimonides had one leg of the three-legged stool which holds up my solution to the problem of evil—his one leg is our own bad decisions. He wrote this Guide for those who were confused between the teachings of the faith and those of philosophy. He said, "The object of this treatise is to enlighten a religious man whom they have trained to believe in the truth of our holy law... and at the same time has been successful in his philosophical studies." He was a precursor of the great European classical rationalists—Descartes, Spinoza and Leibniz—in the sense that he believed the use of reason could discover knowledge. Thomas Aquinas studied him, and both studied Aristotle—the last man to have known everything that was to be known in his time.

Another to study Aristotle was Averroes, the Arab scholar. He labored to synthesize Aristotelian rationalism with Islamic Theology. Thomas Aquinas likewise studied Averroes and quoted him often in his **Summa Theologica.**

Julian of Norwich, who lived from 1342 to (about) 1416, wondered why the great foreseeing wisdom of God did not prevent "the beginning of sin." She heard Jesus say to her, in a series of sixteen revelations in May 1370, "Sin must need be, but all shall be well. All shall be well; and all manner of things will be well." Her account of her visions is available in many modern translations. Translators usually title the book either **Showings** or **A Revelation of Love**, and it has become something of a bestseller lately. Julian of Norwich's major contribution was her thought that, "we have in us, for the time of this life, a marvelous mingling both of weal and woe: we have in us our Lord Jesus uprisen, [and] we have in us the wretchedness and mischief of Adam's falling, dying." This is a person working from instinctual life toward freedom and compassion.

Or as Shakespeare said in *As You Like It*, revised slightly by me:

Useful are the uses of evil,
Which, like the fairy frog, ugly and venomous,
Wears yet a precious jewel in its head;
And thus my life, spent behind prison bars,
Finds tongues in trees, books in running brooks,
Sermons in stone, and good in every thing.

Billy Graham, in **Facing Death**, reminds parents that they do not

Evil in Mirror Lake

own their children. God has given them only in trust. "However," he says, "God may transfer our children to His home anytime. If Jesus were to come today and say, 'I want to take over the teaching and training of your little boy,' you would gladly let go of his hand and place it in the hand of Jesus, would you not? This is what happens when He takes a child to heaven." This is a soothing slant on the all-powerful, all-responsible, age-old idea of God.

Frank J. Tipler in his **The Physics of Immortality** (1994) claims that, "The Omega Point (God) is absolved of moral responsibility for evils, both natural and moral, because it is logically impossible for Him/Her to eliminate any evils at all from the totality of histories that actually exist. I cannot blame even an omnipotent being for failing to accomplish a logical impossibility."

Western secular and religious minds are inclining to believe that all future outcomes, whether good or evil, are a human community responsibility. John F. Kennedy said in his Inaugural Address, "Here on earth, God's work must surely be our own."

Whereas, Abraham Lincoln said, a century earlier, just a month before the Civil War ended, and a month and eleven days before his assassination, in his second Inaugural Address:

> *If we shall suppose that American Slavery is one of those offences which, in the providence of God, must needs come, but which, having continued through His appointed time, He now wills to remove, and that **He gives to both North and South, this terrible war, as the woe due to those by whom the offence came**, shall we discern therein any departure from those divine attributes which the believers in a Living God always ascribe to Him? Fondly do we hope—fervently do we pray—that this mighty scourge of war may speedily pass away. Yet, **if God wills that it continue**, until all the wealth piled by the bond-man's two hundred and fifty years of unrequited toil shall be sunk, and until every drop of blood drawn with the lash shall be paid by another drawn with the sword, as was said three thousand years ago, so still it must be said "the judgments of the Lord, are true and righteous altogether."*
> (Emphasis is added to point out the belief that God did will the war, despite our free wills.)

Lincoln went on to conclude his address with the now famous last paragraph that is always worth rereading:

Old Solutions to the Problem of Evil

*With malice toward none; with charity for all; with
firmness in the right, as God gives us to see the right, let
us strive on to finish the work we are in; to bind up the
nation's wounds; to care for him who shall have borne the
battle, and for his widow, and his orphan—to do all which
may achieve and cherish a just, and a lasting peace,
among ourselves, and with all nations.*

Will Durant in his **History of Civilization**, gives us the Eastern
view of how to solve the problem of suffering. By total uninterrupted
self-denial, suffering or evil becomes a nonissue. I cannot summarize
Durant; we must experience him.

Let us swim together in his boundless lake of ideas:

*Let us look to the East. The law of Karma—the Law of the
Deed—is the law of causality in the spiritual world.
Karma is one of those many inventions by which people
have sought to bear evil patiently, and to face life with
hope. To explain evil, and to find for people some scheme
in which they may accept it, if not with good cheer, then
with peace of mind—this is the task that most religions
have attempted to fulfill. Since the real problem of life is
not suffering but undeserved suffering, the religion of
India mitigates the human tragedy by giving meaning and
value to grief and pain. The soul, in Hindu Theology, has
at least this consolation, that it must bear the consequences only of its own acts; unless it questions all
existence it can accept evil as a passing punishment, and
look forward to tangible rewards for virtue borne. But in
truth the Hindus do question all existence.*

*Oppressed with an enervating environment, national
subjection and economic exploitation, they have tended to
look upon life as a more bitter punishment than an
opportunity or reward. The **Vedas**, their sacred scriptures,
written by a hardy race coming in from the north, were
almost as optimistic as Walt Whitman, Buddha, or
Gautama, the Aristotle of India, representing the same
stock five hundred years later, already denied the value of
life; the **Puranas**, five centuries later still, represented a
view more profoundly pessimistic than anything known in
the West except in stray moments of philosophical doubt.*

55

Evil in Mirror Lake

*The East, until reached by the Industrial Revolution,
could not understand the zest with which the West has
taken to life; it saw only superficiality and childishness in
our merciless busyness, our discontented ambition, our
nerve-racking, labor-saving devices, our progress and
speed; it could no more comprehend this profound
immersion in the surface of things, this clever refusal to
look ultimates in the face, than the West can fathom the
quiet inertia, the "stagnation" and "hopelessness" of the
traditional East. Heat cannot understand cold.*

*"What is the most wonderful thing in the world?" asks
Yama of Yudishthira; and Yudishthira replies, "Man after
he dies. Seeing this, men still move about as if they were
immortal." "By death the world is afflicted," says the
Mahabharata, "by age it is held in bar, and the nights are
the Unfailing Ones that are ever coming and going. When
I know that death cannot halt, what can I expect from
walking in a cover of lore?" And in the Ramayana, Sita
asks as her reward for fidelity through every temptation
and trial, only death, "If in truth unto my husband I have
proved a faithful wife, Mother Earth, relieve thy Sita from
the burden of this life!"*

*So the last word of Hindu religious thought is Moksha,
release—first from desire, then from life. Nirvana may be
one release or the other; but its fullest is both. The sage
Bhartrihari expresses the first: "Everything on earth
gives cause for fear, and the only freedom from fear is to
be found in the renunciation of all desire. Once upon a
time, the days seemed so long to me when my heart was
sorely wounded through asking favors from the rich; and
yet again the days seemed all too short for me when I
sought to carry out all my worldly desires and ends. But
now as a philosopher I sit on a hard stone in a cave on
the mountain-side, and time and again I laugh when I
think of my former life." Mahatma Gandhi expresses the
second form of release; "I do not want to be reborn," he
says. The highest and final aspiration of the Hindu is to
escape reincarnation, to lose that fervor of ego which
revives with each individual body and birth. Salvation
does not come by faith, nor yet by works; it comes by such*

Old Solutions to the Problem of Evil

*uninterrupted self denial, by such selfless intuition of the
part-engulfing Whole, that at last the self is dead, and
there is nothing to be reborn. The hell of individuality
passes into the haven and heaven of unity, of complete
and impersonal absorption into Brahman, the soul or
Force of the World.*

This Eastern philosophy has some good points, like release from
too many desires, as I said before. I, as others, have come to appreciate
the many benefits of the simple life style. Nevertheless, total release
into nothingness is a simple escape from pain. It is not the finding of
happiness that can be found, as many of us do experience. Nirvana
offers no possibility of the presence of Mystery in the events and encounters of life. Both Hinduism and Buddhism sound too much like
what Peter Kreeft calls, *spiritual euthanasia*. It is like killing the pa-
tient (myself) so I can cure my disease (suffering). Nevertheless, the
love of any God, even a false god, is valid and redeeming.

Harold Kushner, in his bestseller, **When Bad Things Happen to
Good People**, attempts to put to rest any necessary relationship between suffering and sin.

*Let me suggest that the author of the Book of Job takes
the position which neither Job nor his friends take. He
believes in God's goodness and in Job's goodness, and is
prepared to give up his belief in a proposition (A): that
God is all-powerful. Bad things do happen to good people
in this world, but it is not God who wills it. God would
like people to get what they deserve in life, but He cannot
always arrange it.*

The Bible also gives no straightforward answer to this mystery of
evil, except to say that God permits it. It does talk about the fall (Genesis 3:7 and Psalms 51:5) and the perversity of human nature (Romans
3:23), but no explanation as to the role played by an all-powerful God
who is responsible for this evil, which is not good.

Possibly this duality, recognized by so many cultures, is really our
battle with our dark side. If much of the power of the unconscious
resides in the so-called reptilian brain, or brain stem, which knows
only the need to survive, then the life force, through it, is harnessed to
whatever the outer cortex interprets as a threat to our safety. The outer
cortex is the later development, and we are still learning how to use it.
I may ultimately learn to use this instinct for fight, flight, or love by

Evil in Mirror Lake

making love a more comprehensive concept of life than simple protection of my separate self image—my ego. Could not creation be the ongoing emergence of spirit from nature? Could God's love, for whom time does not exist, have arranged it so from the beginning?

There are many traditional proverbs that address the problem of evil with a quick turn of phrase. I have several of them here: "God never closes a door that He does not open a window. God sends us tests as stepping stones to faith and greatness. God never sends us a cross too heavy to carry. God's ways are not our ways. The devil had his time and God will have His. We must think of the good things that God also gives us. It was his time to go. God wanted to save her from more evil later in life. God never puts more on you than He puts in you. This is God's will, etc." None of these proverbs answers adequately the problem of evil though I often turn to them for something to say in awkward moments. Mostly, these are just attempts to make excuses for God.

The apparent paradox of how evil can exist if God is all-powerful is what provoked Stendhal, the novelist, to say, "God's only excuse is that he does not exist." Or as our fatalistic friend once claimed: What has been the greatest objection to existence so far? *God.* "What is the meaning of it, Watson?" said Holmes, solemnly, as he laid down the paper. "What object is served by this circle of misery and violence and fears? It must tend to some end, or else our universe is ruled by chance, which is unthinkable. But what end? There is the great standing perennial problem to which **human reason** is as far from an answer as ever."

I have just given many explanations (answers) to the mystery of evil: from two opposing gods (war), the Greeks (fate), the Hebrews (God), Jesus (unknown), sages (good from evil), and Orientals (escape). Even error serves humanity for a time. I find Spinoza closest to my solution to the problem of evil in that evil comes from not following Right Reason and the law of Nature. Unlike Spinoza, though, I believe that God is very much involved in our lives—by persuasion.

My priest friend Fr. Ray gives me a word of caution: "Your answer to evil is your answer, your determination… that which defines you. You may teach this to college students, helping them to think, but I do not think you would say this as you are standing silently with the woman who has lost her child." I respond, "The truth (with love) will set you free." And surely I would not want the woman to leave thinking that God made the decision to take her baby, when it was indifferent nature which did it.

So far, I have led or flogged you, dear reader, through a forest of opinions. We are coming out of the woods, now, upon a beautiful, still

Old Solutions to the Problem of Evil

lake in which I can now see the reflection of my life's experiences mirrored back to me. Is it a mist, a fog, or a haze that arises from this stillness? Through this haze, the Spirit reveals the mystery of evil. At this very moment when I am rejoicing in this discovery, a crowd of questions overwhelms me. Maybe more questions than my simple solution to the problem of evil can ever answer.

METHODOLOGY

My explanation for the problem of evil is philosophical in that I have built an idea on common experience. This finds an echo in the famous dictum of the holy philosopher and theologian, although somewhat anti-intellectual, Augustine, "Do not wander far and wide but return into yourself. Deep within man there dwells the truth." This is my mirror lake. I do not use theologies because not much revelation is available to explain adequately the problem or mystery of evil.

My approach cannot be scientific because doing the necessary scientific experiments are impossible—one cannot simply control all of life's variables. A single subject (myself), multi-manipulated, is about as close as I can come to a scientific experiment. This process of learning is common in all my life experiences. Like all ideas, I must test insights in the laboratory of life where I attempt to isolate the causes of evil by discovering those things that impair my good living. I wish to digest my experiences, including my misdeeds, as much as I digest my meals, even when I have to swallow some tough morsels.

I use the inductive method first made popular in England by Francis Bacon in his **The Advancement of Learning** (1605). In inductive arguments, the premise may be true but the conclusion false. Aristotle's deductive reasoning claims that if the premise is true, then its conclusion must be true. I begin with experiences and end with an explanation. I *mirror* (reflect) my and others' *lake* (reservoir) of experiences. I am looking not just at *evil*, but also at life overall. Evil is found only where people or the devil is. Experiences in themselves can be misleading, therefore I need many of them—and they need to be analyzed in life. This is why my book encompasses all of life's experiences. I believe or feel that this is necessary to understand the mystery of evil.

Allow me to attempt to prove in this book a hypothesis derived from the empirical data of life. Throughout my life, I have re-examined this data to see if my hypothesis is valid, or to detect the ways in which I may need to modify it. If I deem modification necessary, I go back to the empirical data of life's experience. A continual oscillation between my hypothesis and the data of life will prove mutually enlightening.

Evil in Mirror Lake

"Pure logical thinking cannot yield us any knowledge of the empirical world; all knowledge of reality starts from experience and ends in it. Propositions arrived at by purely logical means are completely empty regarding reality. Because Galileo saw this, and in particular because he drummed it into the scientific world, he is the father of modern physics—indeed, of modern science altogether," Albert Einstein said of Galileo Galilei.

I will suggest a new paradigm to the reader—a window through which to view God and Evil. The process of passing from one paradigm to another is not always rational discourse, but sometimes a gestalt switch—like the rabbit-duck or witch-old lady picture in which I can see it either as a duck, or as a rabbit, a witch or an old lady, but not as both at the same time. Some plaques contain the name of Jesus which can and cannot be seen. Examples of extraordinary paradigms include Newton's **Principia** and Darwin's **Origin of the Species**, Galileo's **Dialogue**, and Einstein's **Relativity**.

In my case it worked like this: The old paradigm (God in total control) no longer worked for me because I saw the anomalies (a child dying of AIDS) that did not fit. This caused a theological revolution (God as not all-powerful) which led to a new paradigm (my solution).

This has been found true in the scientific world as well according to T. S. (Thomas Samuel) Kuhn's **The Structure of Scientific Revolutions** (1962, revised 1970). Other people like Karl Popper thought that paradigms would change only for logical reasons—intuition or inner vision would not be the determining cause. I have found that life consists of more than logic and reason. Life also contains intuition.

> *Intuition is the voice of the nonphysical world. It is the communication system that releases the five-sensory personality from the limitations of its five-sensory system, that permits the multisensory personality to be multisensory. It is the connection between the personality and its higher self and its guides and Teachers.*

Writes Gary Zukav in **The Seat of the Soul**—a remarkable treatment of thought, evolution and reincarnation. It is more than New Age gobbledegook.

A government information official once said privately that the job of government agencies is to present information so a logical person will draw a wrong conclusion. Logic is only a tool, and a very helpful tool if it is not used as a replacement for experiences.

I owe my first understanding of logic to Euclid and his book, **The**

Old Solutions to the Problem of Evil

Elements (c. 280 B.C.E.). This book's reliance on pure abstract reason appealed to me—and left me, as a teenager, feeling satisfied with my own capacity for reason. Euclid, although he was teaching geometry, taught me how to build up an edifice of truth. The idea that I could deduce everything within a discipline from a few basic principles was intriguing to me and still is. In fact, Euclid wrote **The Elements** to prepare students for philosophical studies.

The shy twelve-year-old Einstein picked up a geometry textbook and read it cover to cover. He later called it a *holy booklet* which led him to believe he could "get certain knowledge... by means of pure thinking." For both Euclid and later Einstein who improved upon Euclid, science is more than just an assembly of accurate ideas and observable facts. It is a mixture of thoughtful experimentation, careful analysis, and reasoning rigorously exercised together. This type of thinking will be part of this book.

John Locke's assertion that "the natural liberty of man is to be free from any superior power on earth," might explain my insistence that "reality starts from experience," and "not intended to be under the will or legislative authority of man, but to have only the law of Nature for his rule." Yet, unlike Adam and Eve, I freely submit to the *Superior Power* in heaven. However, everything must jibe with my experiences.

Not by piling book learning into my intellect, but by examining the experiences in my soul, shall I discover the meaning of evil. I must look to myself as the center of knowledge. I need to accept myself as becoming. I will look to my heart for intuitive leadership, and aspire to God as my rightful goal. My sign reads not as Dante's over hell, "Lasciate ogni speranza," or "Abandon all hope!" but rather, "Abandon all presuppositions, all ye who enter here!" My only presupposition is that God is both all-perfect and all-good. I cannot prove this presupposition, it must be a self-evident principle.

In logic I must go back to some presuppositions. These presuppositions must be self-evident, that a true God must be all-perfect—and if all-perfect, then also all-good. Having accepted this logic, it must then correspond with the teachings of life.

As James Joyce has Mr. Deasy say in his great but nearly unreadable book, **Ulysses**, "To learn one must be humble. But life is the great teacher." To understand Joyce, I had to first read an introductory book to tell myself how to read his books. Faulkner is the same way. It is like seeing **The Rocky Horror Picture Show**, a cult movie of the 1970s. It, too, makes no sense the first time you see it. Nevertheless, a few can see it a hundred times, and always get something new out of it. Some say **Ulysses** is like that. I struggled through this unique book

61

Evil in Mirror Lake

like a Lenten penance. Yet, was it worth it? As I said, "No," I found myself rereading the first section not once but twice more, and with an unabridged dictionary. It has artistry all of its own. I must read the book, so they tell me, on at least two levels. Ulysses is the Latin name for the Greek Odysseus. These two books are supposed to be parallel. I missed most of this. They both, however, were searching for the meaning of life.

Joyce named the hero, Stephen Dedalus, after the Greek hero, Daedalus, who built a labyrinth on the isle of Crete and then found himself unable to escape. He then built wings to fly to the mainland of Greece. Stephen was trying to escape his island of Roman Catholic Ireland and fly to the mainland of Europe. The Jesuits educated Joyce, Voltaire and René Descartes, to mention a few.

Later, Joyce also realizes that he himself must also flee from his own egotism. Eastern mysticism also enters the story, "When you hear the students yelling at their hockey game," Stephen says, "that is the voice of God." He is into pantheism. He rejects a personal God apart from created nature. He rejects a personal God who cares and has a purpose for me. All life is ever changing and simply going around in cycles. Our only hope is to enjoy the present moment.

Like all great works, it has a bit of truth in it. It recognizes people as free, but has no idea why. This introduces the philosophy of the absurd. No wonder the Catholic Church condemned this book— **Ulysses**!

My point is that we should learn from life. I have adopted a philosophical doctrine called pragmatism (from the Greek word *pragma* or *deed*), not pantheism. Its test of truth is in the result. Never mind what I say or think. The thing that counts is what I do and how it works out. Of course, I would not do some things; some principles I would not break. To do so would give pragmatism a bad reputation. What I am trying to do is to see if my hypothesis adequately explains the reality of evil. When I see proof of my hypothesis in an immediate result, what could be better? The achievement of my desired result, in the end, is what I want. My goal is, after all, to explain the origin of evil. This is the good pragmatism taught to us by the Greeks, based on a few sound principles.

Having begun a course of reading to satisfy his burning curiosity, David Hume discovered "little more than endless dispute." He decided to find a "medium by which truth might be established." He injected the strongest dose of common sense into philosophy that it had yet received. He developed the idea of empiricism (derived from the Greek word for experience). Unlike most of the Europeans who based most

62

Old Solutions to the Problem of Evil

of their thinking on theory, Anglo-Saxon philosophy resisted this. Empiricism denies that there are any innate ideas in the mind of people at birth. Real knowledge is acquired piecemeal. The process is gradual, frustrating, difficult, and always experimental. He proposed, with the scientific method in mind, to consult human nature itself, and not just theories or sheer fantasy. His masterpiece, his first book published, is **A Treatise of Human Nature** (1730-1749). I style myself as an empiricist with some few principles.

Sinclair Lewis displays the difference between people seeking the truth, as opposed to those seeking approval from others of what they already believe, in an insightful social commentary book, **Babbitt**. This satire of the upper middle class contains the memorable statement of Mr. Babbitt to his son, Ted, "I've never done a single thing I've wanted to in my whole life." Sinclair Lewis, in his surreal book exposes the hypocrisy of people not really interested in the truth—good or evil. He intertwines social life and the business world with truth. A cloud of sadness covers all these characters—Babbitt is without a real soul, he is a cardboard front. The joy of belonging to and contributing to the world (to love and to be loved) is absent from these people's lives. Also, their business lives are lacking social responsibility. Babbitt gleans his opinions from newspapers or from business peers, not from his experiences, which leaves him discontented.

I must hold most of my present truths tentatively—they must jibe with my experiences. Yet, if I have no absolutes, I have no basis for determining the truths of experience. The unexamined life is not what I can afford, unless I want to be like the shallow George Babbitt.

In pondering the problem of evil entering my life, I have looked at the many faces of evil. I have seen it as elusive, addictive, aggressive and everywhere. Both moral and physical evils exist. I have noticed that some people admit of no terrible things in their lives, and so they have no problem with evil. A few people made God out to be not-all-good. I contend that this would not be a perfect God.

Darla Kaye Loos counters me with, "You ask the readers to be open-minded. Will you not be the same? If you are an empiricist, as you claim, and truth is based in your experiences and the experiences of others, have you or they experienced the *only all-good God?* Our experiences suggest the opposite, yet you cling to this notion despite your life experiences! What is so terrifying in just contemplating the possibility that we are created more in God's image than the church is comfortable enough to consider? Perhaps God does change His mood and mind and emotions as we do. Perhaps He is both good and evil as we are. The first person who suggested the world was round was ridi-

63

Evil in Mirror Lake

culed for his suggestion." My answer to this is that it simply must be self-evident that God is all-perfect and so all-good.

Peering through the haze, near Mirror Lake, the words of Dr. Henry Faust come to me:

> *The Rainbow mirrors human aims and action,*
> *Think, and more clearly will thou grasp it, seeing*
> *Life is but light in many-hued reflection.*

(Faust L 4725)

To understand life in its many-hued aspects, we will travel around life's lake of knowledge stopping at nine viewpoints—all of which mirror human aims and actions. Let us then today circle this lake at the end of the rainbow. After all these centuries, I have found this knowledge not on a tree, but in a lake. I have tasted it and it is sweet, not bitter. All good journeys are refreshing, and I trust that this literary pilgrimage will be also. Bring on the problems of life, I now know how to handle them, and from where they come. Come, journey with me around Mirror Lake.

My solution to the mystery of evil may just save you from some perceived grief with God. The Buddha said, "This cannot be taught." By this he meant that for me truly to understand, I must experience his truths, not simply to believe them because the Buddha (Church) told me. This is what I will attempt to do as I plumb the depths of my experiences, as well as the experiences of many others, in the abysses of this mirror lake.

Come travel with me as the pilgrims did with Geoffrey Chaucer. We will travel to heaven, not down to Canterbury. We will stop at nine inns along the way as we circle Mirror Lake. Each stop will impart to us different facets of reality especially as it relates to the evil in our world. So come read my stories with an open mind.

A theologian's job is to write something with the least amount of error in it. It is the reader's job to point out any error remaining. Theologians are to revise, so that no error remains. Come help me! We have seen other peoples' explanations of God's role in evil. My methodology calls for me to first look into nature. Let us travel to the first scenic view or view point overlooking Mirror Lake. Oh! By the way, my name is Leo. *Leo* in Spanish means *I read*, in case you did not know.

Old Solutions to the Problem of Evil

A SHORT GUIDE TO COMPARATIVE RELIGIONS

Taoism	Evil Happens.
Confucianism	Confucius say, "Evil happens."
Buddhism	If evil happens, it really isn't evil.
Calvinism	Evil happens because you don't work hard enough.
7th Day Adventist	No evil on Saturdays.
Zen	What is the sound of evil?
Mormonism	This evil is going to happen again.
Islam	If evil happens, it is the will of Allah.
Moonies	Only happy evil really happens.
Stoicism	This evil is good for you.
Protestantism	Let the evil happen to someone else.
Catholicism	If evil happens, you deserve it.
Hare Krishna	Evil happens rama rama.
Zoroastrianism	Evil happens half of the time.
Christian Science	Evil is in your mind.
Judaism	Why does this evil always happen to US?
Existentialism	What is evil anyway?
Andrew Greeley	We deserve suffering but God suffers with us.

CHAPTER III

NATURE AND ITS LAWS

It was early in the morning. It was early spring. I was visiting my former missionary pastor, Padre Vincente, in southern Illinois. We noticed the tops of the gum trees swirling in circles. The clouds were whizzing overhead, and then we saw the black funnel cloud forming in the west. As we saw a house from the neighboring town twirling in the turbulent sky, we headed for the basement and I prayed. But for what? Was it God or nature or fate that sent this tornado? It would take at least one home from our town, surely, but which one? "Why should it be ours, Lord?" I prayed. "Let it touch down on another sacrificial lamb! Or better, let it hit the ball diamond where it will do little damage."

> *Do the skies themselves send down showers? No, it is you,*
> *O Lord , our God.*
> *Therefore our hope is in you, for you are the one who does all*
> *this. (Jeremiah 14:22)*

The laws of nature are often hidden to the casual observer. We are at the first stop on our scenic tour around Mirror Lake. The dogwood trees are in full white-pedaled array on this damp, spring morning. Mirror Lake, our place where our experience will be reflected to us, tells us that nature is an exacting science, and not subject to the whim of God. Science and religion are our friends, but nature is no saint and can be a formidable enemy. Nature, acting according to laws of her own, does at times cause physical evils.

"Yeah, tell me about it. I've experienced it!" I say to no one. Everything in nature has a cause and effect, and God is not an immediate cause although God did create all of nature (I Kings 18:41 and Job 5:10). Exceptions to this law of nature are miracles which I will discuss later. If God were constantly tinkering with nature, we could never understand it. Think of a scientist going to work wondering whether

Nature and Its Laws

today God would want H_2O or H_3O to make water, and I am not talking about the hydronium ion. Nature must be consistent if we are to apply our intelligence to understanding and predicting nature.

"God is the all-sufficient explanation, the eternal rapture glimpsed in every Alchemist's cry of Eureka," says Bernard Lonergan, the Catholic cardinal. He continues, "This is so much more mathematically satisfying than wallowing in the metaphysical speculation that we are just one of many universes." My theological question about nature is, "Is nature reasonable?"

"Nevertheless, why not a divine intervention for me in an emergency?" people plead. "What is God really trying to achieve with the human race? Why is nature so difficult and why does it cause physical evils? If God created nature and its laws, then why is God not responsible for these physical evils?" I ask. "Why do tornadoes always seem to enjoy playing with trailer courts?"

Homer, in an attempt to interpret nature, showed in the **Iliad** and **Odyssey** his belief that all nature was under the control of different gods. When the ships under Agamémnon would not leave for Troy due to the lack of wind (nature), he thought that the gods were unhappy. As a result, he sacrificed his daughter, Iphigenia, to appease the goddess, Artemis. That was not a good idea (bad decision)! Agamemnon's wife, Clytemnestra, never forgave him. After he returned victorious from the Trojan war, she threw a net over him while he was taking a bath and chopped off his head. He had a total misunderstanding of nature—and women!

I must ask: How can I write meaningfully about God in a scientific world? Ian Barbour in **Religion in an Age of Science** calls this a *theology of nature* and, more specifically, an attempt at what he calls a *reformulation* of Christian Theology in the light of contemporary scientific insights. For example, where did the ascended body of Jesus go? Remember he was no ghost. He had flesh and bones as you and I do. We do not even know which way is up.

The Greek essayist and charming biographer, Plutarch, a pleasant minor gossip, in his early 2nd century A.D. work entitled **De Superstitiones**, tells us that families would cut a child's throat as if it were a lamb or a young bird to placate the gods of nature. Meanwhile, the mother stood by, sometimes without a tear or a moan, as a priest placed the dead child on the outstretched arms of a statue of Ba'al. As the infant's body was rolling into a flaming pit—entering the company of the gods—flutes, tambourines, and lutes drowned out any of the parents' cries. Later, as at Carthage, the ashes and bones were collected in a small urn and placed with thousands of others in the sacrificial

Evil in Mirror Lake

precinct, or tophet, of the goddess, Tanit.

The Greek playwrights gave us the idea of *deus ex machina*, or *God from the machine*. As their play was going along and the plot was becoming so intricate that the hero could escape only with the intervention of a god, the god would then fly down onto the stage by means of cables connected to a harness strapped to the actor. This god would then straighten out the plot.

When all else fails in nature, we still have a great tendency to turn to God in hope of a divine intervention in our lives because of our prayers. The brothers Jakob and Wilhelm, in their collection of **Grimm's Fairy Tales**, relate many folk stories that usually contain a wicked stepmother. (I wonder why the father did not intervene. Then, I have never met a wicked stepmother.) Some magic potion or animal or a fairy godmother's wand or a princess' kiss usually thwarts evil, as in **Cinderella** and **Snow White**. This is a version of *deus ex machina* inherited by many of us through these German tales. W. H. Auden, in taking a strictly analytic view of these folk tales wrote, "Broadly speaking, the fairy tale is a dramatic projection in symbolic images of the psyche." No wonder people pray for divine intervention; we have been programed to it.

Isaac Newton, the wannabe farmer, demonstrated in his **Philosophiae Naturalis Principia Mathematica** (1687) the three laws of motion governing nature—an object will remain at rest unless moved by a force, an object's acceleration is equal to the net force on the object divided by its mass, and for every action there is an equal and opposite reaction.

Scientific law simply describes a set of observations, not necessarily cause and effect—if I do A, then B has always followed. Cause and effect cannot be demonstrated logically or mathematically, only experienced. Educated people, though, overreacted to this science which did not need a providential God and said, "Who now needs God except for creation?" Newton simply presented a stoutly scientific picture, elaborating on the discoveries of Galileo and Kepler. Mathematically calculating the laws of light, he designed and built the first reflecting telescope in 1668. Nonetheless, he made the deism of men like Voltaire almost inevitable. The poet Pope composed a famous ditty:

Nature and Nature's laws lay hid in Night;
God said, "Let Newton be!," and all was Light. . .

Spinoza said, "The more we understand individual objects, the more we understand God." This statement struck Goethe as one of the

Nature and Its Laws

most profound in all literature. (I feel that I know God better each time I watch a nature program on TV because afterwards I know more about an individual object of God's creation.) According to Spinoza, science and religion are not in conflict; they are one. I agree, both come from God.

I believe that we need an image of God that does not separate God from creation. God is in nature, and nature operates as an extension of God, although nature is not God. Nature is neutral. It is never evil in itself, just as God is never evil. Yet, evil (terrible things) can come from nature by people being in the wrong place at the wrong time.

Nature is not even cruel as Lt. Col. Gordon Tall says to Capt. James Staros in **The Thin Red Line**, a movie about World War II in the South Pacific (Guadalcanal). The book is by James Jones, and it is interesting that the movie changed the Jewish Capt. Stein to a Greek Capt. Staros. The question about the meaning of life is continually being asked by all thoughtful people in the movie. Is the meaning of life (and war) really only about property, as 1st Sgt. Ed Welsh continually asserts, as he does his duty? Are individuals totally irrelevant, as Sgt. Welsh tries to convince Pvt. Will? Is not nature, at times, cruel?

At times when nature impedes our happy living, nature can cause physical evils (terrible things) to happen to us. Sometimes we perceive that nature is cruel, but it is only neutral. Without people present, there is no cruelty. Our perception of nature depends on how close we focus. Reality lies beyond what you can see.

Friedrich Nietzsche in his hard to understand **Beyond Good and Evil** mocks the noble Stoics who wish to live *according to nature*. "Imagine a being like nature," he continues, "wasteful beyond measure, indifferent beyond measure, without purposes and consideration, without mercy and justice, fertile and desolate and uncertain at the same time; imagine indifference itself as a power—how *could* you live according to this indifference? Living—is that not precisely wanting to be other than this nature? Is not living—estimating, preferring, being unjust, being limited, wanting to be different? And supposing your imperative 'live according to nature' meant at bottom as much as 'live according to life'—how could you *not* do that? Why make a principle of what you yourselves are and must be?" (**On The Prejudices of Philosophers** Chapter I #9.)

Many thinkers in the 18th century such as Washington, Jefferson, Franklin, Paine, and Voltaire became deists realizing that God does not interfere with nature. Thomas Jefferson said, "I am a sect myself." Thomas Paine, author of **Common Sense** and **The Rights of Man**, claims "My mind is my church." Deists left God alone in heaven, not

Evil in Mirror Lake

realizing God's presence in our lives through the power of influence and relationship. Deism did not last long in competition with God as a loving Father who protects us all. Even by the time of Jefferson's death, the Christian religion overtook the cold detached Deism. Yet, many of our most influential figures in American culture did not find a religion to call their own, though the religious teachings of several traditions attracted them. I think of Ralph Waldo Emerson, his friend and one-time houseguest, Henry David Thoreau, and the manly poet Walt Whitman.

Bram Stoker, in his late nineteenth century bloodsucking novel **Dracula**, has vampires and not just God in charge of nature. In one long sentence he says, "Vampires within limitations, appear at will when, and where, and in any of the forms that are to him; he can, within his range, direct the elements: the storm, the fog, the thunder; he can command all the meager things: the rat, and the owl, and the bat—the moth, and the fox, and the wolf; he can at times vanish and come un-known." For some this vampire mythology is not limited to the realm of fiction.

When our parish picnic is coming up, I still sometimes pray that God will not let it rain. I should be praying that I will be prepared whether it rains or not. God does not interfere with nature. Nature operates strictly according to her own inherent laws. Tornadoes, floods, and earthquakes have nothing to do with God's decision—neither does raining nor running out of gas.

Consider what Will and Ariel Durant say, in their world-renowned **History of Civilization**, about this natural evil that happened in Voltaire's time:

> *All of Europe was shaken on November 1, 1755, at 9:45*
> *a.m., on All Saint's Day. While most of the population*
> *were worshiping in the churches, four convulsions of the*
> *earth laid half of Lisbon, Portugal, in ruins, killing over*
> *15,000 people, destroying most of the churches, sparing*
> *most of the brothels. Many inhabitants ran in terror to the*
> *shores of the Tagus River, but a tidal wave of 15 feet high*
> *drowned thousands more. The fires that broke out in every*
> *quarter of the city claimed additional lives. In the*
> *resultant chaos, the scum of the populace began to rob*
> *and kill with impunity.*

This became a great theological problem. Why should God allow such an evil to happen? And it led many into deism and some into

Nature and Its Laws

atheism. Now we know the answer. Earthquakes happen when the pressures on the continental plates, rubbing against each other inside the earth, becomes greater than their resistance. It is then that the plates slip by each other thus shaking everything. Some day we may understand the weather in the same way. At any rate, it is not God who determines when earthquakes or rains are going to happen; it is nature. Remember when nature is violent and even seems destructive, nature is always creating something new and good.

People, who work to unite us with God, like rabbis, priests, ministers, shamans and imams, like to give God credit for as much good as possible. Nevertheless, this can lead to problems. In the book, **The Thorn Birds** by Colleen McCullough, lightning started a fire in the dry shrubs of a hot Australian outback. It went on to burn most of the buildings on the Drogheda Ranch. Just as the beautiful home place was about to burn, it began to rain.

Later, Meggie is angry with God for having done this. The fire also consumed her father, Paddy, and her favorite brother, Stew. She is venting this anger on her friend, a priest, who has come to console her. Father Ralph feels that he must say something in defense of God, and so he calls to her attention that God did send the rain to save her beautiful home. Meggie listens and retorts, "If God sent the rain, then who sent the lightning?" The scene, in the TV version of *The Thornbirds*, as well as the book, fades away with no answer given.

My answer to Meggie is that God sent neither the rain nor the lightning; both happened according to the laws of nature. Who wrote the laws of nature? No one, they just are. God created nature, but the laws of nature come from nature—both of lightning and of rain. Neither are arbitrary.

Who created God? No one, God just is. Nature comes from God. Both just are. The relative question is, "What do we do now?" Nature caused the lightning because the earth on that dry, hot, windy day had built up too many electrons. The earth's surface then released these electrons, and this brought the lightning that produced heat, and so fire. The rain came because it was nature's need to rain.

Another example of how we tend not to be evenhanded with God is how we interpret good and evil in our lives. As a prison chaplain, I had an inmate tell me his story of how he was shot six times in the chest, left to die in the street, and then was lost in a hospital waiting room. Despite all these misfortunes, he lived. Now he is grateful to the point that he wishes to do well and so to thank God for saving his life. I found it very difficult to tell him that God did not guide those bullets that missed all of his vital organs; he was simply fortunate. Being a man

Evil in Mirror Lake

of God, I like to give God credit for as much good as I can. This good, however, did not come from God unless, of course, God worked a first class miracle and redirected those bullets. Yet, God can use this situation to call forth goodness from the individual involved, which is exactly what happened here. What other people do to me, I do not regard as necessarily God's will for me. I think of bad situations simply as the arrival of circumstances to which I have choices only about how I choose to respond. How I choose to respond should be God's will for me. I hope I can find it in my heart to act accordingly. I need to take the lemons of life, sweetened by God's love for us, and turn them into lemonade.

To be consistent, what do I say to a mother whose teenager ran into their house in St. Louis to escape the *drive-by* shots fired by a rival gang member? A 45-caliber slug flew through their picture window and splattered her baby's head as it slept in its crib. Where was God to direct that bullet? I say that God does not direct any bullets. Nature acts according to its laws of ballistics and the person who is aiming the pistol. This evil event—a terrible thing—did not come from God. "But I canna change the laws of physics, Captain!" (Scotty to Captain Kirk, innumerable times in **Star Trek.**)

The perennial argument says: "If God created nature and nature causes evil, then God created evil and is not good." In Mary Shelley's gothic, science-fiction novel, **Frankenstein**, was not Victor Franken-stein responsible for the actions of his creation? Was not the creation turned into The Monster by the rejections he received by everyone, including his maker? Was I not taught that I can delegate authority but not responsibility? Is God not yet responsible for the acts of nature? Are parents not responsible for their children?

I say, yes, God did create nature, but nature does not directly cause evil, though physical evil can come from nature. Nature causes physical effects that are neither good nor evil in themselves. They just are. In the animal kingdom there is neither good nor evil, just efficient hunters. The excess of one species is food for another species. One life disappears inside another.

For example, a volcano can cause either physical good or physical evil. The volcano relieves the pressure in the core of the earth. That is good. If the volcano goes off in the bottom of the Pacific Ocean, that is good. If it creates the Hawaiian Islands, it is very good. If people choose to live near the volcano, and it goes off destroying their village, this is a physical evil caused by people unknowingly choosing to be at the wrong place at the wrong time. God does not cause this nor does nature. This is true despite Martin Luther's prayer in Litany 1528, "Take

Nature and Its Laws

under your care our dams, dikes, and locks, and in your grace hear us, dear Lord God." Nature, like feelings, just is. Nevertheless, some effects of nature can be physical evils, just as some effects of feelings can become moral evils. Nature, however, is different from people because people have free will.

But what is nature? What are its laws? I am still not quite sure. It is, in part, our calling in life to probe the depths of nature. Thales, the first Greek philosopher, began with observing the many and the one. He concluded, "Everything is one." The more we know about nature, the easier it will be to avoid those physical evils—the unanticipated results of our decisions.

When Albert Einstein looked at the universe, he said that God did not throw dice. He meant that everything had a cause and effect, like car accidents. If someone stops suddenly in front of me and I hit that car in the rear, it is because I made a bad decision to drive too fast or too close to him. When his colleagues challenged him, Einstein responded that he believed in Spinoza's nature-driven God—all three being Jewish: Einstein, Spinoza and God.

For thirty years, Einstein argued against Niels Bohr and his Copenhagen Interpretation (CI) about quantum mechanics, which is small scale physics concerning the atom's inner structure. It is based on a different mathematical model. The subatomic world of quantum physics appears to be a crazy Alice-in-Wonderland world. Einstein could never come to terms with the Uncertainty Principle formulated in 1927 by Werner Heisenberg to help explain the quantum physics world. Whenever we observe something, in that very observation, we change it. Heisenberg felt that physics henceforth should confine itself to "a formal description of relation between perceptions" and abandon the search for the truth underlying the perceptions. The Uncertainty Principle gave free will to the particles involved, and Einstein could never reconcile himself with the notion that it was now necessary to give up a deterministic view of nature. In the end Einstein admitted he was wrong. Newtonan and Relativistic, or large scale physics, with its cause and effect, simply do not explain the small scale physics of the atom.

This is why Niels Bohr responded by saying that God did play with dice when it comes to small scale physics. We cannot simply explain this physics by our understanding of cause and effect. "What else is there?" we ask. Some people answer by attributing free will to certain physical particles. I oppose this solution on theological grounds, but this is not a very good reason. Another possibility is the parallel universe theory or the string theory that involves ten or more dimensions in our universe. I only know that nature causes, and God knows

Evil in Mirror Lake

everything.

Maybe Ian Stewart said it best when he countered with "God does indeed throw dice, and he throws them where we cannot see them." I add, "…at least for now." We know that the laws of cause and effect are even in the roll of the dice. Just try playing with loaded dice! Unless I bounce them off a wall, I cannot not make the winning pair roll out.

The big scientific quest now is to find the Grand Unifying Theory (GUT) or the Theory of Everything (TOE) which would discover the laws that govern everything. So much is in the world that I do not fully understand. Why does cause and effect explain large scale physics and not small scale physics?

So far, no one in the scientific world has had the insight into a coherent model that would integrate both the large and small scale physics of nature. This insight will come someday to someone as a finished perception. That is what such highly productive persons as Goethe and Helmholtz tell us, "that the most essential and original parts in their creations came to them in the form of inspirations, and reached their perceptions almost finished." This leads some people yet today to believe in Plato's self existing Ideas.

Most scientists are deists—like Einstein and Hawkins. They hold to an uncreated Creator, but fall short of a personal Being who cares about us, numbering the hairs on our head and calling each of us by name. They believe, as I do, that God does not determine nature, but they do not understand, as I do, how God works in the world through influence. We need to look to revelation for this insight.

We have explored the relationship between God and nature. We have seen that nature has its own set of laws, even when we do not fully understand them. To attribute the working of nature to God, as the ancients did, is still a tendency today. This leaves God to blame for acts of nature that at times can cause physical evil. Marcel Proust (1871-1922), a French author, remarked that "the highest praise to God is the unbelief of a scholar who is sure that perfection of the world makes the existence of gods unnecessary." In other words, even though God created and sustains nature, God is not needed to determine how nature will work. We have seen in our metaphorical lake of knowledge that it is up to us to understand nature. It is up to us to understand and use nature more as our benefactor thus avoiding many physical evils.

A deeper understanding of nature may help here. A trinitarian God created nature. All nature, including people, are created like God is. Once I understand the nature of God as relational (each divine person in God is a subsisting relationship), then this suggests that the fundamental nature of all reality be relational. It is communion that causes

Nature and Its Laws

things to be. Nothing exists without it—not even the inner life of God. Reality springs from Persons-in-Relation. *God* has no ontological content without communion. Nothing is conceivable as existing only by itself. True being cannot exist without communion. See John Zizioulas' book, **The Doctrine of the Holy Trinity: The Significance of the Cappadocian Contribution.** Denis Edwards in **The God of Evolution** sums this up:

> *The God of trinitarian theology is a God of mutual and equal relation. When such a God creates a universe it is not surprising that it turns out to be a radically relational and interdependent one. When life unfolds through the process of evolution, it emerges in patterns of interconnectedness and interdependence that "fits" with the way God is.*

As civilization has advanced we have long striven and gradually improved our ability to manage nature. History reveals an increasing and astonishing display of human power to overcome obstacle and bring about conscious change. This is not to say that all the resultant changes have been wise or desirable. "From its tiny beginnings in repeated struggles to master nature, for instance, by shaping a stone or an antler into a tool, or by striving to light or merely keep alive a fire, human history is a story of change brought about by human manipulation of the natural world," says the noted historian, J. M. Roberts, editor of **Prehistory and the First Civilizations** (1999). In 1968 we even shut down the American side of Niagra Falls for a year.

There are no exceptions to the laws of nature except:

MIRACLES

Miraculous cures are for the sake of the bystanders—not primarily for the benefit of the person healed, I say. To deny that God works miracles—exceptions to the laws of nature—as do the deists, atheists, agnostics, pantheists, and rationalists, is unacceptable to me. This would forsake part of our human experience. At times miracles have changed nature. It is interesting, though, that the New Testament never uses the Greek word *thauma* or *miracle*. Instead, it uses the word for *sign* to describe Jesus' healing and other proofs of power.

I divide miracles into three classes. The third class of miracles encompasses what we call amazing coincidences. The doctor gives a child

Evil in Mirror Lake

a shot of penicillin while I have gone to the chapel to pray, and the child gets better. I am out in the desert starving, and quail fly over the Red (Reed) Sea and land, exhausted, on the shore at my feet. These are miracles of amazing coincidences from the two words *co* and *inside*—two things fit together—managing *co-incidences*. These can be life-altering experiences.

In the second class of miracles are acts of nature that are difficult to understand. Augustine of Hippo said that the birth of a baby is a miracle. Gravity is a mystery as it forces the swirling clouds of sub-nuclear gases to form huge clumps of elementary matter in space. In Barbree and Caiden's **A Journey Through Time**, they say, "No one has any idea of how gravity became, nor do we know today what gravity is. We measure its effect, we rely upon gravity as the engine that drives the universe, we know what it does, but we have not the faintest idea of what it is or why it works the way it does."

Light itself is a mystery, it may have no mass. Since light, or photons, change back and forth from quanta (particle) to wave (pure energy), nobody knows whether it has any mass at all. It travels at its only speed, which is 186,273 miles per second—the speed of light. Electricity is another such miracle and mystery. "These miracles arise from our ignorance of nature, not from the essence of nature," says Michel de Montaigne, a 16th century essayist.

A first class type of miracle is one where God changes the laws of nature in a particular instance. The Gospels report thirty-five miracles directly and allude to twelve others. Let us take the cases of Jesus curing the man born blind and his raising Lazarus from the dead.

The man born blind is presented as a court case (John 9:1-38). His parents testify, "Yes, this is our son," and "Yes, he has been blind from birth." The man himself testifies and gets thrown out of the synagogue. Jesus cured the blind man for the sake of the Pharisees. "How could a man do a miracle like this if he were not from God?" asked the once blind man. Remember, many more people were blind, crippled, and dying that Jesus did not cure. He did not clear out the hospitals.

Even if faith were a prerequisite, would it be fair to say that these other people did not have this faith, even after they had witnessed such a miracle? Also, Jesus did not cure this man simply because of his faith or that he had the disability or evil of blindness. Remember that our definition of an evil is anything that seriously disrupts our good living. Jesus never worked a first class type of miracle on his own behalf, nor simply to help a friend in need, but only **for the sake of the bystanders**. The bystanders here were mainly the Pharisees, whom Jesus had hoped to convert.

76

Nature and Its Laws

Take the example of Lazarus, Jesus' friend (John 11:1-45). Word comes to Jesus from Mary and Martha for him to hurry. Jesus tarries for two days, and then decides to go when it seems too late. When he calls Lazarus from the grave, scripture tells us that many Jews were there from Jerusalem, and upon seeing this they believed in Jesus. Jesus did not work the miracle for the sake of his friend Lazarus, but for the sake of the by-standing Jews who then believed. The same is true for today.

Look through your gospels and you will not find a single miracle that did not include the bystanders. Even the miracle of the *Woman with an Issue of Blood* did not end up being a private miracle. Jesus saw to that (Matt 9:20-22; Mark 5:25-34; Luke 8:43-48). "The woman must not be allowed to obtain healing by stealth, so she was brought to an open confession and was cheered by Christ's commendatory word," says Herbert Lockyer in his **All the Miracles of the Bible**. This miracle could have remained private, but Jesus made sure that it was also for the bystanders.

Most people still feel that they want a divine intervention for themselves when they need it to avert some physical evil. Dostoyevsky says of people in **The Brothers Karamazov**, "When man rejects a miracle, he rejects God too: For man seeks not so much God as the miraculous." And he says of Jesus, "Thou wouldst not enslave man by a miracle, and didst crave faith given freely, not based on miracle." Goethe says in Faust, "The miracle is Faith's most cherished child." (L 1766) But, this is not God's chosen way to react to nature and its laws.

Let us now move around Mirror Lake to the next view point where we can examine the role that thinking, free-willed and emotional people play in moral evils.

CHAPTER IV

THINKING, FREE-WILLED AND EMOTIONAL PEOPLE

"What other people do to us, is not always God's will for us.
What we think we should do in return,
Should always be God's will for us."

Leo J. Hayes

"If you want to WIN in life,
Always do What's Important Now."

Lou Holtz

"Take under your care our dams, dikes, and locks,
And in your grace hear us, dear Lord God."

Martin Luther

"Thinking should always precede doing," I say as I stand along the grassy bank and peer down into the clear blue water of the mirrored lake. The morning dampness still hovers in the air. How is it that I at times make evil decisions? As I look deep into the lake of my experiences, I search the depths of my soul. I will move from knowledge to judgment to reason—the right way of knowing things, or science.

Next, I will delve into free will that is the source of our bad and good decisions—the right way of deciding what to do, or prudence. Finally, I will try to tie this together by examining the role our emotions play, along with our intellect and our free will in achieving the right way of living, or wisdom.

The importance of wholeness was first insisted upon by Hippocrates (c. 400 B.C.E.). In Plato's *Phaedrus*, Hippocrates asserts that we can understand nothing about parts of the body unless we understand the body as a whole. In the Oath named for him, physicians promise, among other things: to devote themselves to their patients (not to their

Thinking, Free-Willed, and Emotional People

HMOs), not to enter into sexual relations with them, never to give a poisonous drug, never to help to cause an abortion, and always to maintain confidentiality. So much for the good old days and the Oath.

THINKING

In explaining this decision-making process, I reflect about how at times in the past I have made decisions that I was sure were correct, only to find out later that I was wrong. How does that happen? This decision-making process, or thinking, is how I go about making my choices. Both the right way of knowing things and the right way of doing things need examination.

First, in knowing things, my five senses bring electrical sensations to my brain/intellect which I use to interpret reality. My senses themselves color what I perceive, or with color blindness, discolor what I see. This input from my senses then becomes a thing for my mind to abstract. The process is simple apprehension or knowledge. I know the concrete objective thing that I perceive as *res reales*, or the real thing. I know the mental subjective image of the thing, as I perceive it to be, as *res rationis,* or the thing of the mind. These two realities are not always the same, but their identity is the goal of thinking.

The importance of this most basic distinction, between reality in the mind and reality in the physical world, is the question of observation. Can something exist if I cannot see it? "From this question has sprung the most enduring thought question to have probed the dark realms of quantum weirdness," says Timothy Ferris in **The Whole Shebang**.

Scientists know this test as *Schrödinger's Cat*. They put a live cat inside a box with a device that has a 50/50 chance of killing the cat in one hour. After this hour and before I open the box, the Copenhagen school of thought says that the "cat is neither dead nor alive but exists in a superposed state of dead/alive." In fact, I say, the *res realis*, or real thing has already been determined. Nevertheless, I just do not yet know it, or *res rationes*—the thing of the mind. Making a distinction can solve most questions. Epictetus said, "Your problems are not bothering you. It is the way you are looking at them." Nevertheless, the problems are real!

One book on this topic of mind/body relationship is a popular paperback by David Burns called, **Feeling Good: The New Mood Therapy**. He lists ten deformative ways in which "we use illogical pessimistic attitudes of mind to destroy our self-image, weaken our

Evil in Mirror Lake

bodies, paralyze our wills, and generally defeat our hearts from attaining their goals and from reaching out to new aspirations." On the other hand, a great insight of our generation is that our mind is in control of how we feel, generally. Most people are about as happy as they want to be.

We must not reduce all knowledge to sensations, as John Locke, the British empiricist, did in his **An Essay Concerning Human Understanding** (1690). He makes all ideas **only** the effects of external objects—electrical sensations—and that inevitably leads to materialism and atheism—there is no need for the spiritual. Instead, we must hold on to the spiritual reality of ideas and consciousness, and not see them only as a part of matter. I can think both abstractly and concretely.

I agree with the poet Samuel Taylor Coleridge, who says that all thoughts give us merely the raw materials that the self—the remembering, comparing, continuing personality—molds into creative imagination, purposeful thought, and conscious action. I record all my experiences, consciously or not, in my memory. This then becomes the storehouse from which my mind, conscious or not, draws up material for the interpretation of present experiences and for the illumination of present choices. Coleridge intimated that there is something inherently mean about *matter*. It is the spirit that counts. It is probably impossible to perceive a real thing—all perceptions are interpretations by my mind, which applies my beliefs to the stimuli.

John Locke, known for his common sense, taught us, "The actions of men are the best interpreters of their thoughts." As I think, so I will be. The ancestor of every action is a thought. What I think about, I become. Wayne Dyer puts the sequence this way in his video, **How to Get What You Really, Really, Really, Really Want**: I **wish** and then I **ask** which leads to **intending** and lastly with **passion**. He also describes how my negative thinking can similarly get me exactly what I do not want. Do not think about being overweight, think about being healthy. I become what I think about—I must put my energy into what I want, not into what I do not want.

To draw memories out of this storehouse in my passive intellect or subconscious, I need an image of it currently stored in my imagination. My imagination is dependant upon physical brain cells that deteriorate, and so I forget. Sometimes I do something quite similarly to what I have done before and have since forgotten. With the coming of this new but similar experience and the new image I have of it, this new image vaguely recalls the old experience. So, we have the feeling of having been through this before—déjà vu. No one needs to invoke a previous life to explain this common feeling of experiencing *having*

Thinking, Free-Willed, and Emotional People

been through this before.

"Experience is the oracle of truth; and where its responses are unequivocal, they ought to be conclusive and sacred," said James Madison in **The Federalist** #20. This is true even if the experience is negative. For an extreme example, if a child gets slapped regularly for crying because he is hungry, the child will eventually learn what will follow if he cries again, or maybe even if he gets hungry again.

Or, on the other hand, as William James, the psychologist and philosopher, told us in his minor masterpiece **The Principles of Psychology** (1890): "The greatest discoveries in our generation are that human beings, by changing the inner attitudes of their minds, can change all the other aspects of their lives." Whatever the experience that had produced this inner attitude, it was not conclusive. Any attitude can be changed. James pioneered both introspectionism and the basic elements of behaviorism. For him introspection could know consciousness. In **Principles** he pioneered the notion of the *stream-of-consciousness*.

Revolting against the American philosophy that had become almost entirely divorced from practical experience, James wished to make a definition of truth that would be above all *useful*. His pragmatism amounted to this: "The ultimate test, for us, of what a truth means is the conduct it dictates or inspires." We see everything in terms of the consequences that will flow from it. I must ask myself: "How will this or that of my beliefs or conviction *function* in the real world?" James denied that absolute truth was knowable. At the same time, he also argued just as vehemently against skepticism. He would have been against the modern nihilists. His famous saying is, "truth is in its results." He apparently did not mean to, but some have taken his philosophy to justify using any means to a desired end. Truth and good for him are interchangeable. Pragmatism amounts to this: "The ultimate test for us of what a truth means is the conduct it dictates or inspires."

Henry James, William's younger brother and novelist, tells us in **The Portrait of a Lady**, "The reason (for my previous marriage proposal) that I wouldn't tell you—I'll tell you after all. It's that I can't escape my fate." This theme of fate runs through most of the old but great literature. To take it literally would be to nullify any decision-making process. Besides free will, the intellect/brain also performs mechanical/physical duties—optics, motor skills, nerve-ending interpretations.

"To form a correct idea of the operations whose result is thought," Pierre Cabanis says, "it is necessary to regard the brain as a special organ whose particular function is to produce thought, just as the stomach and the intestines have the special function of carrying on the work

81

Evil in Mirror Lake

of digestion, the liver that of filtering bile, etc." In this sense, Cabanis, a little known physician/philosopher, agreed with Kant that the mind is not a helpless *tabla rasa,* or blank slate, upon which we impress our sensations. It is an organ for transforming sensations into perceptions, thoughts, actions, and feelings. The brain is not an instrument of fate. The brain is the final frontier. Cabanis' book is **The Relations of the Physical and Ethical in Man** (1802).

Though the outside world sticks the intellect/brain with beliefs about itself, the intellect can change those beliefs if they do not work well. Just as I made up these beliefs, so I can make them over—into something that better fits the reality of the outer world. This is the first part of the process of thinking—to make the realities of my mind correspond with the reality out there.

I do not agree with George Berkeley's excessive idealism concerning ideas and things that he says exist **only** in the mind—sometimes called *immaterialism.* He was in revolt against John Locke's excessive material vision of the universe as a great machine—with engines and pulleys and strings. Locke called this the *visible beauty of creation.* Berkeley called this *false imaginary glare* in, **The Principles of Human Knowledge** (1710, revised 1734). Berkeley was wrestling with the problem that things might really be utterly different from how we perceived them. His solution was to deny their existence. He concluded that matter *could not exist. We could only perceive it.* For him reality is the existence of an infinite and eternal God communicating with finite beings by means of ideas. Ronald Knox, a Roman Catholic theologian and Bible translator, wrote a famous limerick about Berkeley's immaterialism:

> *There was a young man who said, "God*
> *Must think it exceedingly odd*
> *If he finds that this tree*
> *Continues to be*
> *When there's no one about in the Quad."*

This was witty but missed Berkeley's point. The answer is in the riposte:

> *Dear Sir:*
> *Your astonishment's odd:*
> *I'm always about in the Quad,*
> *And that's why the tree*
> *Will continue to be,*

Thinking, Free-Willed, and Emotional People

Since observed by
Yours faithfully,
God.

Things **only** exist in someone's mind, he insisted. Take out the word *only*, and he had it correct.

Kant's great contribution to thinking is his **Critique of Pure Reason** (1781, revised in 1787). Before Kant, most philosophers like Locke, Berkeley, and Hume assumed that all our knowledge of the world must conform to the object in it. Kant says that things-in-themselves are quite simply not knowable. He wrote, with my annotations in [brackets]:

> *All our intuition [knowledge] is nothing but the representation of appearance [accidents]... the things we intuit [know] are not in themselves what we intuit [know] them as being [substances]... As appearances [accidents] they cannot exist in themselves [real things], but only in us [mental things]. What objects may be in themselves [real things]... remains completely unknown to us [mental things].*

Kant called the unknown thing-in-itself a *transcendental object*. Unlike Berkeley's *immaterialism*, experience convinced Kant that matter does exist. Our mind just cannot get beyond the appearances that feed our senses. This was his contribution to epistemology—the study of knowledge.

Kant is basically correct; we can know only the appearances of reality. The substance evades our direct detection. I can see the appearances of trees. Their substance (treeness) is but a mental image, usually agreed upon by most people. Nevertheless, the substance is real. It is the underlying reality that hold the appearances together into a oneness. When enough appearances change, the substance will also change—burning trees turn into smoke and ashes—different substances.

Substance and accidents (appearances), of course, come from Aristotle in his attempt to explain change. His remarkable gift was for defining terms, making distinctions, and categorizing thoughts. Thomas Aquinas used his distinction of substance and accidents to explain the transubstantiation of the substance of bread and wine into the substance of the body and blood of Christ the Risen Lord. Jesus is not a cramped-up prisoner in the tabernacle. I do not break his bones if I chew the host. What the substance of anything is, I cannot know, but I

83

Evil in Mirror Lake

can accept it on faith—accepting an agreed upon common mental image. *We can never know substance directly, yet it is real.* I can encounter only the accidents of a thing.

Kant's other great contribution was in the field of ethics. He gave us the *categorical imperative.* His ethics are based on the idea of duty. A common form of this categorical imperative is this: we must judge every action in the light of how it would appear if it were to be a universal law of behavior. This reminds me of George Marshall the great Secretary of State under both Roosevelt and Truman. He informed his staff not to do anything that they did not want to appear in tomorrow's headlines.

Good thing the people who hid the Jews in Germany did not follow that advice. Sometimes the right thing to do is not something that conforms to society's law of behavior.

As a disciple of his beloved Kant and a contemporary of his detested Hegel, Arthur Schopenhauer pried his way into Kant's difference between the knowable world of phenomena and the unknowable one (the thing-in-itself). His path led through the will, but not in its ordinary sense. His way into the unknowable (substance) is no more nor less that through the living body. Thus, his major work is **The World as Will and Idea** (1819). *Idea* is sometimes translated as *Representation.* I experience my body as both phenomena and as a thing-in-itself—outwardly and inwardly. I, like others, can see myself eating a banana split, but only I can experience the act of eating it. In this way, by being my introspective self, I have a special knowledge of my *own willing*—into the thing-it-self. My experience of eating the banana split indicates its real existence. The body being the way into the otherwise unknowable, is Schopenhauer's great contribution.

Will, then, for Schopenhauer, is *will to live* and *motivation.* All motivation begins with the willing of a end result. Its end is in its beginning since all its urges are to relieve itself from suffering. His world, like the Buddhist and Hindu philosophy that influenced him, is blind and irrational. Schopenhauer, who loved his dogs more than the women who erotically attracted him, was very pessimistic. He was angry with his mother, it seems, from birth, and for the last fourteen years of his life he never saw her. He missed the meaning of life when he obstinately refused to ascribe more to love than lust. He almost seems to glory in his gloomy pessimism, ignoring the yearning in the will for the divine.

David Denby says it well, "Ideas, or the self, may be a myth, but it is one of those myths, like God and objectivity, without which we cannot live. We must act as if it existed. The striving for it ennobles us.

Thinking, Free-Willed, and Emotional People

The absence of it, as Saul Bellow has said, makes us easier to kill."

Samuel Johnson, author of one of the most influential books ever written—**A Dictionary of the English Language** (1755), easily refuted this idea of excessive idealism by famously kicking a stone that really hurt his toe in a way that ideas—such as evil—can never hurt. Yet, I agree with Viktor Frankl's **Logotherapy** that tells me that my feelings and actions depend on my attitudes—my vision of reality. Both my external and internal worlds are realities to me. Thinking attempts to bring these two realities together into an intelligible whole.

Speaking metaphysically, ugh, I ask the question, "Do I see anything out there that isn't a projection of my own mind?" Dow or Tao, of the Eastern philosophy, says truth waits for eyes unclouded by longing. Or, I only see the projection of my own desires—if I am hungry, I see only food; if I am amorous, only the appealing; if in love, only the loveable. What I see is what I am. Scholastic philosophy says that I receive everything according to the mode of myself the receiver. Some philosophers take this to its absurd conclusion. When it is too much for me to worry about the meaning **of** reality overall, and if I feel I cannot handle that big stuff, then I am at least always concerned about the meaning **in** life—what I do day-by-day, hour-by-hour, while I am doing whatever it is that I do. "What counts is not what I do," Robert Fulghum continues in, **It Was on Fire When I Lay Down on It**, "but how I think about myself while I'm doing it."

So the first step in good and true thinking is to test our senses by judging if they do reveal to our mind what really is in the outside world. We must simply apprehend reality as it is. However, our senses condition our knowledge and space. I have made a few mistakes in this regard: Sometimes, I still think the world is flat, until I sit on the seashore and watch an ocean liner coming in. I always see the stack first. Or, I see the departing ship coyly tucking the blanket of the sea over its head until the horizon is straight again.

One final problem with *simple apprehension* is that we communicate by means of language. The study of linguistics looks into how the mind (whatever that means) interacts with the brain (a physical organ). This interaction is what distinguishes me as a human, and is therefore crucial to my understanding. The truth usually lies in the middle. The middle lies somewhere between the *mentalistic* self-existing Ideas of Plato and the linguistic behaviorism expressed by B. F. Skinner in his **The Behavior of Organisms** (1938).

Noam Chomsky, in his **Syntactic Structures** (1957), made clear that nature endows people at birth with specific faculties that both enable them to act as free moral agents, as well as being affected by

Evil in Mirror Lake

stimuli. Besides being born with my mind or intelligence as a *tabla rasa*, a blank page, (this I hold, not Chomsky), I also have an innate creativity for language. The writer coming closest to explaining this linguistic theory is James Peck in his, **A Chomsky Reader** (1987). The crux of the matter is this: How do I learn language? In part, it comes from a rich innate biological endowment, and in part it comes from the proper stimuli. This is the first stage of thinking.

The second step in good and true thinking is making judgments. I can judge whether the desk I have just touched and looked at is wood or Formica. I can judge its value. I can judge whether I should sell it or burn it or keep it. Sherlock Holmes tells Dr. Watson in **A Scandal in Bohemia** that, "It is a capital mistake to theorize before one has data. Insensibly one begins to twist facts to suit theories, instead of theories to suit facts."

"The mind is an active participant in the conception of reality," Kant taught in his **Critiques**, "free will is an active element in the determination of actions; moral conscience is a basic ingredient in morality." These establish the philosophical basis of Christianity as an effective moral code. We are responsible for choosing what we judge to be best.

What I judge as best for me is always at least the **apparent** best. If I make a mistaken judgment, my choice can actually turn out to be really an evil, that is, something undesirable. In judging something good or evil, two schools of thought persist. One is that I subjectively choose what I, and probably the current mores of my group, judge to be good. The other school calls for some metaphysical objective criteria by which to judge present actions. For example, how many wives may I have? Is *Greek love* okay? Can I drop atomic bombs? Smart bombs? Etc.

Third, we have the reasoning process. From the knowledge of two things we can come to the knowledge of a third truth previously unrealized. This is a dangerous process, for I can incorrectly use reason as a tool, and I can seem to prove most any conclusion I wish. Martin Luther called reason "the clever whore." Nevertheless, if used correctly, reason can gain me more truth, more insight into reality.

When Dante reached the Empyrean of Paradise, Sts. Peter, James and John quizzed him about the virtues of faith, hope and love. In **The Divine Comedy**, he answered to their approval by saying that his love was based on both reason and revelation.

"Two modes of knowledge lead to truth in all its fullness—Faith and Reason," says John Paul II in his (1998) encyclical **Fides et Ratio** (Faith and Reason). Also in this same document, the Pope says, "Intel-

Thinking, Free-Willed, and Emotional People

ligence is not confined to observable data alone. It can with genuine certitude attain to reality itself as knowable, though in consequence of sin that certitude is partially obscured and weakened."

For example, if I observe the intricate order in our universe, I can conclude that all intricate order comes from an intelligent being. This most intelligent being, or Supreme Being, I call God. We know this as the *argument from design*. It is not overpowering reasoning. Some people may still opt for chance, selective mutations, or pantheism as an alternate conclusion. On the other hand, there also is no overpowering reasoning to prove that a God does not exist. Our ability to reason will lead us, we hope, to the truth—reality (that which is).

God does not play with dice as Einstein said, nor does the Omnipotent throw them where we cannot see them. Or, as Emerson said, "God's dice are always loaded." Within nature, chance does not exist. All is cause and effect, although it may not always seem so. For example, in human reproduction the sperm may seem to fertilize the egg by chance. In reality, though, it is the strongest and quickest swimmer in the best position that first reaches and breaks into the egg.

Some things in life, like gravity or electromagnetism, are found in the quantum field of the non-spatial, non-temporal, non-local and invisible. Yet, we all believe in gravity and electromagnetism. We know these phenomenons by their effects. They call this empirical science. Yet, nobody knows how either gravity or electromagnetism works. Scientists can measure the effects of gravity and predict its future behavior, yet they have no idea *why* two objects attract each other. Likewise, we know God only from effects although we know little about the Almighty Force itself. In everyday life, we usually go from effect to cause. For example, I see a light bulb, and I trace its cause to electricity, a generator and coal.

As I sit in my beautiful 1899 home, I tell my friend this story, "Once upon a time, a delivery person left a stack of bricks, some mortar, some lumber, and some glass panes piled up on this spot. A tornado came and sucked up all these materials into the sky, mixed them up, and set this house down on its foundation as it is today." My friend finds the story unbelievable because tornadoes simply do not do such intricate work, only intelligent beings do. My friend is thinking from effect to cause.

John Polkinghorne, priest-scientist author of **Quarks, Chaos, & Christianity**, calls this argument about my home's construction the anthropic principle: a world can produce *consequences* comparable to people producing them. Our very finely tuned universe is such an example. Considering all of the variables that have to be just right, it

Evil in Mirror Lake

might be one in a trillion chances that a ball of energy would turn into a world containing human life. This is a reason for believing in a God whose will and purpose lie behind the universe. Behind all order there must be an intelligent being. "To the mind of a believer, it is the mind of the Creator that is being discerned in that way," says Polkinghorne.

This argument about order coming from an intelligent being is parallel to the one about my home being constructed by the tornado or construction workers. God's intelligence and will power lie behind nature. From before the Big Bang, God knew exactly how it would all evolve—at least until free willed people entered the picture. If our world had only one in a trillion chances of being within the few degrees of what is necessary to produce this environment, then there well may be a trillion other planets out there. We have already found almost a dozen so far (2000 A.D.). At least one such world evolved that hot matter into life, into thinking and willing life, in the image of the Creator.

Anselm, the Archbishop of Canterbury, made this argument, "We conceive of God as something that which nothing more perfect can be conceived." Therefore, he deduced that this perfect God must exist. Of all the beings (being is the lowest common denominator word we have in our language) that exist, one must be the uncreated Supreme Being or God. Although we can imagine that there is more than one uncreated being, more than one cannot be all-powerful. Nevertheless, this is precisely what some philosophies have done to express the source of good and evil—two gods at battle with each other. I cannot disprove this, but I think I have a better way of explaining good and evil using just one all-powerful God.

By just sitting under my favorite pecan tree by the Mississippi River and observing the intricate order of the world, I conclude that there must be an intelligent Being behind this complex order. Knowing that there must be a Supreme Being, I can move more comfortably into faith, which is taking someone's word for divine things.

For example, I could never know on my own, by reason, that the Supreme Being, or God, loves me. I must accept this on faith. Even if I believe only because, "God said it," I only know that God said it because someone told me that God said it. If I believe it is true because it is in the Bible, the Word of God, I only know it is the Word of God because some people have told me so. Is the Book of Esther, which never mentions the word *God*, supposed to be in the Bible? Who can authoritatively tell me? Before I answer that, I wish again to run through **knowledge, judgment and reason**—the process of thinking, as described by Thomas Aquinas.

The Bible says in the **Book of Wisdom** that the first step is to

Thinking, Free-Willed, and Emotional People

gather knowledge. All types of knowledge are important to making wise judgments. One piece of knowledge, known to all bankers, is the *Rule of 72*. Some brilliant mathematician figured out that if I receive compound interest on my deposit, and I leave all that interest with the bank to get interest on my interest, then I can figure out how many years it will take me to double my original investment. For example, if I am getting 6% compound interest, then 72 divided by 6 tells me that it will take 12 years for me to double my money. This is **knowledge**. Thinking people always begin with something they know or believe.

The next step is **judgment**. Say, in 1996, I have just inherited $30,000, and I need a new car. I look at a Lexus for $30,000, and I look at a Chrysler LeBaron for $15,000. I like both, and I figure that each car will last me twelve years. If I purchase the Lexus, at the end of twelve years I will have a twelve-year-old Lexus car. If I purchase the LeBaron and invest the other $15,000 at 6% compound interest, at the end of twelve years I will have a twelve-year-old LeBaron car and $30,000. Of course, there may be other factors such as status, resale value, a foreign manufacturer, a local dealer, not buying a BMW, that I may wish to consider as I choose. I may also wish to show a preferential option for the poor, etc., This is **judgment** based on reference to personal values, desire, expectations, as well as facts.

Finally, there is the third step of **reason**, that leads to wisdom. When I consider eternal values in my reasoning process, then I enter the realm of wisdom. What would God want me to do in each decision? With at least some of my inherited money, do I have in mind what the Catholic bishops call—a *preferential option for the poor*? Am I exercising this option by not buying a more expensive BMW? Or, by buying from a poorer dealer? What other options do I have? Could I buy a used car? Wisdom, the highest form of reasoning, is deciding with eternity and God taken into consideration. Wisdom is the art of living in rhythm with my soul, my body, and the Divine Other.

I want to point out that there is mystery-dimension beyond this problem-solving functional mode that I have just explained. When my mind reflects on experience in search of its mystery-dimension, I must be willing to step back and transcend my present moment and look for the God that dwells in the *cloud of unknowing*. "A god who is understood is no god," said a classical scholar. I believe that God loves me, but why does God not actually tell me, thus removing all doubt?

Besides problems to be solved, there are also mysteries to be lived. I must learn to integrate the intuitive heart and the thinking intellect. I need to honor and delight in the intellect without being trapped. The analytical mind is a beautiful servant and a lousy master. The best of

Evil in Mirror Lake

my intellect will not solve all of my problems. I must be careful not to worship knowledge. Wisdom has in it a very deep compassion without which life cannot be lived to its freest.

As Carolyn Gratton says in **The Art of Spiritual Guidance**:

> *Indeed we do need to make decisions, find solutions, accomplish goals and pass judgments, but never in total isolation from transcendent possibilities. Otherwise our problem solving can deteriorate into a mechanical attempt to manipulate the flow of life.*

> *There has been among Western cultures a totalizing of the operations of functional mind and will. Put into religious terms, that tends to the belief that if we just set our minds to it and exert our wills hard enough, we can become holy; we would automatically be leading a spiritual life. We might call that "totalized yang"—and it brings a negative dynamic to spirituality. The dynamics of an authentic approach to the Mystery are the dynamics of receptivity, of yin. We can only discern the purposes of the Holy Other and cooperate with them by being open and receptive to the initiatives of that Other.*

This is wisdom, the queen or foremost of all virtues. Wisdom is the power of making wise decisions with total awareness. Let us pass from thinking to free will.

FREE WILL

After the intellect has decided with all its wisdom, then the free will comes about to execute its orders. Which has the final say? Thomas Aquinas' teacher, Bonaventure, said it is our free will. Thomas said that the practical judgment (when I say this is my good) of the intellect has the final say because the free will **must** carry out this decision. The practical intellect acts after the passive intellect (undecided thinking) has considered all the possibilities and consequences. However, Thomas admits that the free will has the final say about which side of the argument a person allows the intellect to consider most. The final decision, however, still lies with the practical judgment about what we think is the best thing to do at the time. Bonaventure's teaching that free will has the final say is the way it feels to most of us.

When anyone asks you why you did some stupid thing, you can

Thinking, Free-Willed, and Emotional People

always quote this, "At the time it seemed to me like the best thing to do." This is inevitably true. We always choose what we think will make us happy. Always! This may sound like egoist philosophy, but it is always true nevertheless. If I choose to commit suicide, it is only because I think that the results of suicide will make me happier because it will end the present pain.

Sometimes we choose what we think is right or best, for others and ourselves even though it involves immediate pain, problems, sacrifices, and so on. For example we do work, study, military duty, charitable donations, religious vocations, etc., because we think it will make others and ourselves happier, and may even please God. I also use happiness in this very broad sense to include the happiness that virtue, altruism, and such brings, and not just the presumed pleasure of wine, women and song.

So, I must be conscious of my decision-making process. Once I make a practical judgment, Joseph Gredt, a German philosopher, assures me that I will infallibly carry it out. However, usually I allow myself to consider more fully the side of the decision that I really wish to make. Ralph Waldo Emerson echos this in stating that each of us sees in others (including their decisions) what we see in our own hearts.

There are many ways to explain why people choose things. One popular explanation in the early nineteen hundreds was that people's actions were due to chemistry, naturalization, a kind of predestination caused by one's genes and environment. Theodore Dreiser describes this in, **An American Tragedy**. (This book was the basis for the movie *A Place in the Sun.*) What he fails to explain is how two brothers, with almost the same genes and almost the same environment, turn out so differently. He passes over freedom of choice. While genes and environment unquestionably play a part, it is a distortion of reality to ignore the key role of free choices.

This naturalization contends that fate predestines me, and I can do little about my fate. If I feel cheated by the material world, I blame the lack of things for my deviant lifestyle in pursuit of worldly gain.

Theodore Dreiser, revealed the dark side of the American dream. We are chemical machines, he said, whose behaviors are a result of our environment, and how we react to it. This chemism is social Darwinism—free will has no part in it. We are simply controlled by the chemistry in our bodies. It is something like getting cancer.

This chemism is most obvious in some forms of mental illness, where a chemical imbalance does at times exist. Some doctors say that trying to cure this with will power is like trying to cure diabetes with will power. The body needs certain chemicals in addition to free will.

Evil in Mirror Lake

In most cases, however, free will plays a larger role. I am attracted to certain people. Might there not be a chemical reaction between us. Yet, but I do not have to react to it. That is the essence of free will. I need to be able to distinguish the different roles that both nature and my will power play in life.

The use of a simple plot, common language and good easy drama tell the story of a failed American dream. This is the natural setting for **Of Mice and Men** by John Steinbeck, the political and social philosopher. Life catches some people up in tragic combats as they innocently pursue the raw and elusive promise of America.

The best laid plans of mice and men go astray at times. And so it happened in the proletarian novelette which gives us a sympathetic portrayal of the lives of two hardworking men. Somehow, the reader is left with the feeling that society is responsible for the seeming injustices and economic inequalities of lives.

The two main characters, George and Lennie, have reasonable plans for getting a piece of the land to live off, and to raise rabbits. But fate won't have it, says the story. And yet, George takes the situation in hand, and dispatches things in a totally unacceptable way. It leaves me crying murder. And that is about the way the story ends. I am not in total control of my future. Other people likewise play a part.

Poets say that Cupid's arrow carries a chemical of love potions that cast a spell upon us. Who of us has not been so struck in life? Sometimes I do not think clearly and so get myself into trouble. I think of Susie Johnson.

Dido in Virgil's **The Aeneid** did not think clearly after her lover Aeneas rejected her. She then committed suicide—which was not her fate. The gods in these classics are comic book heroes acting out human feelings on a large canvas. This Dido and Aeneas episode has genuine high pathos. However, their first chemical attraction for each other was in the end overcome by Aeneas' need to continue his pilgrimage to found Rome. First things, first.

It was well understood in Publius Vergilius Maro's own time (70-19 B.C.E.), Virgil to us, that **The Aeneid** was in its first half an *Odyssey* and in its second an *Iliad*. He used predestination to deify his friend and patron Augustus Caesar. In his poem Virgil foretells Caesar's greatness from the very founding of Rome. He also sets the stage for the eventual conflict with Carthage and its subsequent destruction. For Virgil, predestination or fate triumphs free will.

Jack London explains the evolution of human nature and free will in reverse. In **The Call of the Wild**, a dog, Buck, goes from being a household pet in the lavish home of Judge Miller's Santa Clara Valley

92

Thinking, Free-Willed, and Emotional People

estate, through a series of changes, all the way back to the call of the wild. The dog reverts from civilization to his original animal wolf nature. In Buck, London endows all of the cunning and savagery that he feels lurks not only in animals, but in human beings as well. London, in attempting to argue his *survival of the fittest* philosophy, goes from Charles Darwin to Arthur Schopenhauer. The potential primitive beast he feels lies within each of us. The lesson is that with determination and adaptability to change, we can all survive—in going either up or down the ladder of civilization. The human brain, however, distinguishes itself in its ability to solve problems. London is another one of the long list of great authors who committed suicide.

George Orwell in his **Nineteen Eighty-Four** (1948) shows free will going down the ladder of civilization. (Note how he transposed the year-numbers.) It depicts the wretchedness of individual life under the imagined totalitarian state of Oceania. It shows that under a heartless socialism, an individual is not only diminished, but destroyed. Orwell intended it as a warning, not a prophetic account of what was to come. He adequately warns me about *Big Brother* government that seeks power entirely for its own sake. Power is not a means, but an end in itself—the great substitute for love. How sad it was to hear Governor George C. Wallace say, "The only thing in life is money and power, and I don't give a damn about money." At the end of his life he found out that the only thing that really matters is love.

Orwell introduces us to Winston Smith and his lover Julia. They did not find their love—only betrayal by each other in Room 101. Mr. Charrington, an elderly antique shop owner, betrayed them, and also an Inner Party member named O'Brien who worked at the Ministry of Truth. Orwell introduces us to *Newspeak* (where words are so abstracted from events and action that they take on their exact opposite meaning) and *Doublethink* (the power to hold two contradictory ideas simultaneously). Both of these mental tricks to mislead our free will are still barriers to understanding evil today. The trick is to present evil as a good. The devil is the expert at this, with Naziism coming in a close second.

Orwell's other great book was **Animal Farm** in which he satirizes and condemns the Stalinist methods in Russia. Orwell would similarly condemn the drab and tyrannical *political correctness* of our time and for the same reason: It dehumanizes me—it limits my free choices.

Conversely, Charles Dickens develops going up the ladder of civilization in the historical fiction, **A Tale of Two Cities** (1859). Sydney Carton, the morose law clerk, is the look-a-like of Charles Darnay, a former French aristocrat who has repudiated his title and left France to

93

live and work in England. In the end, Carton escapes from his self-imposed prison of constant failure by choosing to rescue Darnay from his Paris cell and going to La Guillotine in his place. On that fateful journey he utters to himself those haunting words: "It is a far, far better thing that I do than I have ever done; it is a far better rest that I go to, than I have ever known." He chooses love by laying down his life for his love—Lucie, Darnay's wife.

John Locke in his, **Concerning Human Understanding,** teaches why people choose what makes them miserable (Chap. XXI # 58). The causes of these bad decisions are the *various uneasinesses* that determine my will. First, there is the uneasiness of *bodily pain* such as want, disease, or outward injuries. Without the removal of these bodily pains, focusing the intellect on remote and future goods is difficult for my will.

Second, *wrong desires spawn wrong judgments.* My judgment of present good or evil always seems correct, for I would never choose anything for myself that I had judged to be bad. My judgments about future good or evil, however, are at times mistaken. My voluntary actions cause my present happiness, but also cause the good and evil that come down the road. This is creating my karma. Wrong judgments are not about present good or evil, pleasure or pain, but the things that come after present pleasure and pain. This is the point at which the problematic good and evil enter my life. No one chooses misery willingly, but only by wrong judgment. People may err in comparing present and future good.

The first reason I judge amiss is *the weak and narrow constitution of my mind.* "If the headache should come before drunkenness, we should have a care of drinking too much: but pleasure, to deceive us, marches before and conceals her train," says Montaigne in his **Essays.** Why do people not remember what comes after and not drink to excess because they **know** what comes after? Why does the drinker not avoid the problems that his excess causes him? Has the addict's will become too weak, or does he not think correctly? The answer is that he uses his will to direct his decision to what he really wants—to drink. Usually, I judge a present happiness better than an *absent* good. However, sometimes my desire looks beyond my present enjoyment, to an *absent good,* which I feel is more necessary to me than my present happiness. When any new uneasiness comes, it disturbs my present happiness, and I pursue afresh another happiness.

Wrong judgment results from not considering the consequences of my actions. When I believe this present good will never lead to an evil, I will take a chance. I believe I can change the outcome of my decision

Thinking, Free-Willed, and Emotional People

and so avoid an evil outcome—such as, by an extra effort, ingenuity, luck, repentance, etc. I misjudge the consequences. We call this immaturity if I do not even consider the consequences.

Another cause of wrong judgment is not to choose. When I have eliminated present pains and have relapsed into my accustomed pleasure, I sometimes fail to realize that I can yet achieve even greater pleasure. Making myself unhappy to be more happy seems so preposterous. It is like writing a book when I am already happy, or working your way through law school when you are already making a comfortable living. Why put myself through it? We call this *delayed satisfaction*; doing it is hard. How many people do not complete their education because they are already happy?

A final cause of wrong judgment is that some people choose to do bad things—as in Littleton, Colorado. Another example, this time from literature, is the sickly Lise, who says to the saintly Alyosha in **Brothers Karamazov**, "It's simply that I don't want to do good, I want to do evil, and it has nothing to do with illness." Alyosha sadly reflects, "There are moments when people love crime."

Yet, as said above, a person always does what increases pleasure (or reduces pain). All action is motivated. In Lise, and in Colorado, I would look for anger with a desire to get even. Just walk the galleries in any penitentiary and listen to some inmates talking (bragging) about their crimes. The love of revenge similarly falls into this category. Hitler incited the German populace to start World War II by seeking revenge against their defeat in World War I and the subsequent Treaty of Versailles, that impoverished them. Captain Ahab in **Moby Dick** is a study in revenge.

My happiness depends on my intellect and free will working together happily. John Locke, a founder of liberal democracy, says, "Without liberty, the understanding would be to no purpose; and without understanding, liberty (if it could be) would signify nothing." Our Founding Fathers enshrined Locke's ideas in the American constitution—limited, small government, separation of church and state—or more accurately the prohibition of an official established religion.

John Stuart Mill in his radical work, **Utilitarianism** (1863), in talking about happiness being the end all of life says, "When people who are tolerably fortunate in their outward lot do not find in life sufficient enjoyment to make it valuable to them, the cause generally is, caring for nobody but themselves." On the negative side, he assures us, "Yet not one, whose opinion deserves a moment's consideration, can doubt that most of the great positive evils of the world are in themselves removable, and will, if human affairs continue to improve, be in the

95

end reduced within narrow limits." For example, we have poverty, disease, terrorists, wars, ill-regulated desires and unfair social institutions—all of which we can change.

Mill's most influential book, **On Liberty** (1859), promotes the ethical system known as *utilitarianism*—the best-known form of *consequentialism*. He also called it the Greatest Happiness Principle or Utility. President Franklin Roosevelt was America's great utilitarian. If one program did not work, he would simply try another. This is why most politicians take polls today—they want the greatest happiness for the most voters. It is not right or wrong, but what works best that I do.

Utilitarianism is very different from Calvin in Geneva who prescribed inner as well as outer conformity. The Hegelians of Germany violently objected to it because it is far too individualistic. Utilitarianism has probably helped more human beings find happiness than it has hindered. Nevertheless, are there no principles?

Some principles are worse than no principles depending on where the principles lead me. Herbert Spencer, both known as the *philosopher of evolution*—a word he coined some years before his contemporary, Darwin—and the *father of sociology*, wrote **First Principles** (1862). He attempts to explain the principles of biology, education, history, sociology, psychology, etc. People, who read this most influential book in the nineteen hundreds, thought they had their eyes opened "to a new heaven and a new earth." Spencer overconfidently decided to present everything—stars, the universe, civilizations, individuals, countries, ideas, systems of government—as in the process of an inevitable development upward. His principle was that everything was in a state of continual improvement—social Darwinism. His fallacy consists of deducing conclusions about what *ought* to be, from what *is*. Spencer, attracting Mussolini and Hitler, deduced that since the fittest in a given environment survived in biological terms, so the strongest and most morally ruthless would and *ought to* survive in social terms.

Spencer put into social terms the old religious principle that good would come out of evil. He pointed out that the *stern discipline* of *nature* was only a *little cruel*, and in the end would be *very kind*. Exploited workers, impoverished widows, starving children, war, famines were in fact *full of beneficence*. To have him bless his ill-gotten riches, Andrew Carnegie brought him to America as the Apostle of the Rich. Both used philanthropy as a smoke screen for evil. We seldom read and almost never discuss Herbert Spencer today.

Still, from where does evil come? "If we begin by presupposing that in the creation of the world, God is the absolute positive, then, turn where we will, we shall never discover the negative within that posi-

Thinking, Free-Willed, and Emotional People

tive, since to talk of God's *permitting* evil is to ascribe to him a passive relation to evil which is unsatisfactory and meaningless," said G. W. F. (Georg Wilhelm Friedrich) Hegel in his **Philosophy of Right** (1821), (Additions #90).

So, Georg Hegel said that by nature man is evil, and man's freedom extracts himself from evil to good—thus God has no part in the evil: (But, who created man?)

> *The Christian doctrine that man is by nature evil is loftier than the other which takes him to be by nature good. This doctrine is to be understood as follows in accordance with the philosophical exegesis of it: As mind, man is a free substance which is in the position of not allowing itself to be determined by natural impulse. When man's condition is immediate and mentally undeveloped, he is in a situation in which he ought not to be and from which he must free himself. This is the meaning of the doctrine of original sin without which Christianity would not be the religion of freedom.* (Paragraph 18 **Philosophy of Right**.)

The problem here is that a good God created man evil, and not good. Hegel's academic writings are murky and hard to understand. Nietzsche is not usually balanced. However, he is when he says, "In man *creature* and *creator* are united: in man there is material, fragment, excess, clay, dirt, nonsense, chaos; but in man there are also creator, form giver, hammer hardness, spectator divinity, and seventh day: do you understand this contrast?" (**Beyond Good and Evil** #225)

If instead of the fall of humanity as an explanation for the evil in people, I can look to the rise of people from a lower society (which God had also created good). God can then infuse free will and human intelligence into a being that can then freely choose evil or good. Almighty God does not have to *permit* the evil, except that the Omnipotent One did give free will. Having given me free will, God interferes only by persuasion.

What about our free will in our decision-making process? How can we be free and yet accept the truth that God already foreknows what we will choose to do? It is a perennial mystery. I have not yet solved this mystery, but I do have a way of looking at it. We must concentrate or focus one eye on our experience that we are free and not blink. Focus the other eye on the theological truth that God knows all things, even the future since no time exists in God, and again do not blink. Then, without blinking either eye, these two truths come together

Evil in Mirror Lake

into focus and they do not contradict each other. It is not like I did do it, and I did not do it simultaneously; that would be an intrinsic contradiction. We simply have to come to a way of satisfying these two truths. If I blink either eye, I will have trouble understanding reality that contains both our free will and God's foreknowledge. I am the captain of my life. I decide my own future, at least to a certain extent, even in the midst of a sinful situation. I am responsible for my decisions; God simply knows them before me.

Geoffrey Chaucer, in the fourteen hundreds, tells us in the *Second Nun's Tale* of the **Canterbury Tales:**

> *But that which God foreknows, it needs must be,*
> *So says the best opinion of the clerks.*

Or, as it says in the original Middle English:

> *But what that god forwoot mot nedes be,*
> *After the optinioun of certeyn clerkis.*

Flavus Josephus, the first century Jewish historian, tells us in his **The Antiquities of the Jews** that the three Jewish parties held different opinions on free will:

> *As for the Pharisees, they say that certain events are the*
> *work of fate, but not all; as to events, it depends upon*
> *ourselves whether they shall take place or not. The sect of*
> *the Essenes, however, declares that Fate is a mistress of all*
> *things, and that nothing befalls men unless it be in*
> *accordance with her decree. But the Sadducees do away with*
> *fate, holding that there is no such thing, and that human*
> *actions are achieved in accordance with our own power, so*
> *that we ourselves are responsible for our well-being, while*
> *we suffer misfortune through our own thoughtlessness.*

Dante opens his poem**, The Divine Comedy** with:

> *Midway the journey of this life I found I was 'ware*
> *That I had strayed into a dark forest, [the world of ideas]*
> *And the right path appeared not anywhere.*
> (Translated by Laurence Binyon)

Thinking, Free-Willed, and Emotional People

Or as Ralph Parlette repeats in **The University of Hard Knocks**:

But we are not compelled to walk in the right path. We are free to choose. We get off the right path. We go down forbidden paths. They seem easier and more attractive. It is so easy to go downward. We slide downward, but we have to make an effort to go upward.

Anything that goes downward will run itself. Anything that goes upward has to be pushed.

And going down the wrong path, we get bumped harder and harder until we listen.

We are lucky if we learn the lesson with one lump. We are unlucky when we get bumped twice in the same place, for it means we are making no progress.

I once paid a palm reader two dollars to look into my honest palm. She said, "It's not your fault. You weren't born right. You were born under an unlucky star." You don't know how that comforted me. It wasn't my fault—all my bumps and coffee spills! I was just unlucky, and it had to be.

How I had to be bumped to learn better! Now when I get bumped I try to learn the lesson of the bump and find the right path, so that when I see that bump coming again I can say, "Excuse me, this has a familiar look," and dodge it.

Free will at times gets clouded. Jane Austen in her classic, intricate novel **Pride and Prejudice**, shows how our vanity shapes our assumptions in a way that life tricks intelligent people even more than the dull. I need to understand that life is not always what it seems. Life has its duplicitous ways. I need to understand how my vices of pride and prejudice affect my judgments and mislead my free will. I have a hard time seeing this in myself, but it stands out clearly when I see it in others. With Elizabeth's eventual engagement to Mr. Darcy, prejudice dissolved, and pride was humbled. Love prevailed for one of the most intriguing and admired heroines of English novels—Elizabeth Bennet.

How could a good God, presumably foreseeing all *the fruit thereof*, have allowed the temptation of Eve? Pierre Bayle, a French scholar and controversialist, wondered this in his **Historical and Critical Dic-**

Evil in Mirror Lake

tionary (1697). Gottfried Wilhelm Leibniz answered: to make people moral, that is answerable. God had to give people free will and therefore freedom to sin. It may seem that free will is incompatible with both science and Christian theology. Science sees everywhere, except in first-class miracles, the rule of invariable law. Human freedom seems lost in God's foreknowledge and predestination of all events. "But," concluded Leibniz, "we are obstinately and directly conscious that we are free."

How could a good God, presumably foreseeing all the evil to come into the world, have allowed the creation of evil people? Why did God not create only the people he knew would be good—not evil? I answer by a distinction: Time exists differently in God's world than it does in my world. Time exists before I choose and act. I say, that before I act in human time God does not know what I shall do—otherwise I would not be free. But in God's time all time is present time. However, God would never have known what I would do if I had never existed. Therefore, God could not pick and choose only those who would choose good. Creation, indeed, was a Divine Gamble. Future generations exist in God's time only if future generations exist.

For example, does God know if JFK would have bombed Hanoi in Vietnam if he had not been assassinated on November 22, 1963? At 2:30 PM. It was a Friday! Remember President Richard M. Nixon did send the B-52's to bomb Hanoi in 1972. In 1962 God knew what Nixon would do because he actually did it. However, I say God still does not know hypothetically what Kennedy would do since he never was here in 1972 to decide.

If God could know what you would decide even if you never decided, then you could not be free. So God could not have eliminated bad people before they had an actual choice to be bad or evil.

"We **know** our will is free, and there's an end on it… All theory is against the freedom of the will, all experience for it," Boswell quotes Samuel Johnson. Yet many great novelists decry free will as a delusion. **Moby Dick** is a book about evil. Melville wrote it, and we should read it, as a metaphor. We must think double. The story line is thin, but the metaphor of evil is haunting. Herman Melville has the narrator, Ishmael, say in **Moby Dick**:

> *Though I cannot tell why it was exactly that those stage*
> *managers, the **Fates**, put me down for this shabby part of a*
> *whaling voyage, when others were set down for magnificent*
> *parts in high tragedies, and short and easy parts in genteel*
> *comedies, and jolly parts in farces—though I cannot tell why*

Thinking, Free-Willed, and Emotional People

*this was exactly; yet now that I recall all the circumstances, I think I can see a little into the springs and motives which being cunningly presented to me under various disguises, induced me to set about performing the part I did, besides cajoling me into the **delusion** that it was a choice resulting from my own unbiased **free will** and discriminating judgement.*

(Emphasis is added to show the tug between Fate and informed free will.) My solution for this tug is to substitute the Holy Spirit for Fate or Providence, and to keep free will. The Holy Spirit comes to us with the plan of God the Father. It is a plan that we can follow, or we can refuse. Choice is no delusion, not even in hindsight.

Moby Dick is a powerful allegory dealing with the archetypes of good and evil struggling together within the tenets of eighteenth-century Calvinism. Melville wrestles with our place in the cosmos, attempting to expose the unseen forces of nature and its effects on the individual. He recognized the power of both God and the Devil, and strains to comprehend their invincible source. The great white whale symbolizes evil. However, Ahab's obsession to destroy the whale becomes an even darker manifestation of evil. The rope from Ahab's harpoon is coiled about his neck, and wrenches him from his boat—to forever follow Moby Dick but never conquer it (evil). As his first mate Starbuck pleaded with him to do, Ahab could have turned back and headed home with his ship full of expensive whale oil. He freely chose otherwise. (Starbuck is the person after whom the coffee houses are named. It is the place to go to get good advice.)

"For Prayer," says St. Gregory, "is the Means that God useth to execute the Designs of his eternal Predestination." I took this quotation from a 1730 book, **The Lives of the Saints** by Peter Ribadeneira. It is used in *The Life of St. Joachim, Father of the B. Virgin Mary*. The author recorded that Joachim made a presentation of Mary to the temple when she was three years old. He did not record what his wife St. Anne had to say about this.

If I understand that prayer is conversation with God, and if I believe that God has a plan for me, then my cooperation with God's plan is my predestination. Most Christians, including Paul, believed in predestination only when good is done—not evil.

The Bible mentions predestination only three times. The first is in the *Acts of the Apostles* (4:28) where Herod the anointed, along with Pontius Pilate who was in league with the Gentiles and the people of Israel, caused or brought about Jesus' crucifixion. The Bible describes

101

Evil in Mirror Lake

Jesus' crucifixion as, "They have brought about the very things which in your powerful providence you planned [predestined] long ago." The other two are in Romans (8:29-30) where we are assured that God will make all things work together for the good of those people whom God has called according to God's decrees: "Those whom he foreknew he predestined to share the image of his Son, that the Son might be the first-born of many brothers. Those he predestined he likewise called... and justified... and glorified." And also "If God is for us, who can be against us?"

Talking about predestination, Will Durant relates some historical nonsense in his **History of Civilization,** which is worth reading:

> *Meanwhile, the hard theocracy of Calvin was sprouting democratic buds. The efforts of the Calvinist leaders to give schooling to all, and their inculcation of disciplined character, helped the sturdy burghers of Holland to oust the alien dictatorship of Spain, and supported the revolt of nobles and clergy in Scotland against a fascinating but imperious queen. The stoicism of a hard creed made the strong souls of the Scottish Covenanters, the English and Dutch Puritans, the Pilgrims of New England. It steadied the heart of Cromwell, guided the pen of blind Milton, and broke the power of the backward-facing Stuarts. It encouraged brave and ruthless men to win a continent and spread the base of education and self-government until all men could be free. Men who choose their own pastors soon claimed to choose their own governors, and the self-ruled congregation became the self-governed municipality. The myth of divine election justified itself in the making of America.*
>
> *When this function had been performed, the theory of predestination fell into the backwaters of Protestant belief. As social order returned in Europe after the Thirty Years War, in England after the revolutions of 1642 and 1689, in America after 1793, the pride of divine election changed into the pride of work and accomplishment; men felt stronger and more secure; fear lessened, and the frightened cruelty that had generated Calvin's God gave way to a more humane vision that compelled a re-conception of deity. Decade by decade the churches that had taken their lead from Calvin discarded the harsher elements of his creed.*

Thinking, Free-Willed, and Emotional People

*Theologians dared to believe that all who died in infancy
were saved, and one respected clergy announced, without
causing a commotion, that "the number of the finally lost . . .
will be very inconsiderable." We are grateful to be so
reassured, and we will agree that even error lives because it
serves some vital need. But we shall always find it hard to
love Calvin who darkened the human soul with the most
absurd and blasphemous conception of God (predestination),
in all the long and honored history of nonsense.*

The anti-Christian Martin Seymour-Smith in his **The 100 Most Influential Books Ever Written,** *The History of Thought From Ancient Times to Today,* writes "(Calvin) was a cruel and anxious man hankering after earthly power—which he obtained. In due course Calvin established a reign of silent terror in Geneva."

Senator John Glenn, the astronaut from the Calvinistic Presbyterian faith says both, "Ambition can go hand in hand with God's plan." And he also says, "You cannot change fate."

It was even confusing for Napoleon who once said, "I have always imposed my will upon destiny," and yet he also claimed, "One depends upon circumstances and events... my master is the nature of things." He may have been thinking of an old Roman saying, "The gods lead them who will; he who will not, they drag."

Or consider this cop-out that a medieval Spanish monk wrote in his journal, "I am confident that, after my death, I will go to heaven because I have never decided anything on my own. I have always followed the orders of my superiors. And if I ever erred, the sin is theirs, not mine." Some religious Orders have taught, "Obedience is the greatest virtue, not love." Some are still doing this—they call it blind obedience that sees. See St. Ignatius of Loyola on *Obedience.* Still, it is remarkable how important a place obedience, and disobedience, play when truth and love are at stake.

A teenager voluntarily drinks and then drives killing himself and his best friend. His parents come to me distraught and ask, "Why did this happen?" I find it difficult to say to these parents that this happened because their son freely decided to drink and drive. This evil came, in part, from a free will bad decision to drink too much. Faced with this misunderstanding of evil, or perhaps, this unwillingness to acknowledge evil, I have often avoided my responsibility by saying, "It was his time," or "I do not know"or worse, "It was God's will."

Although my present understanding—of how evil manifests itself through free will— takes away the mystery from an evil happening;

Evil in Mirror Lake

nevertheless, those grieving over horrific loss see it less sympathetically or satisfying. This honesty is responsible, mature, and truthful, but I must temper it with an understanding that those affected by such poor free will decisions are not able to accept it at the time. This is being in denial—one of the five steps of grief.

As Alvin Plantinga observed, "Nobody is more insistent than A.A. (Alcoholics Anonymous) that alcoholism is a disease; nobody is more insistent than A.A. on the need for the alcoholic to take full responsibility for his disease and to deal with it in brutal candor." When a cynic asked Mother Teresa, "Where is God when a baby cries in a Calcuttan alley?" she responded, "God is there, suffering with that baby. The question really is, 'Where are you?'"

Evil patterns in society (my *second body*) can lead me astray. Besides my physical body influencing me, society also propels me. But as a spirit person, my environment can never totally determine me. When evil comes into my life, though, I like to make excuses—Adam blamed Eve, and Eve blamed the snake; whom am I going to blame? How about blaming my secretary? "The fault, dear Brutus, is not with the stars, but with ourselves…" (Shakespeare, **Julius Caesar**).

Sometimes bad luck is simply used as an excuse. "Fate has dealt unfairly with me," said Dorian Gray, a character of Oscar Wilde, "so I will give my life over to pleasure." "Let the portrait bear the burden of my corrupting soul," Dorian said. Youth is the only thing worth having, Dorian believed, and then entered a Faustian deal to sell his soul to the Devil for worldly vanity. In the end, in an attempt to kill his conscience, he killed himself as he stabbed the picture—**The Picture of Dorian Gray**.

Evils are often all threats, not blows. Threats can be a terribly effective sham from beginning to end. Threats emanate from the unseen dark powers whose terrors are always on the brink of triumph. Ask any consiglio for the Mafia. Only steadfastness of will can prove triumphant.

My temptations come from the world, the flesh, and the devil. (See **Summa**, First Part Q 114, A 3.) They only have access to my imagination, the final free-will decision is always mine to make. Evil is never the decision-making process itself; it can be only the result of it.

How and why did this free will come to me? Scientists tell me that the dinosaurs lived here on this planet for 149 million years. I imagine, anthropomorphically speaking, God looking down on this fabulous zoo of huge and small dinosaurs. One day God came to the conclusion that the park was pleasant, but wanted some animals that could know and love. So, poof, off go the dinosaurs in a hail of meteoric, dust-raising

Thinking, Free-Willed, and Emotional People

rocks to make way for this rational animal we call human. I make it seem like God intervened and destroyed the dinosaurs, but it was nature.

The reader may wonder why I speak anthropomorphically when I have been speaking so much about reality. A writer may use any metaphor if both the writer and the reader understand what the writer is saying. Herein lies the problem. When we read about "God walking in the cool of the evening in the garden" (Genesis 3:8), beginning a discussion about what type of shoes she was wearing, is not appropriate.

I, however, am more than just an accident of nature. I am more than a bubble on a wave of energy floating through time and space, as said Joseph Campbell, one of the most brilliant mythologists of our (or any) time. I was created in God's image: knowing and loving—destined to be coeternal with the Divinity. God took a Divine Gamble in giving intelligence and free will to me. I can use these powers to love or hate, and indeed I do both. And that is why there are two states of being for me at the end of human time.

Remembering this is helpful: instead of needing to go out to find this love, I need to be still and let love discover me. Love is the nature of my soul, and I am a soul in clay form. Pablo Neruda describes this recognition in a beautiful line, "You are like nobody (else) since I love you."

"The body is much sinned against, even in a religion based on the Incarnation," says John O'Donohue in **Anam Cara**:

Religion has often presented the body as the source of evil, ambiguity, lust, and seduction. This is utterly false and irreverent. The body is sacred. The origin of much of this negative thinking is in a false interpretation of Greek philosophy [and some of the saints]. The Greeks were beautiful thinkers precisely because of the emphasis they placed on the divine. The divine haunted them, and they endeavored in language and concept to echo the divine and find some mirror for its presence. They were acutely aware of the gravity in the body and how it seemed to drag the divine too much toward the earth. They misconceived this attraction to the earth and saw in it a conflict with the world of the divine. They had no conception of the Incarnation, no inkling of the Resurrection.

When the Christian tradition incorporated Greek philosophy, it brought this dualism into its thought world. The soul was

*understood as beautiful, bright, and good. The desire to be
with God belonged to the nature of the soul. Were it not for
the unfortunate gravity of the body, the soul could constantly
inhabit the eternal. In this way, a great suspicion of the body
entered the Christian tradition. Coupled with this is the fact
that a theology of sensual love never flowered in the
Christian tradition. One of the few places the erotic appears
is in the beautiful canticle the* **Song of Songs**. *It celebrates
the sensuous and sensual with wonderful passion and
gentleness. This text is an exception; and it is surprising that
it was allowed into the Canon of Scripture. In subsequent
Christian tradition, and especially among the Church
Fathers, there was a deep suspicion of the body and a
negative obsession with sexuality. Sex and sexuality were
portrayed as a potential danger to one's eternal salvation.
The Christian tradition has often undervalued and mistreated
the sacred presence of the body. Artists, however, have been
wonderfully inspired by the Christian tradition. A beautiful
example is Bernini's Teresa in Ecstasy. They catch Teresa's
body in the throes of an ecstacy where the sensuous and the
mystical are no longer separable.*

And yet, Teresa of Avila treated her body so badly that she was ill much of her life because of it.

Too often I try to hammer changes into my life by using my will to beat my life into proper shape. My intellect tells me my goals, and then my free will tries to force my life into subjection. This way of approaching the sacredness of life is externalist and violent. It brings me too much outside myself, leaving my temple where the divine also resides. I must learn to trust this oblique side of my inner self.

Martin Heidegger, the twentieth-century successor to Georg Hegel, says that true listening is worship, and the senses are generous pathways that can bring me home to the divine. William Wordsworth, careful of the senses, wrote that, "pleasure is the tribute we owe to our dignity as human beings." My senses link me profoundly with the divine within and around me. And yet, I should not limit myself to a five-sensed being. There undoubtedly is more.

Meister Eckhart, a Middle Age mystic, says there is no such thing as a spiritual journey. According to Eckhart, I don't have to travel outside myself to come into a real conversation with the mysteries of the spirit world. The eternal is not elsewhere; it is at home, within me. There is nothing as near as the eternal. **If the spiritual life were a**

Thinking, Free-Willed, and Emotional People

journey, it would be a quarter inch long and miles deep.

This is the way I look at life. By means of this book, I am looking into the depths of life's experiences so it may mirror back to me the meaning of life, and the part that the Fundamental Person—God— plays in it. Besides this probing of the depths, life is still a journey—if only a quarter inch long. My life span of seventy some years is important to me, but when plotted on a continuum of the fifteen billion years of this universe, my life span is less than an inch. And yet, I am the only type of creature promised eternal life. Now, **that is** miles deep.

The eternal and mortal worlds are not parallel, but fused. The Irish people have a phrase for it, *fighte fuaighte* or *woven into and through each other*. The Irish brought this unity of creation out in what we have believed to be the first poem ever composed in Ireland. Amairgen, chief poet of the Milesians, composed it as he stepped ashore to take possession of the land of Eire for his people:

> *I am the wind which breathes upon the sea,*
> *I am the wave of the ocean,*
> *I am the murmur of the billows,*
> *I am the ox of the seven combats,*
> *I am the vulture upon the rocks,*
> *I am a beam of the sun,*
> *I am the fairest of plants,*
> *I am the wild boar in valor,*
> *I am the salmon in the water,*
> *I am a lake in the plain,*
> *I am a world of knowledge,*
> *I am the point of the lance of battle,*
> *I am the God who created the fire in the head.*

> (Ed. P. Murray)

There is no dualism here; all is one. The helplessness of the father of modern philosophy, René Descartes' *Cogito, ergo sum*—"I think, therefore I am," or "Je pense, donc je suis," Amairgen replaces this with, *Ego sum*, "I am," because everything else is. I am in everything and everything is in me, Amairgen is saying. The Irish reject the Cartesian split—between soul and body. Personally, I believe God created us good and not with a sinful nature as Martin Luther taught. The Catholic Church has always taught that Original Sin weakened human nature, never that it became sinful. Many people have wondered about this split in our personality—about our being both good and evil:

Evil in Mirror Lake

*As with wine for sick men, since it is rarely good and often
bad, it is better not to use it at all, than in the hope of a
doubtful benefit to incur a manifest risk; so I hardly know
whether it would not have been better for the human race if
this swift movement of thought, this acumen, this cleverness,
which we call reason, had not been given to man at all, since
it is a plague to many and salutary only to a few, rather than
given so abundantly and so lavishly.*

Cicero

And:

*Be more concerned with your own character than your
reputation, because your character is what you really are,
while your reputation is merely what others think you are.*

John Wooden

Recall Henry Fielding's Man on the Hill in **Tom Jones**. He describes creation in two long sentences in answer to his own question:

*On what object can we cast our eyes which may not inspire
us with ideas of His power, of His wisdom, and of His
goodness? It is not necessary that the rising sun should dart
his fiery glories over the eastern horizon; nor that the
boisterous winds should rush from their caverns, and shake
the lofty forest; nor that the opening clouds should pour their
deluges on the plains: it is not necessary, I say, that any of
these should proclaim His majesty: there is not an insect, not
a vegetable, of so low an order in the creation as not to be
honoured with bearing marks of the attributes of its great
Creator; marks not only of His power, but of His wisdom and
goodness. Man alone, the king of this globe, the last and
greatest work of the Supreme Being, below the sun—man
alone hath basely dishonoured his own nature; and by
dishonesty, cruelty, ingratitude, and treachery, hath called
his Maker's goodness in question, by puzzling us to account
how a benevolent Being should form so foolish and so vile an
animal. Yet this is the being from whose conversation you
think, I suppose, that I have been unfortunately restrained,
and without whose blessed society, life, in your opinion, must
be tedious and insipid.*

Thinking, Free-Willed, and Emotional People

(The Man on the Hill was a recluse!)

If we only watch the evening news, we would think that the world is getting worse all the time. But the media perceives that its business is to give us news—which by definition is the exception. Good is harder to be noticed than evil.

Colman McCarthy, a syndicated columnist, tells how difficult it was getting the news media to cover the 1993 National Caring Awards Ceremony held in the Senate Caucus Room. The Caring Institute, founded in 1985, promotes Albert Einstein's belief that, "only a life lived for others is worthwhile." A reporter at a news magazine, when asked to cover the event, snorted that her shop did not trade in warm stories about do-gooders. One newspaper did care about caring—**USA TODAY**—with a half-page spread which included pictures.

How boring it would be to watch on your evening news Mr. DeMonge going to work as a telephone technician, and then coming home to his loving wife and five children. But good people are still in the majority, and I believe this silent majority is growing. Be careful of what conclusions you draw from watching the evening news. Walter Cronkite's famous sign-off on CBS, "And that's the way it is," Dan Rather has now correctly changed it to, "And that's part of our world tonight," and more often than not, the evil part.

Some people think that the current situation in the United States gives little support to such a positive belief. Frank Morris, in **The Wanderer** (7-22-99), asserts:

> *America... is assessing where it has been these past decades ... The results fall into two general categories—one, the optimistic... the other the pessimistic, by my judgment the realistic one.*
>
> *The optimistic is based almost entirely on materialistic values—technological, scientific, medical advances; unparalleled wealth; reduction of the danger of global war; greater racial justice; and so on...*
>
> *On the pessimistic side, there are the disintegration of commonly held norms of decency, morality, and cultural values; the coarsening of entertainment; the increasing dominance of money in athletics...; the disintegration of the traditional family...; the acceptance of sexual perversion; and on and on.*

Evil in Mirror Lake

The Trial (1925), by Franz Kafka, has affected the ways in which people think—negatively. The book is a bleak metaphor written on two levels. As I read it I could not imagine "anything like that could happen to us," whereas on the other hand the very subject of the novel is that this is what is already happening to us—we are the servants of nameless masters who themselves have no purpose. We could sum up this negativity of Kafka as "the continuing and inevitably increasing indifference of human beings for one another's welfare." This proved true during World War II when all three of Kafka's Jewish sisters perished in Hitler's camps.

To be able to see how the human race is becoming ever more loving through its free will, it helps to view the world by each preceding hundred years, or even by each preceding thousand years. The Divine Gamble is paying off. God gambled when deciding to give us a free will—necessary for good or evil. Cornelius Plantinga Jr. argues that *on the whole* God puts up with evil. John Stackhouse Jr. claims that God uses a *cost-benefit ratio* to deem that the cost of evil is worth the benefits of loving, dependent human beings. Remember that love, the highest good that God seeks in this Divine Gamble, is the important thing. It is not freedom *per se*. Freedom is simply a requirement of love.

But how much evil is acceptable? Walter Hasker raises an interesting idea in, **On Regretting the Evils of This World**. "I do not regret my own existence nor those whom I love, and yet our lives all have some evil in them—indeed, probably much evil—and nevertheless *on the whole* I prefer this world, evils and all, to another possible world with fewer evils if that other world would not include me and my loved ones." Apparently, God thinks the same way. Remember that I have never *known* nonexistence.

Though we still have illegal drugs, terrorism, biochemical warfare, land mines, church burnings; nevertheless, virtually nowhere in the world today do we have legal slavery or cannibalism, and even segregation is disappearing. In another millennium, I predict, such things as racism, murder, crime, abortion, divorces, etc., will mostly be things of the past. Though human nature has not changed much during the past millennium, people are learning to bridle it. We call this civilization. Don't let the evening bad news nor single Bible quotations steer your reflection of history off the course. "Because of the increase of evil, the love of most will grow cold," (Matthew 24:12). The end of the world/universe(s) is not destruction in the Big Crush, but rather all matter returning to pure energy—God's love.

William L. Shirer, the author of **The Rise and Fall of the Third Reich**, asked in an interview with Bill Moyers on PBS, "If there is a

Thinking, Free-Willed, and Emotional People

Christian God, i.e. a God as defined by Christians, how could this God allow fourteen million people to die in World War II? If there is a Jewish God, how could this God allow six million Jews to die in concentration camps? This is a great problem for me."

Perhaps these millions of people died because of the bad decisions or choices of many people? Although I am sure that God used some persuasion here, God would not directly interfere with these free will decisions because then people would not be free to love. This is the Divine Gamble, and I believe that even during WW II, which was a great setback for civilization, there was more love than hate or fear. To appreciate good done in the midst of this great evil, see the movie, *Schindler's List*.

Edward Gibbon, in his philosophical analysis of history, reached this conclusion in his more tolerable moment, "We may acquiesce in the pleasing conclusion that every age of the world has increased, and still increases, the real wealth, happiness, knowledge, and perhaps the virtue of the human race." His **Decline** wished to discover the nature of things—to discover if the universe has laws and, if so, what these laws are. He paid immense attention to the effects of the climate, and did so systematically. Is there, he asked, one great natural law that lies behind all man made laws? He answers that there is, and he concludes that by understanding this, people can make their own destiny. Gibbon was himself a deist who had little native appreciation of the genuine side of religion. But in his case it was to his advantage as a secular interpreter of history. What has confused us for many millenniums is our belief, or definition, that God is *all-powerful*. Here again is the crux—the pivotal question.

We, of course, still have a long way to go to total goodness. Some two thousand years ago the father had the *right* to kill his baby if he did not want the child. Now the mother has that *right*, or choice–especially to kill baby girls as in China. Some might call this progress—I call it a temporary setback to pre-Christianity. Another misuse of free will can be seen in the relationship between the sexes.

"In sexuality and maternity a woman can claim autonomy; but to be a *true woman* she must accept herself as the *Other*, (Other than the man), wrote Simone de Beauvoir in **The Second Sex** (1948). Up to its date, this was the most distinguished book on the liberation of women since John Stuart Mill's **The Subjection of Women** (1861). Beauvoir's purpose was to communicate a sense of how it was to be alive as a thoughtful and reflective woman in her era. She had the acuity to observe that making oneself passive "was different" from being a "passive object." She was an existentialist, and so she assumed that people

111

Evil in Mirror Lake

must choose to become what they are. This notion is the way in which I achieve authenticity in a purposeless universe. The problem with many women is that men force them to "play at being themselves." De Beauvoir accused women of being just as "inauthentic" as men because they play the male game. She was scornful of "female mysticism" since the female mystic "(put) herself into relation with an unreality." Despite her atheism, she gave a balanced approach to the two sexes. The serious weakness of her book is that it fails entirely to explain—let alone dismiss—religious feelings.

Society can, and has, limited free choices. **The Feminine Mystique** is not only the title of a million-selling book by the gestalt psychologist Betty Friedan in 1963, but this title describes a society that has built fences around and burnt incense to the female sex. The worst mystique is in old Spain where young men courted, serenaded, protected, desired, and at times fought over the young females—even to their delight. Shortly after the festive wedding, she became a baby-producing mother and household manager. Her husband began his search for a mistress.

In America up until the 1960's, the feminine role was limited before marriage to a school teacher or a nurse. After marriage the homemaker could continue working on if they needed the income. Frustration surrounded women. Friedan's polemic, warlike, controversial book espousing the cause of feminine freedom moved millions of stifled women out of the home into the marketplace where they could use their talents as they freely wished. Frustration had broken loose.

Friedan goes on to show that women can be quite as foolish as men, but women can be similarly just as human as men. Women no longer have to deny their minds. With jobs opening to them, they have gained independence. Possibly her feminism has turned into pseudo-feminism, but she did ask the correct question: "Who knows of the possibilities of love when men and women share not only children, home, and garden, not only the fulfillment of their biological roles, but the responsibilities and passions of the work that creates the future and the full human knowledge of whom they are?" Her balance extended to informing women that "man is not the enemy" and that "female chauvinism is highly dangerous and diversionary."

Recently I went to a Promise Keepers meeting in Louisville, Ky. They told the men to treat their wives as queens. Hardly a thing for women to object to, I thought. However, when I related this to a female, she told me that women do not want to be treated as queens but as co-kings (Informed Partners). Simone de Beauvoir has insisted that to be a true woman, she must accept herself as the "Other"—a queen,

112

Thinking, Free-Willed, and Emotional People

not a king.

When we look to the future, and if we humans are here as long as the dinosaurs were, we will have about another 144 million years to go before we are really good. The sun will not burn out for at least four more billion years. Sometime after that the world as we know it will end; if with a bang or a whimper. Actually, it will be first a fire ball and then a snowball.

This is how our decision-making process and free will works. The Divine Gamble is paying off. We are using our decision-making intellect and will to make this world a better place century-by-century, I think. This is despite the last century's WWI and WWII, the holocaust, Hitler, Stalin, worldwide communism, or constant wars. But there are strong emotions influencing us to do good and to do evil. What about our emotions and the decision-making process? How do emotions tie in with our intellect and will? I should trust my feelings to some extent.

Successful people call this instinct, and say I should trust my instincts. Unsuccessful people have also trusted their instincts, but I do not hear from them. Instincts are the summation of all my past experiences and judgments that subconsciously tell me what I should do.

Jean-Jacques Rousseau said that God was unknowable (I disagree), but he feels that God is there and everywhere. In his **Confessions** (1781), he says of his chief benefactress and lover, Mamma, "for, instead of listening to her heart, which led her right, she obeyed her reason, which led her wrong." It is as Blaise Pascal said in his **Pensées**, and acknowledged by many modern philosophers with the greatest difficulty, "The heart has its reasons which reason knows nothing of." As one of the greatest mathematical scientists, Pascal investigated the meaning of *chance*—of randomness, of processes now often called stochastic. He also denied the supremacy of reason. Reason can be just a way of being wrong with more confidence.

The question arises whether the passion of the sensitive appetite will move the intellect. Thomas Aquinas, in his **Summa** (I of II, Q 77, Art. 2), answers in the positive with a twofold distinction. The first is by way of a kind of distraction. Thomas says that if feelings so take up a person, feelings will dissipate the power of the will.

Second, this may happen by the will's object—my good apprehended by my reason. Aquinas claims that people who are experiencing some kind of passion do not easily turn their imagination away from the object of their affection (or affliction). The result is that the judgment of reason often follows the passion of the sensitive appetite. As a result, the will's movement follows the reason, having been afflicted by passion. Right or wrong, the will "has a natural inclination

Evil in Mirror Lake

always to follow the judgment of reason," says Thomas Aquinas. Inordinate desire of good is the cause of every sin. The good is what I believe will reduce pain or increase pleasure. It is my truth. I have learned it somehow. And I, created good by God, have learned it in a sinful world—original sin.

"People are not naturally cruel. They become cruel when they are unhappy—or when they succumb to an ideology. If religious people had always followed the instinct of their heart rather than the logic of their religion, we would have been spared the sight of heretics burning at stakes, (Oriental) widows walking into funeral pyres, and millions of innocent people slaughtered in wars that we have waged in the name of God. Compassion has no ideology," says Anthony de Mello in **The Song of The Bird**.

Compassion seems to be the key word. Serial killers and terrorists don't have compassion, but they will nevertheless speak of love of God. Love can mean so many things; compassion is more specific. I cannot kill innocent people and still claim to have compassion. My inner life tells me that God is compassionate.

"We cannot know God until we stop telling ourselves that we already know the Great Unseen," says Neale Donald Walsch in his irreverent book, **Conversations With God, Book I, An Uncommon Dialogue**. The All of Everything says:

> *Listen to your feelings. Listen to your Highest Thoughts. Listen to your experience. Whenever any one of these differs from what you've been told by your teachers, or read in your books, forget the words. Words are the least purveyors of Truth.*

This is also true for this book. Look to your experiences in your Mirror Lake.

Or as Jean-Jacques Rousseau says in another place in his **Confessions,** "From how many mistakes would reason be preserved, how many vices would be stifled in their birth, were it possible to force (our) animal economy (nature) to favor moral order, which it so frequently disturbs." Throughout the **Confessions** Rousseau examines himself. It was he who promulgated the idea of the noble—or innocent—savage who later became corrupted by civilization and property. He did not believe in Original Sin, but his unbelievably frank **Confessions** reinforced the idea of original sin. Rousseau was no saint.

This line of thinking led to Rousseau's other two notable books— **Emile** and the **Social Contract** (both 1762). The first describes, in a

Thinking, Free-Willed, and Emotional People

novel, the ideal education of the innocent child. All liberal modern educational experiments derive from this. In the **Social Contract**, he illustrated what kind of state into which the properly educated child should emerge. He thinks of people as good, and people should just let their goodness flow out into the community. And the community should expect this goodness, rather than expecting people to be evil.

"Doubts of all things earthly, and intuitions of some things heavenly; this combination makes neither believer nor infidel, but makes a man who regards them both with an equal eye," says Herman Melville in **Moby Dick**. In the middle stands virtue. "En medio stat virtus."

The Jewish Holocaust is an example of where intuition or feelings could have saved people from some very bad decisions. The Holocaust incensed many people in Germany, but the German people suppressed their feelings because it was not the *reasonable* practical way to react to Hitler. To say the least, it was not politically correct to oppose the Nazies. Yet, Hitler never spoke to anything but their feelings …he never spoke of politics, order, etc. … only to their self esteem! Hitler knew that people usually do what they feel like doing. Feelings can override both goodness and badness. *Intuition* is also an important way to get to the truth or correctness of a matter—I should always listen to my gut feeling, but again I should not trust it either, completely.

Today scientists talk about this in terms of right and left brain. We regard the left brain as the human logic and the right brain as the non-human intuitive connector. I need my whole brain. How do I feel about abortion? I must never forsake compassion. The Muslims teach me that my heart is the seat of my intelligence. I will now talk about these emotions, as I continue to peer into the deep blue waters of my past experiences, and others'.

EMOTIONS

Rousseau offers a helpful insight in his, **On the Origin of Inequality**. To get this book and read or reread it, would be better, but to stimulate our thinking read this passage.

> *Whatever moralists may hold, the human understanding is greatly indebted to the passions. It is universally allowed that it is through the activity of the passions that our reason improves; for we desire knowledge only because we wish to enjoy; and it is impossible to conceive any reason why a person who has neither fears nor desires should give himself the trouble of reasoning. The passions, again originate in*

Evil in Mirror Lake

our want, and their progress depends on that of our knowledge; for we cannot desire or fear anything, except from the idea we have of it, or from the simple impulse of nature. Now savage man (the famous noble savage), being destitute of every species of intelligence, can have no passions save those of the latter kind: his desires never go beyond his physical wants. The only goods he recognizes in the universe are food, a female, and sleep: the only evils he fears are pain and hunger. I say pain, and not death: for no animal can know what it is to die; the knowledge of death and its terrors being one of the first acquisitions made by man in departing from an animal state.

My favorite Christmas classic is Charles Dickens' **A Christmas Carol**. I read this story often and have seen several movies and plays of its dramatization. It is special to me because of all the messages it has to share. It reflects an amazing insight into how I function as an emotional human being.

This is a story about feelings and great beliefs. Charles Dickens was a great psychotherapist. His works show an accurate understanding of human nature. He understands both how my emotions influence my beliefs, and how my beliefs influence my emotions, and then how both dictate my actions.

Ebenezer Scrooge, the villain and hero of the story, is a hard-bitten, stubborn man. He is absolutely sure of his very negative beliefs and resists the many overt attempts by those around him to influence his thinking in a positive way. His standard response is, *Bah, humbug!* We get acquainted with him in the opening scene of the play as we witness his suspicious and unfriendly interactions with his nephew, Fred, who only wishes to invite him to Christmas dinner. When people come collecting for the poor, he responds, "Are there no prisons? Are there no workhouses? If they will die, then let them die and by that decrease the surplus population."

His debtors are poor street vendors who were desperate enough to borrow money from him at high interest rates. His overworked and underpaid employee is Bob Cratchit. Ebenezer begrudges him so much as a handful of coal for the office fireplace unless it is absolutely necessary. He really resents his wanting to take off Christmas Day to spend with his family.

Ebenezer's chosen profession is a money lender. By today's standards, we would call him a loan shark or a credit card company. He is an old man, and we might wonder why he has no bodyguards or

Thinking, Free-Willed, and Emotional People

hit men to collect his money. At this time and location in history, it is unnecessary. There are workhouses and debtor prisons in operation. Most of Scrooge's debtors are hoping to sell their wares to support their families, and they borrow the money from Scrooge with the expectation of being able to pay him back. He designed his high interest rates to keep them paying for many years under the threat of debtors' prison or the workhouse—a predecessor of modern day credit card companies.

Nevertheless, in one night his entire emotional and belief system undergoes a radical change. This change makes a positive impact on the rest of his life and the lives of all those around him. It is a life-changing event. On this night, Christmas Eve, four spirits (psychotherapists) visit Scrooge. Ebenezer's emotional reactions throughout the story are very interesting.

The first is the ghost of Ebenezer's deceased partner, Jacob Marley. He is laden with chains that he must carry with him throughout eternity. He explains to Ebenezer that he had forged each link of those chains during his life, and he warns Ebenezer that he could look forward to the same fate if he continues his life as he is now. He announces that three spirits will visit Ebenezer that night, and will help him to reconsider the path on which he is traveling. Jacob's job in this therapeutic network—intervention—is to get Ebenezer's attention. He does.

Ebenezer's reaction is one of shock and fear. Both are powerful emotions, nothing like it in the world for getting your attention. However, after this apparition of Jacob Marley was over, the certainty and security of Ebenezer's old beliefs and scepticism close down over him. He decides that this was just a nightmare brought on by indigestion, "a bit of beef, a blob of mustard," nothing more. He is not yet prepared or willing to consider what it all might mean.

As for the spirits who were soon to visit him, he seems to have chosen not to believe Jacob's prediction. We do know, though, that at least he kept his mind and emotions open to the possibility because when the next appears he is not shocked. However, he is still fearful and apprehensive.

The second is the ghost of Christmas Past. Though psychotherapy was a new science in the days of Dickens, we can see the Freudian influence. Ebenezer's first trip is into his past. Today, when I think about psychiatry, I think of lying on a sofa and talking about my childhood. This is a commonly accepted route in therapy because it is in my childhood that I form most of my disabling and limiting beliefs. This is a time when I am most susceptible to my emotions because

117

my reasoning skills are not yet sufficiently developed to counterbalance my emotions.

We know from our experience in dealing with children that they tend to be more emotionally erratic than *most* adults. We know from listening to children that they can come up with some very unusual perspectives. We are only aware of what is expressed; we have no idea of all that is happening on the inside because most children have not yet developed the necessary language or communication skills. Likewise, I am not pointedly aware of all of the disabling and limiting beliefs in myself that originated when I was small.

The therapeutic role played by the spirit of Christmas Past is to take Ebenezer back in time to his boyhood and young manhood. There the spirit will help Ebenezer examine and evaluate where his current feelings and beliefs originated. We see young Ebenezer at his boyhood school. We learn about his estranged relationship with his father, and the love between him and his sister. We can see how a lack of money affected his young life, and began to influence his thinking. We see him in happier times in his relationship with his first employer and fellow employees. Then, we see how his feelings begin to create a change in him, and cause his later beliefs about money.

When Ebenezer's sister dies after giving him a nephew, he feels that he has lost the only person who truly loved him. Ebenezer's fiancé tries to influence him away from the negative changes she is seeing in him, but, unable to, she tearfully breaks off their engagement.

Ebenezer is experiencing these events all over again during the appearance of the ghost of Christmas Past, remembering how he was and how he felt then. He is also experiencing how he is feeling now after having lived with the results of those choices and decisions that he had made then. He is feeling the pain of loss and the pain of regret. Comparing what he has now with what he had given up years ago, he is grief stricken. The apparition returns him to his bedroom and leaves him to think about his pain.

Take a moment to consider the therapy that Ebenezer is undergoing. As a biological being, two things motivate me: the need to avoid pain, and the desire to gain pleasure. Of the two, pain is the greater motivator. I will do more to avoid pain than I will to gain pleasure. Even when I choose to do something that is painful for me, I am doing it either to avoid a greater pain or to gain a greater pleasure. The exceptions being those pathological conditions, in which a person finds pain pleasurable.

Now, concerning Ebenezer Scrooge, his psychotherapists know that he is an unhappy man. His disabling beliefs, which he had formed in

Thinking, Free-Willed, and Emotional People

his youth, have created his unhappiness, and these beliefs are currently carrying him toward his present destiny. A disabling belief is a decision that I have made about myself or others that limit or prohibit me from taking a positive action. Every time I say, "I can't," it's like a flag going up, highlighting a disabling belief.

Jacob Marley has shown Ebenezer what his own current ultimate destiny is. This has created much pain and fear in him. This is something that Ebenezer now definitely wants to avoid—if he can. The ghost of Christmas Past has turned up the heat on his pain even more—by showing how Ebenezer began on the path of his present destination.

Now comes the third visitor, the ghost of Christmas Present. This therapist knows that Ebenezer is in much pain. The ghosts have filled him with sadness and regrets for his past, and fear for his future, as described by Jacob Marley. They have racked up Ebenezer.

The first thing that the ghost of Christmas Present does is to show Ebenezer the alternative to his pain. He comes to Ebenezer all jovial and laughing. He gives Ebenezer a cup of Christmas cheer which he identifies as *the milk of human kindness*. When Ebenezer drinks from the cup, he too is laughing and happy, happier than he has felt in many years. The ghost spends a little time with Ebenezer, playing with him and cheering him up. The purpose of this therapy is to balance Ebenezer's emotional network. Ebenezer has changed; no longer is he the man he was—that bitter, mean old man.

But with the pain he is experiencing, his therapist did not want him to become a depressed basket case either. In order for him to evaluate properly what his therapist is going to show him, Ebenezer must be emotionally in a more positive frame of mind. Bringing out all Ebenezer's emotions, first the negative, and then the positive, was the best way to bring his sense of compassion to the surface. Ebenezer knows sadness and want, and now he knows some happiness. Both are very recent experiences for Ebenezer.

Christmas Present then takes him to his nephew's home where he sees what a good time everyone is having. His nephew, Fred, offers a toast to him although he is absent. Ebenezer, now in a kindlier frame of mind, begins to realize how wrong he has been about his nephew. He always thought that his nephew played up to him because he was his heir. Although Fred is not poor, his living was modest. Scrooge, according to his old beliefs, always thought Fred was angling to get something from him before his time. After all, Fred would get everything Ebenezer had when he died, but he could just "jolly well wait till then." Now he realizes that, like his mother before him, Fred genuinely loves and cares about his Uncle Scrooge. He is only trying to be family with

119

Evil in Mirror Lake

him. Scrooge always believed that Fred's wife had married him mainly for the money his uncle had. Now he can see by her protective manner toward Fred and by her own testimony that she could care less whether Fred had his uncle's money or not. All she wants is Fred.

New emotions begin to surface for Ebenezer—embarrassment for having misjudged his family, pride in his nephew for his choice of a wife, and shame for so callously rejecting them in his life. He can definitely see and understand what he has been missing.

Next, they visit the home of Bob Cratchit. He is the opposite of Ebenezer. Mr. Cratchit and his family are poverty stricken, but they are very happy and supportive of each other. Even now, Ebenezer finds this difficult to understand. How could they be so happy when they have so little? He sees the meager holiday meal that Mr. Cratchit spent his entire week's pay to provide. Even so, the food had to be portion controlled to ensure that everyone in the family received a serving.

Again Ebenezer is ashamed. He is this man's employer. Working as long and as hard as he does, he fares no better than this! Then he sees Tiny Tim, a boy that is not only poor, but crippled as well. Yet, he is happy with the love and support of his family. His family regards him as a joy, rather than a burden. The spirit fills Ebenezer with compassion for the boy, and asks about his future. The ghost tells him that he sees a vacant chair and a crutch without an owner. If these shadows continue unaltered, the boy will die. The ghost alarms Ebenezer, and he wants to know if something could be done for Tiny Tim. The ghost attaches more pain to Scrooge's old beliefs by quoting him, "If he will die, then let him, and by that decrease the surplus population." The ghost returns Ebenezer to his bed with a great deal more to think about, both happy and sad.

Now comes the fourth apparitional psychotherapist, the ghost of Christmas Future. By this time, Ebenezer no longer fears the apparitions. A trace of apprehension persists, but a need to know has replaced most of it. This ghost says absolutely nothing to him, and without any fanfare they visit Christmas Future. In the future, he sees two deaths. The town's people receive the first death with a great deal of joy. There apparently is no one to mourn or miss the dead man. They looted his house, and desecrated his memory. The second death is Tiny Tim's. His dying devastates his family with mourning at their loss, and Ebenezer mourns the loss himself.

He feels sympathy for the other dead man also, and wants to know who he is. The spirit takes him to the cemetery and shows him a grave with Ebenezer's own name on the headstone. His final emotional experience of this therapy is one of horror. He wakes up in his bedroom

Thinking, Free-Willed, and Emotional People

screaming as if awakening from a nightmare.

Now, after all the spirits put Ebenezer through, why was it necessary to take him to the point of his own death? Why leave him with these feelings of horror? It was time to motivate Ebenezer to action. The therapists had helped him to review the status of his life, and had shown him the direction in which his life was leading him. They also helped him to see happier alternatives.

What they were striving to create in him was a deep level of commitment or motivation—a powerful *why*. I have positive beliefs that I do not act on, at least not consistently. The reason that I do not is that I still link pain to the effort—laziness. I avoid discovering the secret of success because deep down I suspect the secret may be hard work.

When I think of dieting, I am reluctant because I feel that I am going to put forth all of this effort and sacrifice to gain results that will be only temporary. In fact, statistics show that when most people go off their diet, they gain back all the weight they lost plus a little more. For me, this would create more pain than not dieting at all.

Nevertheless, what if I were absolutely committed to losing weight and keeping it off no matter what? When I did successfully lose weight and keep it off, I did so because I had found a powerful *why*—diabetes. I absolutely needed to associate pleasure, or the avoidance of pain—blindness—with my new lifestyle of slow eating and fast walking.

Down through the annals of history, ordinary people with a deep level of commitment have overcome every obstacle. Abraham Lincoln overcame poverty to become a lawyer and later president of the United States. Helen Keller was deaf, dumb and blind, but she went on to become one of the most famous teachers in history. Could Martin Luther King Jr. have achieved the great strides he made in racial equality in America through nonviolent demonstrations if he were not deeply committed in every fiber of his being, and willing to settle for nothing less? That is commitment—what it takes.

It would have been very easy for Ebenezer Scrooge to try to correct some of his mistakes, and accomplish some good, but then slowly to dissolve back into his old patterns of behavior. That is human nature. Without commitment, all of our results are temporary.

What the therapists were doing with Ebenezer was showing him the absolute certainty of a future that was the direct result of his old patterns of behavior. Ebenezer decided that it was a future that was too painful to accept, and one that he absolutely did not want. He was prepared to do whatever he had to do to prevent it, and he knew what he had to do.

When he awakens and realizes that the ball game is not yet over,

Evil in Mirror Lake

that he does, in fact, have an opportunity to intervene and change it, he is overjoyed with gratitude and wastes no time. He acts on his new commitment immediately and with great gusto. His feelings of joy have become locked with his new beliefs, and a commitment is born. For the rest of his life he will associate joy with giving—and avoid that after-death scene.

Too often I take my feelings for granted without realizing the critical function my belief systems have played concerning them. I have disabling and limiting beliefs. Furthermore, I cannot dismantle them without first changing the way I feel about them, just as four spirits helped Ebenezer to change the way that he felt about his old beliefs.

When I want to replace a disabling belief with a new empowering belief, I must first decide that the disabling belief I have identified **must change** because I do not want the pain it is causing or will cause.

Secondly, I must decide that I **can** change it. Every thought and action that I take, creates a result in my life. The accumulation of all my results carries my life in a particular direction. For every direction there is an ultimate destination, or destiny. Some foolishly call this fate. If it is my fate (as most of the great books say), then it is a fate that I can change—as Dido changed her fate, by suicide, in **The Aeneid**. And Scrooge changed his fate.

In the world's greatest novel, **War and Peace**, Leo Tolstoy uses the vast canvas of 580 characters to tell me that all is predestined—but that I cannot live unless I imagine that I have free will. So far so good, but he fails to enumerate the laws of history to which he so often alludes. Is history a series of events manipulated by *great* men, or is history a series of men manipulated by *great* events? He never reconciles free will with determinism or fate. Tolstoy conveys a sense of inevitability. The notion that I am fated does occur to me at times, but I feel better with the notion that I have complete free will. However, I put these two together by allowing the world's spirit to make my plans, yet I am able to say, "No!" or "Yes!" Out there is a power directing me towards the best way to fulfill my destiny.

How is my disabling belief affecting my ultimate destiny? Our Heavenly Father created me and endowed me with those qualities that make me unique and special (Matthew 25: 15). God created me in the Divine Image and likeness. It is my special privilege and responsibility to complete the creation of myself. I am already in the process of doing this every minute of every day by the choices and decisions that I make. The person that I am today is the person that I have created myself to be. If I am not happy with the results that I am getting, I have the option of making new choices and decisions.

122

Thinking, Free-Willed, and Emotional People

If I consider myself *only human*, then perhaps I am not trying hard enough. As a child of God, the all-powerful One created me to be so much more than **only human**. The annals of human history are full of accounts of ordinary people achieving extraordinary results. The main difference between these people and myself is in **the commitment**. If the results I achieve are temporary, then my commitment to those results is also temporary. Permanent change requires a permanent commitment to the change, e.g., dieting, saving money, worshiping God, associating joy with giving.

When I know what I want to change and why, then I also need to attach enough pain to my old belief so that I want never to return to it—no matter what! To do so would mean ultimate pain. Then I must decide what my new empowering belief will be. I will commit to this belief. It will move me toward the ultimate destiny that I hope to achieve.

For me, I have had a hard time losing weight. Each time I saw a piece of candy I thought how delicious the pleasure would be if I would eat it—happiness. Now that I have the beginning of diabetes, I think that this piece of candy may cause me to go blind—pain. It is a great motivator.

Remember Ebenezer Scrooge on Christmas morning when he realized that he had an opportunity to change his ultimate destiny? His feelings overcame him with joy. I also must attach and anchor an overwhelming positive feeling to my new empowering belief. I can achieve this by focusing my attention on all of the benefits I will gain through this new empowering belief. In this way, through my practical intellect, I will have a positive impact on my ultimate destiny, leading me away from evil. My conscience collaborates between my emotions and intellect as a counselor to my will. Success in happy living is a combination of thinking, choosing and feeling.

If my book is about evil, why am I writing about these things also? This book is also about life, and according to my definition, evil is the absence of the good life. From a positive point of view I find it helpful also to know what ought to be as well as what is lacking. This is the yin and yang of life—a balanced approach.

Well, if these three powers—thinking, free will and emotions— can lead us **away** from evil, then what influences lure me **toward** evil? What influences me in the decisions I make concerning evil? I just threw a rock into Mirror Lake to see the ripple radiate out, but now I also notice a cloud of mud rising from the bottom.

123

Evil in Mirror Lake

INFLUENCE OF ANGELS AND DEVILS

Are there really such things as angels and devils? Unlike God, whose existence I can prove through cause and effect, as I attempted to do in Chapter IV, the manifestation of angels and devils is something I cannot positively identify or prove because I cannot be sure of their effects. However, I can believe (take someone else's word for it) that angels and devils do exist. Apparently, I would not be alone in my belief. The Bible mentions angels some two thousand times, and a *TIME* magazine survey found that 69 percent of Americans believe in the existence of angels.

As Nancy Gibbs wrote in *TIME* magazine (12-27-93):

> *The act of looking for angels is an exacting, exalting gesture.*
> *To the degree that this search represents the triumph of hope*
> *over proof, it may be a good and cheering sign of our times.*
> *For all those who say they have had some direct experience*
> *of angels, no proof is necessary; for those predisposed to*
> *doubt angels' existence, no proof is possible. And for those in*
> *the mystified middle, there is often a growing desire to be*
> *persuaded. If heaven is willing to sing to us, it is little to ask*
> *that we be ready to listen.*

Whether I can explain angels and devils as a cultural way of expressing the arrival of God's messages, is a question that has plagued philosophers and theologians for centuries. When as a Senior at SLUH (St. Louis U. High), I heard God speaking in my heart to change direction in my life. Saying that an angel had come to me with a message would be one way to view this experience.

Thomas Aquinas asked and answered many questions about angels in his **Summa Theologica**. He reasoned that God's creation of pure spirits was logical—to fill out the gradations of creation. On the lowest level God created inanimate things, such as rocks. Next came living things like plants. Then came living things that had locomotion, namely the animals, and finally came the rational animal that we are. Above us humans is God, who is pure spirit in whom intellect and will are one. It is fitting that between people and God there be another species of beings, namely pure spirits, who are without bodies but with intellect and will as separate powers. So, believing that angels do exist is logical.

How did the good angels and the bad angels get separated? The Uncreated Being created these all pure spirits outside heaven, not face

124

Thinking, Free-Willed, and Emotional People

to face with God. The Divine Gamble again came into play. These angels, with their free will, could either choose to love or choose not to love God. The test was inevitable. What the test was we have no idea. Augustine of Hippo suggests the test may have been that the Supreme Being revealed to the angels that in the future God would become a lowly man—a rational animal—and the Father would expect the angels to adore God as a man. Through free will come both evil and good. Augustine required a God to judge and punish and reward. I say the angels did it to themselves.

What is the job description of angels? Clement of Alexandria, a Christian scholar of the second century, Avicennia, an eleventh-century Persian-Jewish philosopher, and Johannes Kepler, the seventeenth-century German astronomer, all believed that the angels moved the stars and thus coordinated the vast and intricate movement of the entire universe. Origen, the third-century theologian tells us that angels are placed over the four elements—earth, water, air, and fire—and over plants and animals. The Jewish Talmud says the same thing. The **Book of Enoch** sets angels over hail, wind, lightning, storm, comets, whirlwind, hurricane, thunder, earthquake, snow, rain, daylight, night, sun, moon, stars, and planets. The Islamic prophet Muhammad said that an angel accompanies every raindrop. John Henry Newman, the nineteenth-century Roman Catholic cardinal, said that angels are "what is called the laws of nature—meaning that they are not separate beings." Protestants have kept fairly quiet about angels, and there are some who regard excessive attention to them as idolatry.

"Though humans no doubt appreciate the acts of the angels in their unending praise of God, in the governing of God's kingdom, and in the regulation of natural law in the physical universe," David Connolly, in his **In Search of Angels**, tells us, "what endears the angels to us most is their personal involvement in each human life."

Philo of Alexandria and Origen both thought that two angels, one good and one bad, watch over each person. Since the time of Thomas Aquinas, though, we more often believe that a single beneficent Guardian Angel watches over each of us.

How did this all come about? In **Paradise Lost,** John Milton addresses the origin of evil. Original sin embeds evil in my nature dating back to the Garden of Eden. Adam's initial mistake was to think (as I do) that what Eve abhorred in her dream, she would not do in her waking hours—but she did. The night before Eve had dreamed that the devil tempted her and she resisted. She confided this dream to Adam. At first, Adam did not want to allow Eve to roam the garden by herself. He relented and she went. The devil came disguised first as a mist.

125

Evil in Mirror Lake

Satan's good would be our evil. Evil will be his good. Mind creates its own place. It can make a heaven of hell or a hell of heaven. It is mind over matter. It is all in how I choose to look at it. Scrooge's mind made up beliefs that made a hell out of his life. Milton's genius for making his devil so alive and intriguing is far more compelling than an abstract analysis of principles.

Mephistopheles describes himself in **Faust**:

> *Part of that Power which would*
> *The Evil ever do, and ever does the Good.*

(L 1335)

Or another translation from the original German:
> *Part of that force which would*
> *do evil evermore, and yet creates the good:*
> *I am the spirit that negates.*

As to the number of angels who fell and became devils, Aquinas reasons that a majority must have remained loyal because a thing tends to its natural end, and only deviates by way of exception. It was John Milton who set the number of revolters at one third in his famous poem, **Paradise Lost**. Herein it is also said, "They also serve who stand and wait."

In both the Christian and Islamic traditions, the devil is a creature of God and not an equal. Therefore, God will prevail. Yet, Satan is real, and does what God allows.

"Both Catholic and Protestant Christianity agreed on a belief in witches," says Anthony S. Mercatante in **Good and Evil**. He asserts, in **The Malleus Maleficarum** (Witch Hammer), that Catholics and Protestants alike, in the persecutions of witches, used a handbook on witchcraft written by two Dominicans and published in 1487.

The best-known legend of the devil in European folklore is a German tale about Dr. Faust who, according to the English poet Christopher Marlowe, made a bargain with Mephistopheles (in Hebrew, *he who loves not light*). Their diabolical pact was to give the devil Faust's soul at death in exchange for an immediate return of his youth. He was willing to trade control over his spirit or soul, his conscious mind or ego—for material things. This temptation, to surrender control over my life or destiny for a bowl of porridge, is everyone's battle, as it was for Jesus—and Esau.

When consciousness emerged from nature's instinct for preservation of the physical being, there came a battle between my standing as an individual against the collective Being (God), or my accepting the

126

Thinking, Free-Willed, and Emotional People

deeper reality of our Oneness—to which the emotional response ought to be compassion, or love, or creativity. This clash between independence and dependence is a continuing subject for great literature—and great evil.

In Goethe's **Faust,** Mephistopheles is going to have to make the discontented professor Henry Faust happy in this life, in exchange for his soul in the next life. "…You shall be the master, and I Bond,/ and at your nod I'll work incessantly;/ But when we meet beyond,/ then you shall do the same for me." Faust, whose *two souls*, has finally torn completely asunder, agrees to the bargain.

Faust, the proud book worm, relies on reason and sorcery rather than faith. This dramatic romantic poem is an allegorical drama of ideas regarding the internal nature of heaven and hell and the personal experience of salvation or damnation which results from each person's journey for meaning. **Faust** is a treasury of ideas about the meaning of existence and the place of God in everyone's life. The story, in summary, is about a person who wants to know the meaning of life. At the end he learns.

Happiness comes from working in the service of my world with my talents. Happiness is oneness with the world. Wisdom is not book-learned, but it comes from examining my soul. I am becoming; I am not finished, and I must look to my heart for instructive leadership. My attention should be on daily life, not eternity. I do not experience happiness because of what I get, but because of how I live each moment. Happiness is not an acquisition—it is a skill.

In **Faust**, the angels sing the universe is perfect, but the sinister Mephistopheles chides God that people are in a state of misery—man's reasoning powers make him miserable. The greatest joy in life is the skill to put knowledge into active use. Faust, at the end, realizes what would have made him happy, but he did not experience it—to love and to be loved. It is interdependence.

Dante, in his massive work **The Divine Comedy,** described the three-faced Satan (who is a parody of the Christian Trinity) as meting out elaborate punishments. Dante's chief rival, John Milton, in **Paradise Lost**, has Satan rebelling because, "Better to reign in Hell, than to serve in Heaven." But what of all the angels serving in Hell, I ask. The poem continues without answering that thorny question. Satan decides to reek revenge on God by spoiling his plans for obedient people—and succeeds.

Just before he died, Dante Alighieri published his **Commedia** (a grateful posterity added the adjective Divine). **The Divine Comedy** (1311), the first great book written in Italian, is the embodiment of the

Evil in Mirror Lake

religious and moral ideals of its age. The details of punishments, which so exactly and subtly reflect the sins handed out to sinners in Hell, is original to Dante. His beloved, but a pagan poet, Virgil, escorts him on Good (Terrible) Friday through a funnel-shaped pit divided into terraces—Hell. At the core of the earth they turn and make their way up the layered path of Purgatory. It was the pure love of his life, Beatrice, who took him into Heaven on Easter. He set out to describe the world in his poem as a mirror lake, reflecting the world of the Christian God of his era. One of his memorable quotations is, "If only the king of the universe were our friend."—that inscrutable all-powerful God!

Maybe what is behind these stories is the same functioning of beliefs (both disabling and empowering) that we detected attached to the emotions (feelings) in the story of Scrooge. Might devils or ghosts represent disabling beliefs as well as empowering ones? Is not the mind a creation of God? The crucial point in my experiences is that something or someone beyond my conscious self influences me.

Gerald Messadie denies the real existence of the devil in his book, **A History of the Devil**. He asks, "How can it be? If the devil had been tempted, then temptation must have pre-existed, and therefore Evil too." As Augustine taught us, neither evil nor temptation exists by itself. Evil is a lack in or of something, and temptation is an opportunity to do or to be something.

Some angels said, "No way would we stoop to worship a mere man even if he were also God." This was their eternal (mortal) sin, and so we have the bad angels, or devils, with Satan, or Lucifer (a Latin name for light), or Beelzebub as their leader. "Sin, by and large, is love gone wrong," says Carolyn Gratton. Charles Baudelaire in his impious French classic, **The Flowers of Evil**, has poem CXLV "Litany to Satan" open by making the point that if Almighty God will not take pity on our pains, maybe Satan will.

> *O grandest of the Angels, and most wise,*
> *O fallen God, fate-driven from the skies,*
> *Satan, at last take pity on our pain.*

Other angels said, "Yes, God, we will worship you wherever you are, even as a man." This was their free choice that forever united them with God, and God with them.

Why cannot the bad angels change their minds and be sorry, and so let God forgive them? Whenever I change my mind, it is always because I come upon newer knowledge. I then change to a more informed practical decision of the intellect. Remember, this practical decision of

Thinking, Free-Willed, and Emotional People

the intellect is the final determiner of what I infallibly do.

This is why society, until the present time, has always guarded against the influence of bad philosophies so strenuously. For example, they put Donatien Alphonse Francois Sade in prison for life because he wrote, **Justine**. Through his characters, this Marquis de Sade espouses good reasons, or sophistry, for types of cruelty that push the envelope of human perception. Today we believe that bad teaching ought to be corrected only by better teaching. As Joseph Campbell counsels, "Preachers err by trying to talk people into belief; better they reveal the radiance of their own discovery." Nevertheless, the practical intellect has the final say in my behavior, whatever the influences.

The problem with the devils is that their superior intellects gave them all the facts they needed to know at the time of their decision. Also, they have no physical body with its emotions to sway them off the course—so the decisions those devils made then, they are still making now. It is a fallacy to think in terms of the good God not forgiving them. God still loves his creatures, even the devils, and wants to be loved in return. God's hand of friendship is eternally extended to them. It is just their nature that devils will not change, just as the good angels will not change in their choosing God. The important thing to remember is that the choice was theirs to make, despite any influences, and both the angels and the devils are eternally making their same free-will decisions or choices.

Later, we will see that we humans, after death, are in the same situation of nonchange. Our bodies have decayed, and so we cannot get any new information to change our fundamental final option or decision—for good or for evil.

To freely choose anything besides God—for whose love I was created—will be my hell forever. Also, to choose a loving, dependent relationship with God will be my heaven forever. The choice is mine to accept God's hand of friendship or to reject it—despite the influences of either the angels or the devils, or the influences of my higher or lower nature.

Why would the devils roam about the world seeking the destruction of souls? Misery loves company or a sense of power over others, are the only reasons I can think of. What power do the devils have over me? It is the power of influence only. They have access to my imagination. They can suggest things and reasons for doing certain things. Devils cannot force me to do anything. They cannot possess me without my invitation. All I have to do is just say, "No!"

Evil in Mirror Lake

Mephistopheles brags in Goethe's romantic poem, **Faust:**

My eloquence should captive every heart,
Since prompting is the devil's special art.

And:

Do not stifle the Spirit. Do not despise prophecies.
Test everything, retain what is good.
Avoid any semblance of evil.

Paul of Tarsus to the Thessalonians
(I Thessalonians 5:19-22)

The devil is indeed trying to influence me to reject this loving, dependent, meaningful relationship offered to me by God. Taste the fruit (apple) and you will be like (equal to) God. They tasted and their eyes were opened. They saw that the devil had deceived them, and they felt their nakedness.

On the other hand, good angels, and according to a particular tradition, my guardian angel, can suggest good things for me to do. *TIME* magazine's survey found that 46 percent of us believe we each have our own guardian angel. All I need to do is always say "Yes" to my guardian angel to be a saint.

Why write so much about angels? Well, they are back in style as they were in the days of Thomas Aquinas. In fact, he wrote so much about angels that he was known as the Angelic Doctor. His most famous question is, "How many angels can dance on the head of a pin?" The meaning is in the answer—an infinite number. Since angels have no body, they are not limited to any point in space including the point of a pin.

All the angels mentioned in the Bible by name—Michael, Gabriel, Raphael, and Uriel—are agents of God. These names all end in *el* which means God. Michael, who is the most powerful, means "Who is as God." (The Jehovah's Witnesses believe that Jesus is Michael made man.) Gabriel, who brought the message to Mary, is "Strength of God." Raphael, who healed blindness with a fish, is "Healing Power of God." Uriel, who drove the first humans from paradise with a flaming sword, is "Fire of God." This latter story in Second Esdras (4:1-11) is not in most Bibles.

Inside each of us there are two voices—each speaking for a lower or a higher nature. This is where the idea of angels and devils really comes from. The apostle Paul speaks about this in Romans (7:15-24)—

130

Thinking, Free-Willed, and Emotional People

sometimes, I do what I know I should not, and vice versa.

Our ancient Hebrew ancestors had no idea of evolution, but they knew that something inside people was not quite right. They opted for the view that people are good but flawed, and used the story of the fall in the garden to explain the goodness and badness in people.

Today, I can explain that I inherited my lower nature from the animals, and thus for survival's sake I am a very self-seeking human being. Whereas my higher nature is God's life in me, propelling me to be a child of God, a brother or sister in the Lord, an heir of heaven. Plato, in his **The Republic** Ch IV, long ago, explained it thus:

> *The meaning is, I believe, that in the human soul there is a better and also a worse principle; and when the better has the worse under control, then a man is said to be master of himself; and this is a term of praise: but when, owing to evil education or association, the better principle, which is also the smaller, is overwhelmed by the greater mass of the worse—in this cause he is blamed and is called the slave of self and unprincipled.*

Whether I opt for the angels and devils as my way of understanding this internal conflict, or for my higher and lower natures, is not terribly important in the outcome. People say that the devils' greatest success is in getting me not to believe in them. I say that there is something imperative for me to remember: It is either the devil or my lower nature that is constantly tempting me in the wrong direction toward evil. Pushing our human nature toward higher awareness and more compassionate behavior is, after all, work that requires attention and effort. Lucifer is, in fact, Mother Nature's alter ego, either way—either as a real person or as a symbol of our lower animal nature.

The prophet Isaiah used the term *Lucifer* merely to refer poetically to the hated king of Babylon. Later, Christians like John Milton would use Isaiah's figure of speech as the proper noun around which to weave an elaborate tale, crafting a devil of impressive proportions.

Howard Bloom says in his **Lucifer Principle**, "It is not an invention of either Western or Eastern civilization. It is not a uniquely human proclivity at all; it comes from something both sub- and superhuman, something we share with apes, fish, and ants—a brutality that speaks to us through the animals in our brain. If man has contributed anything of his own to the equation, it is this: He has learned to dream of peace. But to achieve that dream, he will have to overcome what nature has built into him."

Evil in Mirror Lake

I feel in myself the strong roots of savagery perpetually pressing against the controls of civilization, and I become skeptical of ever expecting perfection. Teilhard de Chardin in his **The Divine Mileau**, on the other hand, believes all of creation will be brought to perfection. I learn that I can achieve only as much as evolution has prepared me for, and human nature will permit. This is the dark spot that I see ever shifting its posture in my mirror lake of experience. Let me be ever vigilant in prayer, for the flesh is yet weak, and evil is tempting.

We now go to the next view point, a shady spot along the bank of Mirror Lake under a weeping willow tree, where I can pray about this.

CHAPTER V

GOD AND PRAYER

One day, as a teenager, I was sitting on the couch in our living room doing my homework when the phone rang. The call was for my dad. After the phone conversation he sat back in his usual chair, but did not pick up his newspaper that he had been reading. Instead, he simply stared out of the window. After awhile, he turned to us and asked if we remembered the phone call he had made the night before to his friend George telling him about a job opening with Swift & Co. at the Stock-yards. We had only one phone and it was in the living room so every-one heard everyone else's conversations. We nodded, "Yes." Dad went on to say that this last phone call was from George saying "thanks" because he did get the job.

Still, that is not all. George had been out of work for six months, and he and his wife had decided to make an *Our Lady of Perpetual Help Novena* at St. Henry's Church. The previous night was the ninth and last week of that Novena (nova in Latin means nine). As he was arriving home and had the key in his front door, the phone was ringing. It was my dad calling him with the news for which he had been pray-ing. Was this phone call for a job offer, coming precisely at the end of a Novena, simply an amazing coincidence, or did God, through Mary, really answer his prayer? Everybody has a story like this.

This is akin to the First Insight in James Redfield's best selling book, **The Celestine Prophecy.** It is an awareness that mysterious oc-currences change our lives. We have the feeling that another process is operating—like the guiding providence of God. Amazing coincidences are God's way of staying anonymous, say our spirit-filled friends.

I sit on a rock dangling my feet in the air. The bees are murmuring. I toss a pebble into the lake. After some time of just feeling comfort-able with myself in timeless silence, I murmur to no one, "Prayer is

Evil in Mirror Lake

conversation with the Mystery."

If God knows what I want or need before I ever pray, why do I need to communicate this to God? Do I need to do this to get God to do my will? What connection does my prayer have to my avoiding evil? Why did Jesus, at times, spend the whole night in prayer? Was he praying all 150 Psalms? Was he listening, maybe even wrestling with God, like Jacob before the battle? Or was Jesus looking for guidance and clarification of God's message that he knew God had called him to relate to the world? Or is prayer just a waste of time and energy? I seldom get what I ask for!

Prayer does at least two things for me. First, it makes God's presence felt and active. It is like my good friends who came to be with me when my father died.

Yes he forgave me for wrecking his beloved car. In fact he never said a word about the car; he was just so happy that I was okay. He simply traded in the wrecked car for a new one. He did wait until I finally asked to borrow the new car before he offered it to me. Then, he simply handed me the keys and said, "Have a good time." What a great dad!

My friends could not change a thing, but their presence made all the difference in my hour of need or sorrow. Dean, my teenage friend, much more mature now, flew back from his important job in Washington, D.C., to be with me. He would tell us only that he worked for The Company.

Also, by praying and listening I can hear some good advice from my friend, God. It is like a friend who advises you, after having lost your spouse, not to sell everything next week and move to Florida to live with your daughter. Instead, he advises, take a trip and visit her, but do not decide for six months to two years. Turn to God in prayer for good advice.

Prayer also takes me out of my problem-filled world and puts me in God's problem-free world. The apostle Paul reminds the Romans, "Do not conform yourselves to this age, but be transformed by the renewal of your mind so that you may judge what is God's will, what is good, pleasing and perfect" (Romans 2:1-2) In other words, I do not pray to change God, but to let God change me.

Prayer should always be a prelude to action. Dorothy Day, the proposed saint who cared for the poor on the streets of New York, once asked, "Why was so much done in remedying the evil instead of avoiding it in the first place? Where were the saints to try to change the social order, not just to minister to the slaves, but to do away with slavery?" I need good advice about my problem-filled world, and I can

God and Prayer

get it in prayer.

However, what I usually want in my prayer is not good advice about what I should do, but for God to produce the results of what I want. I want a push-button prayer life to go with my push-button lifestyle. My tendency is to want my God to be a little more actively at my disposal than it seems. If my prayer does not produce the desired result immediately, I am inclined to quit praying. So many other things are readily at my disposal whenever I want them, why not God?

I would like to deal with God as Aladdin did with his magic lamp. Whenever he rubbed it, a genie would appear and do anything Aladdin requested. I am trying to deal with God in that same way—would it not be nice to have him appear genie-like anytime I wished, ready to do my bidding. Yes, but this is a total misconception. Real religion is not a magic technique for gaining immediate access to Divine Power. It is a relationship based upon mutual trust and respect. It is a dependent and loving relationship.

Sometimes I go to church to get (a more-powerful) God on my side. This notion tempts me to agree with the late atheist, Madalyn Murray O'Hair who said, "Don't pray, do something!" I should pray to know what to do—how to avoid evil and do good.

"Prayers work best when the players are big," is the dry wit of Notre Dame's football coach Frank Leahy, flashed on the cover of *TIME* magazine (10-11-46).

I must admit to my *creatureliness*. This is the import from the story of Adam and Eve in the Garden of Eden. They were perfectly happy; they had only to refrain from eating the fruit of two trees, one of which was the tree of life. Yet for some reason they were not content in their loving dependent relationship with their creator. The devil comes along as a snake. According to John Milton in **Paradise Lost**, the snake told Eve that he had eaten of the tree of life, and now he was mostly human—he could talk. He assured her that if she ate, she would become divine. She ate and Adam followed. Then, their world fell apart. Neither she nor he became a god.

Prayer is not going to turn God into my *super lawyer, super protector*, or *super provider*, but prayer will turn God into my *super friend*. Prayer can help me from making big mistakes—evil. And prayer will keep me humble—the truth of what I am, a creature. I still have a tendency to think that my prayers cause certain things to happen in the world.

The Jungle Book (1894) by Rudyard Kipling, tells the story of the Eskimo priest (angekok) praying in his church or Singing-House (quaggi) that Kotuko's trip to get food for the village would be suc-

Evil in Mirror Lake

cessful. And it was. The priest later prayed, in thanksgiving (or boast-fulness):

> *"Ah," said the angekok, with an important cough, as*
> *though he had been thinking it all over. "As soon as*
> *Kotuko left the village I went to the Singing-House and*
> *sang magic. I sang all the long nights, and called upon*
> *the Spirit of the Reindeer. My singing made the gale blow*
> *that broke the ice and drew the two dogs toward Kotuko*
> *when the ice would have crushed his bones. My song drew*
> *the seal in behind the broken ice. My body lay still in the*
> *quaggi, but my spirit ran about on the ice, and guided*
> *Kotuko and the dogs in all the things they did. I did it."*

This is an example of people who believe that prayer can change nature—my singing made the gale blow. Another example of God (Brahmin) controlling nature is reported in *Letting in the Jungle*, another story from **The Jungle Book:**

> *When that last loss was discovered, it was the Brahmin's*
> *turn to speak. He had prayed to his own Gods without*
> *answer. "It might be," he said, "that, unconsciously, the*
> *village had offended some one of the Gods of the Jungle,"*
> *for, beyond doubt, the Jungle was against them.*

With Jesus I pray, "...but deliver us from evil." Amen. Prayer is not some magic formula for controlling nature. Prayer is saying *amen* to the kingdom. It is being ready, watching, submitting, and willing to accept God's invitations spaced throughout my life. With Michael Quoist, who wrote many prayer books, I pray "Lord, help me to say 'yes' to what you ask of me, and 'no' to all evil."

Gregory the Great taught us about penetrating prayer, or as contemplationists call it today—centering prayer. In meditation I move beyond all passing thoughts, fruits of the evil false self, to go deep into the center of myself, and there I make union with the cosmos Spirit. There I will find my true calling of how to be in service of or to the human family. So it is with prayer that I make life an adventure with a divine partner.

AMAZING COINCIDENCES

Our religious belief must be consistent with our experience if our

God and Prayer

faith is to make sense. If a coincidence such as *answered prayer* happens only once, maybe it is by chance. If it rains after I open a window, my opening the window did not cause it to rain. Nevertheless, when I have many amazing coincidences or mysterious occurrences between my prayers and events, I draw the conclusion that there is a connection, and that connection is God's influence. Of course, there does not have to be a conscious prayer beforehand, but some insight is needed. I see no reason not to believe that God's influence or energy, possibly through the angels or the Holy Spirit or Mary or all of the above, moved my dad's imagination who then remembered and made that call. Of course, dad had to cooperate, George had to go to the interview, and Swift & Co. had to want to hire him as their company buyer.

An amazing coincidence that changed the life of the great Russian writer, Fyodor Dostoyevsky, is reported by Antoinette Bosco in **Coincidences Touched by a Miracle**. She tells how he was about to be shot for treason when five minutes before his execution a horseback rider rides up with a message from the Czar. It is a stay of execution. At the next railroad station on his way to Siberia a woman gives him food and a Bible. These coincidences changed his life, and later gave us his masterpieces. I see free will and God's persuasive activity in this, and not fate.

Coincidence is also a mathematical term. It means that two angles have a perfect fit; it is a perfection. In math a coincidence is not luck or chance. Amazing coincidences can be a perfect fit between God's will and my choice—both operating at the same angle.

God in general works through others, as through his son, Jesus. This is depicted well in the following story. A man of great faith owns a home in the path of flood waters. A National Guardsman comes by in a Jeep and says "Get in, the levee is breaking!" The man thanks the guardsman, but says that he has faith in God. The guardsman says "So be it," and drives away.

The waters come and the man is at his second story window when the Coast Guard comes by in a boat and says "Get in!" The man replies that he has faith in God and will not leave. The Coast Guard says "So be it," and speeds away.

The water rises until the man is on his roof. Sure enough, the Rescue Squad flies by in a helicopter and says "Strap on!" The man shouts back that he has faith in God, and waves them off.

Ultimately, the man drowns, and the flood waters consume his home. Upon arriving at heaven's gates, St. Peter takes him in to meet God. The man is very angry with God for having let him drown, despite his great faith. He demands that God explain to him why he had

Evil in Mirror Lake

not been saved. God responds that the angels had sent a Jeep, a boat, and a helicopter to save him.

God helps those who help themselves, but not always in the way they wish. This is grace building on nature, a partnership adventure. As Jesus said to Peter, "Be on guard, and pray that you may not undergo the test. The spirit is willing but human nature is weak."

The Father helps us in prayer to avoid evil by giving us good advice through the Holy Spirit, and by sending others who can help us. Nevertheless, God does not help us by changing nature. Amazing coincidences, though, do show us that God, by influencing our decisions, is in control of the direction in which our world is going. So, we must constantly attune ourselves in prayer to the activity of God in our lives.

"Or was there, perhaps, an unseen hand at work?" asks Terry Golway upon the birth of his first-born, "For surely there must be such an entity, with practiced fingers working feverishly while we mortals play our assigned roles in drama and tragedy, believing credulously that so much of life is coincidence and happenstance. Oh, yes, there is a hidden hand all right. For mere chance and coincidence, however powerful, could not have presented so precious a gift as Katie and, not long afterward, her brother Conor."—**The Irish in America**. The hidden hand is the Holy Spirit; we must be attuned to it.

From the negative side, there is no such thing as a *curse* placed on someone or some family. Bad things come from bad decisions either on my part or from others, if not from nature itself. Of course, there are such realities as: negative thinking, chronic pain, shortsightedness, and so on, which can propel me into multiple bad decisions. I should not depend too much on luck to make me an exception. Even with a thousand-to-one odds, the one always comes up eventually. There is no such thing as a Kennedy curse—just a series of bad attitudes and decisions, and not necessarily just by the Kennedys.

Patton on the other hand deeply believed in an all-powerful God who was controlling history. He tried to imitate his all-powerful God. May we never need him to be reincarnated in our lifetime. **Despite** and not because of the army Chaplain's prayer, ordered by General George Patton on Christmas Eve of 1944, the bad weather did subside and they were able to relieve the Americans besieged at Bastogne. This was simply an amazing coincidence, in my view. But who am I to say for sure that this was not a first class miracle?

I should not pray to change the weather, I should pray to know what to do no matter what the weather does. Obviously, God will not deliver me from all physical evil—terrible things. But God will always be there as my friend to counsel me as to what I should do in response,

God and Prayer

if I am but listening—one half of prayer. If I am listening or noticing, I will observe many amazing coincidences. They may just be signs to me of God's will and love for me.

I am now going to wander over to the sandy part of the lake, another view point, to see if I can detect God's activity in the depths of our world.

CHAPTER VI

GOD IS ACTIVE IN THE WORLD

B efore a cluster of T.V. cameras, a Honduran man described the terrible consequences the floods and mud slides, brought on by Hurricane Mitch, had caused his family, his community, and their homes. He ended by commenting, "We ask God, 'what bad things did we do to deserve this?' Tell us and we will change."

NBC news 11/3/98

Lying on the sandy beach, propping up my head with my arms, I peer out over the surface of the choppy lake. I feel the sun's warmth beating on me. On this lazy summer morning, I welcome the wafting breeze which cools my sweating brow. I feel two energy fields at work—one above and the other in the lake. I sense a strong analogy to something in myself. This confluence of energies intrigues me. For as the eerie current churns below the surface, and the wind swirls above, so in my soul I feel two turbulent forces—evil and good.

God is present and active in my world today. But how? God is not active in controlling the course of nature, although God sustains nature moment by moment—as electricity keeps the light bulb burning. Likewise, God does not interfere with my free will, although I feel the Spirit's influence swirling about me. How then does God's activity relate to the eerie evils that run deep in my world? It is **my** conception of God that determines **my** view of the Almighty's activity in my world.

Here are some different examples of how people view God's activity in the world: Deism, Theism, Atheism, Agnosticism, Soul Pantheism, Spirituality, Evolution, Trinitarian Creation, New Age, Paganism, Hebrews, Communism, Jansenism, Commercialism, Super-organism, Upanishads, Kabbalism, and Theistic Deism.

Deism is a rational belief, or knowledge, in the existence of a God, but it does not accept the continued presence of God among us outside

God is Active in the World

the continual act of creation. We can also describe deism as a body of thought advocating natural religion based on human reason rather than on revelation. It emphasizes morality, and denies the interference of the Creator with the laws of the universe. Although deism was popular among our American founding fathers, it all but died out even by the time of Thomas Jefferson's passing. Deism was too cold, and the idea of a caring father, as God, swiftly replaced it.

Kant's classic distinction between deism and theism is that a deist believes that God is the *cause of the world*, whereas a theist holds God to be the *author of the world*. Theism is a belief in the existence of a personal God who is actively manifested in the world. In the Jewish religion, the name of God (G-d), Yahweh (YHWH), or Jehovah is too sacred to write, much less to pronounce. Their God is very intimately involved in our world by influencing our decision-making process through the power of God's presence. This is theism.

Robespierre describes atheism (a-theism means *non-theist*) as "an immodest assumption of impossible knowledge." It is the absolute denial of a God. Atheism is the belief that God does not exist, or can be shown not to exist as defined in a particular way. Charles Bradlaugh wrote, in his **Plea for Atheism**, that an atheist is certainly justified in saying, "The Bible God I deny; the Christian God I disbelieve in; but I am not rash enough to say there is no God as long as you tell me you are unprepared to define God to me."

Agnosticism is simply not being sure of the existence of God. Sometimes agnostics worship the *question mark itself* as God. They admire the unintelligible instead of staying quite simply in the unknown. Mystery is better than absolutely nothing. It is like hedging your bet. When W. C. Fields, in his old age, was caught reading a Bible and asked, "Why?" he responded, "I'm looking for loopholes."

Joseph Campbell is a type of soul pantheist. He has interpreted a common thread in mythology as the idea that God or Divinity is a personification of the Energy that informs all life. Campbell tells me that I am a bubble on a wave of energy passing through time and space. He replaces the idea that energy comes from a personal deity with the notion that energy itself **is** the deity.

Spirituality is not the opposite of materialism, but its amalgamation. It is the two working as a whole. It might be well for me to think of myself as a body in a soul, as well as a soul in a body. I need to reach for my soul. The midpoint in the hourglass between energy and matter is where the seat of the soul is. To touch that place is to come of age spiritually—it is to be in communion with the God acting within me.

The evolution of the universe began with a Big Bang, many scientists say. If so, then creation is really divine love's Big Bang evolving. Some early Church Fathers, such as Gregory of Nazianzus in the 4th century, said God's love was so great that it had to break forth. Creation itself, the early Church Fathers say, is nothing but God's love looking for more things to love. In our own times, Dutch theologian Edward Schillebeeckx has observed that "we have not yet probed the depth and meaning of creation—God's activity in the world. God created this world out of love." Campbell does not say this, but his equation of Divinity or God would be $E=mc^2$. E equals God's love which is pure energy. This energy, or part of it, turned into matter which includes everything. God creates to give Godself in love. This is my deduction—$E=mc^2$.

Whenever I ask scientists what they think happened before the Big Bang, or who set off this singularity, they inevitably answer that this is not a scientific question, and move on. Timothy Ferris, in **The Whole Shebang**, says that it is reasonable to ask what cosmology, now that it is a science, can tell us about God. "Sadly, but in all earnestness, I must report," says Ferris, "that the answer, as I see it, is: Nothing."

Yet, if I operate on the premise that every effect needs a cause, then the question of pre-Bang reality is valid. Sometimes I have to begin with hypothetical answers as long as they make sense. Making sense to my mind and being the truth can be different, but it is a start, especially if I do not have anything else to go on.

A trinitarian, all-knowing and all-loving God being the Primary Cause makes sense. Why? Because creation is done out of love, for love. Love is caring about the well being of others. God created me and everything out of love. If I could probe deeper into the nature of this primary cause, it would help. Neither reason nor science can carry me there, only revelation and faith. Nevertheless, this revelation must make sense. Schillebeeckx concludes by asserting "It is a marvel that God reveals God's inner life to us as dynamic, as Trinitarian, as three people in love." "That's remarkable," says Archbishop Rembert G. Weakland in the *St. Anthony Messenger* (June 1999), "we could forever sit and think and not come up with this marvelous image of God as three persons in love and dynamic." "My image is this," continues the Archbishop, "We are the People of God, dancing on pilgrimage." The trinitarian God is operating in our world not as a uniperson (a single person) but as a community of persons.

Denis Edwards in **The God of Evolution** argues for the same view though somewhat expanded:

God is Active in the World

The old popular idea of God as located in the heavens,
understood as the sky, is clearly no longer viable in a
world of the Hubble telescope and space travel. But there
is another common imaginative picture held I think, quite
unreflectively, by many believers and unbelievers alike:
God (usually as a unipersonal individual being) and the
universe are understood as two realities, more or less
over against each other, with God reaching into the world
to act at particular moments. This common way of
imaging the God-world relationship results in an
interventionist view of divine action. God is imagined as
intervening to create and to move creation in the right
direction at certain times.

I argue for another image that is also necessarily
inadequate, but which is less inadequate than those
described above. ***The universe can be understood as***
unfolding "within" the trinitarian relations of mutual
love. (Emphasis added.)

In determining how God is active in our world, the more I know about my God's inner life, the greater expectation I would have to more correctly interpret that activity. Since evil is a lack of what ought to be, and since God would naturally tend to act according to God's own nature, it is important to look into God's being, and this will then help us to understand evil—a lack of what ought to be.

When I talk Trinity, I am talking mystery. It is a bigger mystery than even the universe itself. At most, all I can make is an educated guess. Augustine of Hippo thought the following first: The First Person of the Trinity looks in upon himself and forms an image of himself, much as we do when we are introspective. That image, though, is so perfect that it goes out as a separate person—the Word of God. It is a procession of knowledge. Next, the First Person looks upon this Second Person and loves her. The Second Person likewise loves the First. This love relationship between them becomes so perfect that it spirals out into a Third Person—the spirit of Love. This second procession is one of love. And so, we have a trinity of persons in one God. I must interject here that in God there is no time so there was never a time when only the First Person existed. The inner uncreated life of the Trinity is timeless, unlike our time filled world. How does this translate into humanity? This love relationship in God is reflected in humanity. This is the positive way of looking at God's activity in our world. The

143

Evil in Mirror Lake

absence of this is evil.

"These two did oftentimes do the two-backed beast together, joyfully rubbing and frothing their bacon against one another, in so far, that at last she became great with child."—Gargantua, thus says Rabelais in **Gargantua and Pantagruel**. I mention this to show the whole of human sexuality. For the first thousand years the church taught that the only primary end of sex was the procreation of the human race. Augustine goes as far as to say that after the woman knows she is pregnant, making sexual love until after the birth is immoral. During the second thousand years, recognized in Vatican II, the Catholic Church came to acknowledge two equally essential ends in marriage. The second is the mutual love and support shown between husband and wife sustained by this act of love. I predict that before this next millennium is over, the church will also discover that sex is also fun. Sex is perhaps the most pleasurable and exciting activity that adults enjoy. Of course, for some husbands, it seems to be golf. And for some women, shopping and conversation over coffee.

"Good sex is adults at play. Play is a wondrous activity, a way of celebrating existence. One theologian suggested that next to love, the concept of play best expresses God's life and activity. God is play, at play with the universe, creating in joy and delight. In sex we are God's partners at play," says James and Mary Kenny in *The Messenger* (2-11-00). In the biblical **Song of Songs**, God teaches us that because sex embodies and expresses love, it is beautiful. Sex is pleasurable, important, sacred, and beautiful. We learn all of this from a trinitarian God.

This holistic approach to sexuality makes it as holy as the Trinity. Nietzsche's critique of this was, "Christianity gave Eros poison to drink: he did not die of it but degenerated—into a vice" (#168). The evolution of ideas takes time to develop. In writing this, I am not interested in just evil, but also what ought to be.

The first of the robust authors, who tells us in his lusty animalism that life for its own sake could be made worth living, is Francois Rabelais, an ex-Catholic priest in the fifteen hundreds, in his **Gargantua and Pantagruel**. In laughing, he explores the meaning of seriousness. He explores the serious subject of what life is and what the difference is between our illusions and the reality in which we have them. He asks the most basic question, "How to know God?" The answer is through both reason and faith.

Three reasonable ideas can be drawn from my faith in a trinitarian image of God. First, God's highest activity is knowing and loving. We humans reflect that image and likeness in our being able to know and

God is Active in the World

to love.

Second, creation's maleness and femaleness reflect the first two persons in God. They first get to know each other, and then after expressing their love for each other in their bodies, a third person—a child proceeds from their love. Notice that the first procession was that of knowing, and the second was that of loving. Therein is the prototype of the human family, patterned after the Trinity—father, mother and child.

Third, I have a cause for this explosion of God's energy that in turn becomes equal to all matter, times the speed of light squared ($E=mc^2$). Matter is solidified energy—God's energy or love. The universe coming from God's love avoids the philosophical problem of something coming from nothing. The something is simply God's love solidified into the universe. Everything is one. For a delightful and thought provoking little masterpiece, see **$E=mc^2$** by Davis Bodanis.

"Events unfold in ways that make us think of God. They achieve, in their happening, a symmetry and an order that would be frightening if assigned to Chance," Thomas Lynch says in *Our Sunday Visitor* (3-21-99). The Holy Spirit is my relationship with God as Father, or Mother, or Parent. This Spirit is the love of God that touches and guides my life. This is how God is active in the world.

Epitetus (55-135A.D.), the emancipated slave, a Greek philosopher, who knew nothing of a triune God, nor of Einstein's equation, calls for the presence of God within ourselves. Why then are we ignorant of our noble birthright, he queries. Why are we not constantly aware from where we came? When we say grace before meals, do we remember who we are who eat—whom we feed? It is the divine we feed, the divine we exercise. We carry a God about within us.

This presence of God in the universe is expressed in this ancient Sanskrit saying, "God sleeps in the minerals, awakens in the plants, walks in the animals and thinks in you."

Making a distinction between the uncreated eternal inner life of the trinitarian God and the created participation in this life of God is important. This distinction saves me from pantheism and the fiery stake. Note that there is no problem with matter (the Universe) being eternal as long as God has created it eternally. This universe, science tells me, was spawned only about twelve or so billion years ago. But there could have been an infinite number of Big Bangs before that. We cannot imagine this infinity of time, but we can intellectually accept it.

I say this although the Fourth Lateran Council of 1215 denounced Aristotle's belief that the universe is infinitely old. The Council affirmed that "for Christians, the universe had a beginning in time." This

Evil in Mirror Lake

became a matter of faith. Scientists now believe the same. Thomas Aquinas (1225-1274), however, some few years later answered, "We hold by faith alone, and it cannot be proven by demonstration, that the world did not always exist." (I Q 46 a 2)

This is about as far as I can probe into the mystery of what might have been with the Big Bang emanating from a trinitarian God. I cannot prove it, but it makes sense to me that God is active in the world in this way. Evil, then, is a lack of what ought to be.

George A. Maloney, describing Christic consciousness in a New Age gives us a new dimension in his book **Mysticism and The New Age.** He says, trying to bridge the traditional Christian teaching with the New Age:

> *The Spirit, that the risen Jesus sends by asking his Father, is seen as the loving source of God himself, divinizing all who are open to receive his gift of the Spirit. This holiness given to us to transform us into heirs of God, true children of God (Rom. 8:15), is the very indwelling of God's Spirit taking possession of us Christians, penetrating our minds, our thoughts, and all our actions with the very life of God.*

> *St. John, the beloved disciple of Jesus, cannot get over the miracle of our regeneration, "...not by water alone but by the Spirit..." (John 3:3, 5). "Think of the love that the Father has lavished on us, by letting us be called God's children; and that is what we are" (1 Jn 3:1). St. Paul describes the main work of the Spirit as making us into true children of God: "...the Spirit of God has made his home in you... and if the Spirit of him who raised Jesus from the dead is living in you, then he who raised Jesus from the dead will give life to your mortal bodies through his Spirit living in you." (Romans 8:9, 11)*

> *God's very own Spirit dwells within us as in his temple (1 Cor. 6:19-20). We possess through the Spirit the fullness of the triune God living and acting in love within us at all times. This Spirit of love brings new life to its fullness in the proportion that we allow the Spirit to become our Guide, Teacher and Revealer, as he guides us Christians to make choices according to the mind of Christ.*

God is Active in the World

Pagans see God and their own happiness in the fulfilling of their natural instincts. On the other hand, the Rabbi author, Harold Kushner, tells us that the Bible story in the Book of Genesis found God and happiness in our human ability to control our natural instincts. Besides the devil, whom I have been talking (writing) about at length, I also have my flesh and the world actively influencing my natural instincts towards evil.

The Hebrew community was correct in holding firm to God's working in our world today. The Jews were and are theistic. Spinoza missed the whole picture in saying that he attributes everything **only** to nature and people's decisions. Besides, Spinoza's God is terrible—a God of good and Evil. God works only like a good parent—by influencing me through relationships and advice. When these influences and relationships are bad, it is the world leading me astray into sin and evil. At every moment and in every situation, God is the intimate, attentive, and encouraging friend who is guiding me in the world. It is the silence between the notes that makes the music of my life. I must be listening as well as doing to compose this music. I am creating my own character and destiny.

And yet I must be aware of the heresy of Plagianism. Pelagius was a fourth-century priest who taught that you could will belief. Belief cannot be willed, it is only a free gift. I do not leap into faith, I fall into it much like I fall into love. I am also free to reject the free gift. This would be my sin. I am free to sin, but I am not free to not sin. All credit has to be God's for not sinning. All credit has to be God's for faith. Otherwise it is not faith; it is success.

Communism has its seeds in Georg Hegel. "The history of the world is none other than the progress of the consciousness of freedom," Hegel gives us his most famous quotation, in **The Philosophy of History**, assembled by his associates at Berlin in 1831. The core of his philosophy is that history is the mind (Spirit of God?) becoming conscious of itself. The universe is no more nor less than the revelation or unfolding of an absolute (Idea, Ideal, Spirit, God, Matter?). Hegel's idealism does not entail the Berkeleyan notion of matter as nonexistent. This *absolute* evolves by a constant battle or dialectic between what is, the status quo (thesis), and the ideal of what ought to be (antithesis). His own spirit alienates man. This conflict results in a coming together (synthesis). Hegel himself did not use these three now-famous words.

His neat notion that the State embodies the reality of Mind's Progress toward Unity with Reason is sinister and is not in accord with reality. Also, his idea that such men as Alexander and Julius Caesar were great heroes, probably helped make Adolph Hitler into a hero.

Evil in Mirror Lake

Hegel's philosophical basis for Prussian nationalism and expansionism would be the main cause of two world wars. This is all exposed in his greatest book, **Phenomenology of Spirit** (1807).

Later Karl Marx and Friedrich Engels, students of Georg Hegel, would say that man, who was alienated from himself, was also alienated in his economic life. Marx turned Hegel's philosophy upside down. He simply substituted *matter* for Hegel's *mind* or *spirit*. The result is a becoming (synthesis) which in turn becomes thesis and its continuing, evolving, dialectical progression of changes. This means a movement of perspective (or consciousness) to a point where thesis and antithesis are subsumed in a higher or new understanding of reality. What propels this process of becoming—thesis, antithesis, synthesis—is, "the cunning of reason," or intuitive understanding, or inner knowing. But of whom?

This historical materialism, called dialectical materialism only after Marx's death, is, of course, the philosophical basis for communism. The reason that it does not work is that communism considered neither people's free will nor their selfishness. Communism was a human gamble. It expected people to freely choose to work for the common good. Communism failed because it overestimated people. Most people will not work for the common good—only for their own good. They quashed individual human initiative with a command economy. The State is not the soul of the universe—the Holy Spirit is.

The falsity of Hegel and Marx's explanation of the movement of history is demonstrated by the world's great setbacks—Stalin's crimes, the Holocaust, etc. *"The cunning of reason,* which propels communism, would have more blood on its hand than even God could ever wash off,"* said David Denby. The Spirit has its own reason for allowing tragedies. We simply have to trust the (Holy) Spirit. No, the great setbacks are not the Spirit's working out of creation. The Spirit needs people to cooperate. The setbacks are people saying "No" to the Spirit's plan.

On the other hand, commercialism—things will make me happy—among many things in our pop culture, alienates people from their spirit. It happens this way. Ads tell people what is on the leading edge of *cool*. So, some people wear and drive and drink things that are not really their choices but the choices of some anonymous brand name from Madison Avenue. People have surrendered their right to choose for themselves. Alienation from my spirit comes when I make having and doing the only values in life. If, though, I am working for a better world, then using better things is part of the process, part of my spirit. David Denby says it best in his fine book, **Great Books**:

God is Active in the World

*Alienation is a loss of self: We work for others, to fulfill
other people's goals, and often enough we confront what
we produce with an indifference bordering on disgust.
And so the eternal cry of boredom and meaninglessness;
the impoverishment that so many feel, the hollow
exhaustion at the end of the day; the dull anger, the
internal distancing of oneself, the need to escape ...
Many of us have simply accepted as inevitable the
spiritual condition that Marx considered as perversion of
man's essence. Such is the nature of modern work, we
assume, in factories, offices, corporations, department
stores, gas stations— work that is safer than in Marx's
time, but often no more engaging. Reading the early Marx
is like pulling up a rock covering hidden perceptions;
those feelings are still there, wriggling around in the dark.
He gave them shape once again.*

*Americans might not express their feelings in that way,
but they act on them: They divide their lives in two, work
and play, earning and consuming; they drag themselves
through work to reach the promised land of leisure, the
ecstasy of the defining car, suit, house, or vacation that
settles for all time who they are. The disgust with work
makes the act of buying things an arena of anxiety and
triumph. Alienation exists at all levels of American
society. It is called consumerism.*

My view of how God is active in the world is this: the collective choices of people, who are conscious of their calling, can follow reason, or the call of the Holy Spirit, or can choose otherwise. The world's setbacks are the result of people's bad choices—despite the fact that people always choose what they judge as best for them at the time. The Spirit moves on and in the end is more powerful through her force of persuasion. People move on through their instinct to survive, and eventually learn from mistakes at least collectively since individuals may never give up their ego position. The world gets better century by century, millennium by millennium, because God's Spirit is propelling us upward. What is done to us is not always the will of the Spirit. What we choose to do as a response, should always be God's will.

I think I would like to identify with a little known Neapolitan, Giambattista Vico, whose primary source was personal experience rather than books, although he was profoundly well read. He wrote

Evil in Mirror Lake

The New Science (1725, revised 1730, 1744). He is also important for his notion that history runs not in a straight line from bad to better to best, but in circles—from growth to decay. He saw a society as the product of its literature, myth, language, law, art, types of government, religion, and philosophy. He saw Divine Providence at work in human affairs. He could see the difference between a God of culture and a true God, to whose providence he subtly appealed. People with all their free will are acting to fulfill a divine destiny. His masterpiece did not have a good translation in the English language until 1948.

Howard Bloom calls God a super-organism. In an intriguing and must-read book, **The Lucifer Principle**, he claims that the primary forces behind much of human creativity—both for evil and for good— are: super-organisms, ideas, and the pecking order. This is the "holy" trinity of the Lucifer Principle, also the triad of human evil. He insists, "We are incidental microbits of a far-larger beast, cells in the super-organism." Does this not sound like we are members of the body of Christ? And God is actively acting through us? But there are other super-organisms out there in competition.

It is an idea whose time has come, the *meme*, that determines the victory. It is the best idea that conquers. The best idea explains to me the meaning of my human life and of my evil. Capitalism conquered communism because it works better. Meme comes from the Latin word *mihi* that is the dative case for *to me*. Ideas are the most powerful thing in the world. The pecking order comes from my animal brain. This supremacy has traditionally come from my violence. Violence is the most appalling of human expressions. Yet, I can dream of peace—to fashion a world where violence ceases to be. Nature is indifferent. There is no motherly nature who loves her offspring and protects them from harm or evil—that is my job, my decision.

Yet, I must be careful not to limit my life to simply deciding. I am also caught up in the mystery of God's plan for me and my constant calling to choose to say "Yes" to that mysterious call—"I am the servant of the Lord." "When a great moment knocks on the door of your life, it is often no louder than the beating of your heart, and it is very easy to miss," Boris Pasternak said. Living is the Spirit and I together.

"When you notice that there are particular moments in your life when you are led to introspection, work with them gently, for these are the moments when you can go through a powerful experience, and your whole world view can change quickly. These are the moments when former beliefs crumble on their own, and you can find yourself being transformed," says Sogyal Rinpoche in his insightful book, **The Tibetan Book of Living and Dying**.

God is Active in the World

This new awareness of God's activity in our lives is what one of the Upanishads calls "a turning about in the seat of consciousness," a personal and non-conceptual revelation of what we truly are. It amounts to a new birth, a new me. These Upanishads have been the prime influence on Hindu thought—and on Buddhist and Western thought, the latter through Arthur Schopenhauer, and in more modern times Ludwig Wittgenstein, "the spirit of the snake... is your spirit..." We are all one.

They are called the Upanishads because the pupils had to sit (shad) down (ni) close (upa) to the teacher. There are more than 100 Upanishads, but many of these are afterthoughts. The vital ones are fewer than twenty in number. We know next to nothing about their authors. Although the Babylonian **Gilgamish** and, possibly, the earliest layers of Homer predate them, it is in the Upanishads that people are first seen consciously thinking as well as telling stories and praising the gods and expressing sexual love. See the **Kama Sutra**. This Hindu book on sexuality, targets not just sexual activity, but, also, selfishness within sexual activity. They say that when I choose selfishness, I do not commit evil; it is merely a mistake. The writer of the Upanishads separated pleasure from good. The one true pleasure for them is self-knowledge, the ultimate good. The ego that seems all-encompassing is the chief obstacle to the truth that all is one, identical with Brahman (which I call the Holy Spirit).

Modern authors are writing about the same things but with different languages and different definitions. For example, "You stand between the two worlds of your lesser self and your full self." I would say your higher nature and your lower nature. Modern authors also identify the soul (the source of my life) as part (uncreated and eternal) of the World Soul (uncreated God). They relegate the personality to the lower nature, whereas I would put it as the concrete expression of my (created) soul. They refer to what amounts to the Holy Spirit as *a nonphysical Teacher*. Except for the transmigration of souls, as opposed to my understanding of a one-shot eternal event, most teachings jibe. Neither of these last two events can be proved, just believed or imagined. These ideas can be found in **The Seat of the Soul** and **The Dancing Wu Li Masters**, both by Gary Zukav—one of the modern authors referenced to above.

James R. Newby of Yokefellows International, a Quaker-like group, says in his **Quarterly Yoke Letter** (8-96):

*No matter how much we seek to define God and
"systematize" our process of knowing, there will always*

Evil in Mirror Lake

*be mystery beyond our knowledge. Learning to be
comfortable in the tension between affirming our faith in
one breath, and asking questions about our life and faith
in the next, is to accept our human frailty and admit with
the Apostle Paul that in this life we do, indeed, see
through a glass darkly. The more we come to know God,
the more we will discover there is to know. This mystery
becomes an important aspect of our quest.*

Until recently, the state government thought that the idea of a Supreme Being who watches over oppressed innocents and punishes criminals was essential to its well-being. The police cannot be everywhere, but God is. This is the terror of wrongdoers and the comfort of the virtuous. We now look upon this belief as superstition, and we can see the result as our prisons fill up with wrongdoers.

Jonathan Swift lampooned this authority of Divine Providence in **Gulliver's Travels** by fictionalizing that in the country of Lilliput "the disbelief of a Divine Providence renders a man incapable of holding any public station; for, since kings avow themselves to be the deputies of Providence, the Lilliputians think nothing can be more absurd than for a prince to employ such men as disavow the authority under which he acts."

Nevertheless, in the end of time, the Power and the Majesty will make all things right. Our appropriate response to God's presence and power in our world is, as Albert Einstein once suggested, an awesome reverence that bows our heads and treads on silent feet. Dr. Faust said the same thing:

> *The thrill of awe is man's best quality.*
> *Although the world may stifle every sense,*
> *Enthralled, man deeply senses the Immense.*

> **(Faust L6273)**

Jewish mystics of the Kabbalah or Cabala also seek this Immense. It is not a book but a system of beliefs about how to get to the divine. Their most important book is the **Zohar**, written by Moses de Leon (1250-1305). The very heart of Kabbalism is to know God directly and to pass on the information thus gained only to initiates. Creation came as an accident when God momentarily lost consciousness and let spill out sparks of creation that fell into increasingly lower realms, and evil as well as life was created. Kabbalism teaches that people can perfect themselves, or at least that there is a path toward perfection. The uni-

God is Active in the World

verse as a whole, and all parts of it, are permeated with the energy of the creator. The purpose of existence is to return all the sparks, the souls, to their original place. Out there is a Spirit guiding us to this restoration. We need but to get beyond the sensual and in contact with this Energy. The Kabbalists feel alive in doing their part in this re-creation—and are grateful for their existence. Except for the weird way they go about it—throwing sticks—they are not far from my perception of the truth.

Christianity holds that God is active in the world as a caring Father, Son and Holy Spirit. Anything that God does outside of God's inner life is done by all three persons together. God speaks to me through inspired writings and to me personally through prayer. When I listen and act, I help God cause "Thy kingdom come." Despite what the evening news tells me, the world is evolving into a better place generation after generation in a never-ending improvement, a constant struggle for excellence. However, it always allows for and admits to certain setbacks. Hitler and World War II were big setbacks, or a catharsis.

Deistic Theism is my new category of thinking about how God is active in our world. It has God allowing the universe to run on its own natural powers, but God is also personally interested in my well-being. Christ the God-Man is the center of my personal relationship with God. Whether God as the Holy Spirit extends influence into the world through messengers (angels) or by working directly, it makes little difference. God is still influencing the world through the intelligent and loving decisions of myself and others.

God created a universe that is both good and evolving, and so not perfect. Creation will always be changing. The universe is not divine dualism—but rather, it is my good and bad decisions that affect the outcome of creation along with the impulses of nature. We are free moral agents helping to create the universe.

God influences my free will into making informed and loving decisions. Maybe the instinct to survive, including dependence on the group, accounts for my loving choices while intelligence accounts for my making informed choices. But then, both the instinct and the intelligence have to be attributed to the One source behind all appearances. The ultimate controls and direction of the universe is God's. To believe this, we must believe in the strong force of good influence. I have been in situations where I had no authority, no official power, but I was in the right, or I thought I was. I chose to use energy, will, and intelligence, which proved potent despite the lack of a publicly granted position of authority. And I prevailed. *May the force be with me!* This is the unrelenting (moral) power of God to direct the world.

153

Evil in Mirror Lake

The temptation of people in authority is to want to exchange the position of the shepherd who leads by walking in front, for the position of the cattle driver who walks behind and drives. This is the difference between old style, top down authority as a force in organization vs. leadership using psychological methods. The new way is the idea of serving rather than being served. Something Jesus taught a long time ago.

The world's great substitute for love is not hate nor apathy, but power. Friedrich Nietzsche tells us we are all driven by the *will to power*. Will to power began as a European perspective. To fulfill oneself in power, is to be human. Power is force. This simply, in the end, is true neither for people, nor for the Almighty. "I think I have discovered the highest good," said Martin Luther King Jr., "It is love. Love is the most durable power in the world." Love is the power of influence—attraction to goodness! Again, "I wish people would love everybody else the way they love me. It would be a better world," bragged Muhammad Ali, formerly Cassius Clay. Who won out in the long run—the power of Jesus' love or the Roman legions? Remember Joseph Stalin asking how many divisions does Pope Pius XII have? Who won?

When Michelangelo Buonarotti painted God the Father in human form, mark what robustness, what power is there. Yet, whenever so many other Italian artists reveal the Divine Love in the Son, note the soft, curled or hermaphroditic pictures, so destitute of all brawniness, hinting nothing of any power except that which is love. I am seeing God as all powerful and as loving, and so I, as the artists, vacillate between power and love. My truth is a matter of my perspective. My God is active in the world only through love—the Holy Spirit, who is both feminine and masculine.

The fourth insight in the book, **The Celestine Prophecy,** is that we steal energy from other people. I need to look elsewhere for my energy if I am to be a loving person. This energy of love is available to me in the Almighty.

Through the newly formed haze, I think I see a man walking toward me on the lake. I may not be alone here. Let me examine how God influences the world to good through the loving Jesus.

JESUS IS THE YES MAN

Jesus, the enigmatic preacher from Galilee, said "Yes" perfectly to the Father thus avoiding all personal moral evil as the Father likewise calls me to do. Jesus as man, I believe, was not aware that he was also God, and so he was "like us in all things but sin." Nevertheless, Jesus is

God is Active in the World

the God-Man.

Josephus, the Jewish historian of the first century, wrote about the historical Jesus as a man, "…a doer of startling deeds," and as a teacher who "…gained a following both among many Jews and many men of Greek origin." The Jewish **Talmud** says that, "On the eve of the Passover, they hanged Yeshu… because he practiced sorcery."

The Nicene Creed of 325 A.D. expresses my belief that Jesus Christ is true God and true man. I must focus one eye on each of these two truths (God and Man) and never blink either eye. I also believe that these two natures in Jesus are not intermingled, but are separate, yet united in the one person. The Council of Chalcedon (451 A.D.) described this hypostatic union as divinity and humanity being joined *without confusion*. Still the question remains, was the human side of Jesus aware of his divine side? If he were not aware that he was God, then he faced evil the same way I do.

In my youth, I believed that Jesus knew all along that he was not only the human Messiah, but also the divine God! Despite his agony in the garden, I believed that Jesus knew of his future resurrection as he was on his trek to Calvary. Today I think differently.

The effect of thinking about Jesus in my old way separates me from Jesus because I do not know my future. I cannot read other people's minds; nor do I have the assurance of my divinity that all things will work out well. Yet, if I believe as did Paul that Jesus became like me in all things except sin, then it must be that this Jesus was not aware of his Divine Nature. I think Jesus' divinity is why Mary and the saints became so popular in the early church. Believers could identify better with them and their humanness whereas Jesus was so divine.

I now think that, although Jesus was God, he nevertheless had no human knowledge of his divinity. Even if Mary had told Jesus about his miraculous conception, the angel's message was not clear that he was divine—just the son of the Most High. I, also, am a son of the Most High. The Jews did not expect the messiah to be divine. He struggled like each of us to find and to carry out the will of his Father (Abba). Thus, he spent long nights in prayer. At times, events amazed and disappointed Jesus. He was hungry and angry; he was lonely and afraid; he ran away and stayed behind; he cried, he experienced all things as we do. In fact, in the scriptures, Jesus expressed all of our emotions except laughing, if you wish to make anything out of that. I do not.

This is why a scholar of scripture, Roger Vermalen Karban says:

One of the most unforgivable things we do to Jesus is to
steal his real, historical personality from him. Ironically,

Evil in Mirror Lake

the theft starts the moment we begin to look at him as
God. At that point, some of us give in to the temptation to
think of him as some kind of divine robot, programmed
only to do "God things," while others create such a
saccharin disposition for him that diabetics can't come
within 50 feet of his smiling countenance without fear of
going into a coma. Once we steal Jesus' humanity, we
create a person with whom we can never identify, a real
misfit; someone who does what God wants him to do, but
who doesn't have a relationship with God to do it.

When Jesus was twelve years old, he stayed behind in the temple to ask the teachers a few more intelligent, probing questions. His parents looked for him for three days. Why did he do this?

I will answer this like an Irishman, with a question. "Was it not because he was an immature preteen?" Immaturity means not considering all of the aspects of a situation. Jesus truly was not thinking about his troubled parents. Jesus was like us in all things, including being immature at age twelve (to be immature is not a sin). To sin is to say "No" to God. To be immature is simply to be unaware of all the implications of my actions.

I like to think of Jesus as struggling through life like me, trying to know the will of his Father, and always saying "Yes" to that will. Unlike me, he was always able to say "Yes" to the Holy Spirit. In that way he was a perfect human. I must rely upon the Holy Spirit to help and guide me as I submit to God's will in my pursuit of excellence.

This excellence is to be found in the Beatitudes of Jesus, they tell me. Nevertheless, I have always found it hard, in a practical manner, to understand just what the eight Beatitudes are saying to me today. I happened to be able to see the Dead Sea Scrolls in Chicago, 2000. They contain a beatitude that predates the gospels and does make sense to me today:

> *Blessed (Ashré) is he who directs his heart toward his*
> *ways (the Law of the Most high),*
> *and restrains himself by her corrections*
> *and always takes delight in her chastisements.*
>
> *He does not forsake her when he sees distress,*
> *nor abandon her in time of strain.*
>
> *He will not forget her (on the day of) fear,*

God is Active in the World

And will not despise (her) when his soul is afflicted.

For always he will meditate on her,
and in his distress he will consider (her?).

When I find Jesus in the garden praying that the chalice pass him by, he was praying this Dead Sea beatitude, I think.

I used to think that this garden prayer was about the crucifixion since it happened the next day. He is praying as if his crucifixion (an evil) is God's will. Now, I interpret this differently. The chalice referred to in Jesus' prayer is the message of his preaching that he believes the Father wants him to continue teaching. Part of the message that Jesus is preaching is that God (Yahweh) is the God of all people, and that God loves all people equally, and welcomes them into The Kingdom.

This is one reason the Sanhedrin was upset with Jesus. Jewish religious belief, in that day, was that God (Yahweh) loved the Jews more than anyone else, after all, they were the Chosen People (Romans 11:28-29). It is interesting that the Jews do not send out missionaries to convert the world to Judaism, unlike most every other religion. Still, they do invite people to come to their classes if they get to know you.

The Jews did not realize that the only reason they were chosen was to prepare the world for the coming of the Messiah. I would think that their chosenness ended then, but John Paul II says that God continues to have a special relationship with the Jewish people. That status did not somehow expire with the birth of the Christ (the anointed one). "God made an *irrevocable* Covenant with the Jewish people," insists John Paul II in a recently concluded symposium on **The Roots of Anti-Judaism in the Christian Milieu** (1998). He continues, "and [God] remains faithful to it." The Old Testament is then alive and well today. Possibly, it is like the first born who forever remains such, though he has a dozen siblings. Or maybe it is like a first love, never forgotten! Could this simply have been a political fence-mending statement?

At any rate, today the Jewish people have a difficult time coming up with a plausible answer to why they have been chosen—for what? Christians believe they were chosen to prepare the world for the coming of the Messiah Redeemer—Jesus. In the garden, Jesus was asking the Father that he might be relieved of continuing to teach this universal message of God's love for all peoples because he could tell that both the Jewish leadership and the Romans were getting very upset with him.

Jesus further upset the Jewish leaders by insisting on the heart and

157

Evil in Mirror Lake

spirit of the law, rather than its mere outward observance. Also, his implication that the Kingdom of God was already among us, in this world, differed from the Jewish belief that the Kingdom was to come. Jesus' kingdom was a threatening message, disliked by Rome and the Jews. Ultimately, it was Jesus' clinging to the integrity of his vision of social justice coming in the Kingdom of God, that got him killed by the Kingdom of Herod and Caesar.

His attack on the temple priesthood was similarly detrimental to his safety, and he realized that it would likely get him killed. He sweat so profusely that it poured like blood, being unaware of any three-day resurrection. I would not sweat blood if I knew that all would be well in three days. This is despite the scripture telling us that Jesus would raise up the temple in three days (John 2:19-21 and Luke 9:22). They killed Jesus (an evil) not because God (all-good) willed it, but because the Sanhedrin (chose evil) asked for it, and Pontius Pilate (chose evil) ordered the execution to keep peace between himself and the people he ruled.

"The Romans caused his ultimate downfall because Jesus' popularity was a threat to their regime," says Roberta Harris in her picture-filled book, **The World of the Bible**, which gives us an up-to-date (1995) overview of the archaeological history of the Holy Land or The Levant—its ancient name. During Jesus' youth, the Roman Legions had already wiped out two towns in Israel that had instigated a revolt against the Kingdom of Herod and Caesar. Jesus' Kingdom of God was a similar threat. In fact, Jesus' kingdom involved a call for social justice between the *haves* and *have nots* of this world, which hints a bit of communism. The poor were taxed exceedingly heavy by King Herod and his wealthy friends.

Read the Beatitudes from the point of view that Jesus' Kingdom of God was meant to replace the present Kingdom of Caesar in this world, and soon: Blest are the poor, the Kingdom of God will be theirs. Blest are the sorrowing, they shall be consoled. Blest are they who hunger and thirst for social or contemporary justice, they shall have it. Blest are they who have shown mercy, we will show mercy to them. Blest are they who are single-hearted in this cause, for they shall see the Kingdom of God. Blest are they who work for the common good, they shall be called the sons and daughters of the Kingdom of God. Blest are those now persecuted for their call to the holiness of justice, they shall reign high in the Kingdom of God.

Certain scripture passages speak of Jesus as, "smitten of God" (Rev. 13:8; Isaiah 53:4). Isaiah 53:10 says, "It pleased the Lord to bruise him." Except by way of God's influence through persuasion, I under-

God is Active in the World

stand Jesus' crucifixion as God simply not interfering with other people's decisions, not Jesus', not the Jew's. I, like Jesus, must never flinch from the Father's will even in the face of terrible consequences. The above quotations from Isaiah in the Bible see God in the traditional way as manipulating and controlling destiny directly, instead of just influencing it. It is as the Muslim imam says, "Nothing will ever happen to us that Allah does not allow." Jesus, however, simply did the will of his Father to repair the rupture of our sins, and the sin of Adam (and Eve). While doing this, some unhappy people killed him. This evil was not God's will! This is true even though God foresaw what was to come. God knows the hearts of the people—even in the future.

Jesus' heroism stems from his keeping true to the integrity of his vision of social justice coming in his Kingdom of God which was to replace the Kingdom of Caesar. Jesus did not have to come up to Jerusalem, and he could have fled that night out into the desert. He chose to surrender himself into the hands of the authorities. Why? For years he had told stories without explaining them to the public, he was constantly on the move, he had come to the attention of the authorities, it was time to take his stand. Yet, his kingdom, as he told Pilate, was not totally of this world. His kingdom also had a spiritual dimension to it, and it was time for him to take the character test with his life on the line. Jesus was not just some social reformer, but he was also a social reformer.

Outside of the gospels, **The Annals of Tacitus** informs us, "Consequently, to get rid of the report (that Nero had ordered the conflagration of Rome), Nero fastened the guilt and inflicted the most exquisite tortures on a class hated for their abominations, called Christians by the populace. Christus, from whom the name had its origin, suffered the extreme penalty during the reign of Tiberius at the hands of one of our procurators, Pontius Pilatus, and a most mischievous superstition, thus checked for the moment, again broke out not only in Judea, the first source of the evil, but even in Rome, where all things hideous and shameful from every part of the world find their center and become popular."

Willie Allen, a friend, says, "God's will could be seen as Jesus' internal conviction of the truth as he saw it and of his responsibility to speak it. The *will of the Father* might be the appearance of such convictions in a person's awareness. The trouble with leaving such matter to be understood through metaphors is that people can't use an abstraction in their own lives. Jesus saw a truth and chose to stand on that truth, as he saw it, rather then leave people with the truth as the Jews saw it."

159

Evil in Mirror Lake

Sometimes evil is a judgment based on how things turn out. The Jews (Sanhedrin) were acting in their best interests as they saw it. They lacked a higher vision. Nevertheless, the crucifixion was an evil event, just like the holocaust was an evil event. Neither the crucifixion nor the holocaust was God's will.

This relieves me of the ghastly paradox of a *God on the cross*— that mystery of an unimaginable ultimate cruelty and self-crucifixion of God *for the salvation of man,* as Nietzsche claimed. My vision of this incident is that state officials made an evil decision in condemning a man, who also happened to be God. This was not a self-crucifixion. It was not just the fulfillment of a prophesy.

If I am going to understand evil and from where it comes, I must first understand the foremost of all evils—the crucifixion of the God-Man. God did not do this evil nor any other evils in our world. Other people did it as free moral agents.

Did Jesus have to die to save me from my sins? He could have just been born and then gone right back to heaven! I must never limit God even to the ways that God has already acted. God could simply have forgiven me my sins and told me, "Go in peace and sin no more." It was not Jesus' death that saved me from my ego-filled nature; it was Jesus' love for both his Father and for me, despite his sufferings, that redeemed me in the sight of his Father.

However, I know that God chose differently—the only begotten (come from the Father) Son became man and dwelt among us. Jesus' death on the cross was unnecessary, but it did show me how much God loves me. He totaled himself; gave it all. I need to know that. Jesus had to die to rise, but he did not have to die on the cross, as indeed he did. The blood shed at his circumcision was more than enough "to save us from our sins." Again, it was not the blood, but the love behind the blood that contained all the value. This is not like a bloody sacrifice practiced by ancient tribes. The cross happened—a bad thing happened—and it showed the depth of Jesus' and/or God's love for me. (It also showed what would happen to anyone who defied the temple and claimed to be the Messiah setting up his own kingdom.)

For a fresh and innovative, yet controversial, view of the teacher from Nazareth, see Bruce Chilton's **Rabbi Jesus.** He also assures us that it was the temple episode that precipitated Jesus' arrest and execution.

The human reasons for Jesus' execution are obscure, yet real. We human beings, also, can predict the future. If I often and seriously oppose my bosses, I can predict that they will either fire or transfer me. The question for me to decide is whether it is worth it. Jesus could have

God is Active in the World

foreseen his end, and chose it anyway. Even though Jesus' kingdom was *not of this world*, nevertheless it was already *among us*.

If Jesus were like us in all things but sin, no one was more surprised than Jesus, the human, when he arose on Easter Sunday. Later when the evangelists wrote the gospels, knowing Jesus was divine, they had Jesus saying, "Destroy this temple and in three days I will rebuild it." Picture Jesus believing that God, Yahweh, would take care of him if he only said "Yes" to all that God asked him to do. He had said *"Yes,"* and they led him to the gibbet of the cross. Jesus died, not because he must suffer evil to bring new life, but simply because powerful people condemned him to death. Yet, because Jesus was also God, his death became a sacrifice of a Divine Person, and so has infinite merits. The infinite merits come from the infinite love of the divine Jesus.

This is not true simply because I say it is. Remember my methodology in Chapter II. If the facts fit the theory, then the conclusion is valid. Ask yourself if this is not a better, truer way to look at evil in our world. Who is responsible? God or man or nature or a combination?

"My God, my God, why have you forsaken me?" was just the first line of Psalm 22 (21) which Jesus had memorized from his youth and prayed aloud from the cross. It is a Psalm of deliverance and hope. You can read it in your Bible. In those days, they had not yet numbered the psalms; quoting their first line identified them. God did not forsake Jesus. The evil of the crucifixion was not God's will. It was the result of some people's bad decisions. However, God worked through it. Jesus submitted to evil while submitting to God's will. I must do the same when evil comes because of my doing God's will. I must love, no matter what the consequences.

Why is there so much darkness in the world created by God? Jesus is the answer to the darkness. He is the light of the world which overcomes darkness. But, why is there darkness at all? Is an absence of light, not an absence of love?

God is in control, as we have seen, but not total control. In the 100 Greatest Books ever written, according to Easton and Franklin Presses, most of the great authors of these books describe clergymen in a negative light. Only Michael de Cervantes in his **Don Quixote de la Mancha** has the priest both intelligent and compassionate. I have asked myself, "Why is this?" My answer is that most of these authors have bought into the notion of the all-powerful God, and so God is responsible for the evil in their stories. Clergymen are agents of God and this evil. These authors do not like God's evil nor his henchmen.

The message of Cervantes' book is much harsher than the rosy

161

Evil in Mirror Lake

notion that in madness lies sanity, like in the TV series M.A.S.H. Don Quixote is about living a life based on illusion, a life that engages reality at no point. This too is evil, or at least leads to it. Reading romances just causes Don Quixote's madness as reading similar material has driven Madame Bovary in Flaubert's masterpiece of that name into folly of her own.

In the Bible, I find the same problem of combining made up stories with reality. Let us travel over to the next viewpoint where I see a boulder I can sit on and read my Bible. We can also peer down into the placid lake and mirror our experiences. Our inner soul contains all the knowledge of our experiences. We simply need to make sense of it.

I think someone is following me out of the haze. I am in deep thought now and cannot worry about who is following me—I cannot lose my train of thought.

CHAPTER VII

EVIL AND THE BIBLE INTERPRETED

"If evil befalls a city, has not the Lord caused it?" (Amos 3:6)

*"Everything proceeds from the mouth of the Most High,
whether the thing is good or evil." (Lamentations 3:38)*

*"Joshua conquered the entire country with all their kings.
He left no survivors, just as the Lord, the God of Israel,
had commanded." (Joshua 10:40)*

The haze having lifted, I sit here on this boulder and I ponder. The understanding that evil comes from God may be what we perceive the Bible to teach. We need to know how to interpret the inspired words of our sacred writings if we are to get beyond this. I begin with a story about understanding—words. Words mean only what their speaker intends for them to mean. I close my Bible and begin to reminisce. I have a story to tell which illistrates the importance of accurate interpretation.

Once upon a time, when I was a teenager in the 1950s, I kept a diary. One Friday night some friends and I went out and had a good time. That night I wrote in my diary, "Tonight we went out and had a ball. Everybody was cooking with fire."

Then an atom bomb came and destroyed almost everything. In the year 4072 A.D., an archaeologist digs and finds my diary and an old English dictionary next to it. She begins to translate it, and eventually publishes a paper about what teens did in the 1950s. She claims that they would pass a round sphere around a bonfire before they ate. She offers as proof the words *ball* and *fire* in my diary. However, we know that is not what I meant. How can she learn what I did mean? She must dig up all of the magazines, newspapers, and books in my library, and

Evil in Mirror Lake

spend many years developing the mentality of a teen who lived in the 1950s. Then, when she reads my words from that viewpoint, she can say, "Yes, the teens went out and had a good time. They were probably involved in some fun activities, but we have no idea if they went dancing, roller skating, or cruising."

Other people's words do not always mean what we make them to say. Words mean only what their speaker intended for them to mean *in context*. This may sound like former President Bill Clinton defining the meaning of the word *is*, but you know what I mean. (If they read this book in the year 4072 A.D., how many people will understand this last sentence?)

Note how important it is to date this diary accurately. If the archeologist judged that I had written my diary in the late 1960s, then the word *ball* could have sexual overtones, but not in the 1950s. Also, I ask: Was this story of mine about the diary made up, or did I actually keep a diary?

First, before you answer, realize that this question is not important. The story was to teach the interpretation of words apart from the mentality of the author. I can teach this equally well with a made-up story or a real life incident. A story only means what the author intends for it to mean, no more and no less. You should not put your meaning into the storyteller's words. As John Ruskin said, "Be sure that you go to the author to get his meaning, not to find yours." It is only the author's meaning that is inspired by God.

Second, I did drop a clue. At the beginning of the story I said, "Once upon a time." Now, is this not our way of saying that I made up the story that follows? I never kept a diary in my life. So, I can make the point of the story, no matter whether I kept a diary or not.

The Bible means only what the author intended for it to mean at the time he wrote it and for his particular audience. How can we know what he intended to say? We must develop the mentality of a nomadic, Semitic bedouin of centuries ago. German scripture scholars coined a phrase for this: the *sitz im leben,* or situation in life. Only then can we read their words with proper meaning. Just as we begin our stories with "Once upon a time," they began their made-up stories with, "God said.*"*

A contemporary of Jesus Christ and Saul/Paul was a Jewish rabbi, Philo of Alexandria. What is most important about him is that he gave a new approach to the Hebrew Scriptures. He discovered what was not in them—Greek Platonic philosophy. His allegorical pursuit of the meaning of Scriptures became the accepted manner of a biblical exegesis among many early Church Fathers. He was the first to put em-

Evil and the Bible Interpretted

phasis on the Logos—the word of God—a term going back to the pre-Socratic Greek philosopher Heraclitus, who took it to be the universal reason governing the world. Subsequently, Clement of Alexandria took up this idea, on behalf of the second person (Logos) of the Trinity to help explain the beginning of the fourth gospel. Philo also influenced Augustine in writing the **City of God** as well and Plotinus in his **Enneads**. Philo recommended that people should obey the Mosaic Law but employ allegory to understand its deeper meaning. Philo's revival of Greek notions of the nature of God became the foundation of the common philosophy of Judaism, Christianity and Islam.

Plotinus, an essentially intellectual mystic, left us his **Enneads** (3rd century A.D.). His pupil, Porphyry, rearranged the lectures into six books of nine sections each (*ennea* is the Greek word for nine). We now know his philosophy as Neoplatonism—in his time it was simply known it as Platonism. He saw the universe itself as a living thing. He saw existence in terms of a series of emanations from the One God, the First Principle—sometimes called the Absolute. This Absolute is beyond human understanding, and cannot be thought of in such merely human terms as space, time, or number. I need to remember this. Anything I say of God is only by way of analogy—it is partly the same and partly not. Plotinus holds that evil is really owing to a gradually increasing density—an increasing coarseness, an increasing lack of quality—of matter as it proceeds downward from the Absolute One. God seems imperfect since he is not entirely in control of creation. God sees Godself mirrored in the murk of creation, and cannot but love what is seen. This is the first glimpse of a God not in total control, yet good.

As early as the fifth century, the great Christian theologian Augustine warned against taking the six days of **Genesis** literally. Writing on the **Literal Meaning of Genesis**, Augustine argued that the days of creation were not successive or ordinary days—the sun, after all, God did not create, according to Genesis, until the fourth *day*. This is after light has already been *created*—and had nothing to do with time. Rather, Augustine argued, God "made all things together, disposing them in an order, based not on intervals of time, but on causal connections." Sounding like an evolutionist, Augustine reasoned that some things were made in fully developed form and others were made in "potential form" that developed over time into the condition in which they are seen today.

A story cast in mythic form may be pointing to profound religious *truth*. These truths have significant revelation for us today, but their historic order of events and their ancient cosmology (the view of the natural world) does not. It is important that I make plain the difference

165

Evil in Mirror Lake

between revealed truths and time-honored assumptions.

Denis Edwards in **The God of Evolution** delineates these "salvific truths" told in the Scriptures:

> ...*the preexistence and transcendence of God over all creatures; the ongoing relationship of all things to God as creatures to their Creator; God's delight in creatures; the divine proclamation of the goodness of creation; the blessing that makes creation fecund; the creation of human beings in the image of God; the call of the human being to work with creation but also to take care of it as God cares for it; the social nature of the human person; the insight that male and female represent the divine image; the goodness of human sexuality and marriage; the reality of human sinful rebellion against God, bringing alienation from God, from other human beings, and from creation itself; the enduring divine promise of salvation.*

These teachings of Genesis are the theological "truths for our salvation." This is the difference between revelatory truth and time-conditioned assumptions.

We also must remember that the authors of the divinely inspired Bible were trying to teach us how to relate to God. They are not teachers of history, nor anthropology, nor science, but only of religion. If they thought that the sun rotated around the earth, or that God determined and controlled all of nature, so what? This is not the purpose of their inspired teaching.

We must remember that neither the biblical authors, nor I today, possess all knowledge and total understanding of God—they taught what they knew. Qoheleth, the Preacher, in the book of **Ecclesiastes**, teaches us to eat, drink and make merry for tomorrow we will die; there is no afterlife. (Eccl. 3:20; 5:18-8:15; 12:7) Qoheleth, the inspired, angry, cynical, skeptical author, said this in his *Word of God*, which God had inspired. The Hebrew and Christian ecclesiastical bodies confirm this. The Bible may be the inspired Word of God, but it is not God's final word. As professor Hans Walter Wolff, the world's expert on the Book of Jonah, says, "God doesn't have to be faithful to his word as long as he is faithful to his people."

Revelation can come in stages. Revelation literally means to *re-veil*. We get but a glimpse through the opening of a veil that closes again. As John O'Donohue, an Irish Catholic priest scholar says in **Anam Cara**, "There is no direct, permanent access to the divine."

Evil and the Bible Interpretted

It may seem that Qoheleth's inspiration was not by God—unless God had a change of mind. After all, life after death is a religious truth— I can know it only through faith. Is this book you are now reading inspired? Do not say "No" simply because it is not ancient. Cannot God speak to us today? I, the author, feel inspired—I have been working at this book for nearly twenty years. Is that enough? No! In order for any writing to be **officially** *inspired* by God, it is only reasonable that, at the very least, some ecclesiastical body has had to declare it so. The inspiration of any sacred writing is a matter of faith in that church body which so declares it inspired.

Well, today we believe that Qoheleth was wrong in that religious point. Human life continues after death. Still, we appreciate how he told us to fear God and nevertheless to keep the laws. Keeping God's laws is still the best way to live, even if we do not get a bonus in the next life. He anticipated Shaftesbury (1671-1713) who thought it abject and cowardly to be virtuous from hope of heaven or fear of hell. Qoheleth knew some of God's truth but not all of it. Nevertheless, the church and synagogue say it is inspired.

While reading the Hebrew Testament, which is full of savageries, the British writer J. R. Ackerly once wrote to a friend, "I am half way through Genesis, and quite appalled by the disgraceful behavior of all of the characters involved, including God." So we must be aware of the inspired author's limited knowledge of God.

In the Book of Genesis, the inspired Hebrew writer viewed the world as God not having created it *ex nihil*, out of nothing, as the Greeks came to convince us, but simply as a world of confusion into which God, Yahweh, came to give order. The world at the time of the writing of Genesis was indeed in chaos from people's bad decisions, and seeming chaos from nature. God, through the prophets and eventually Jesus, was to give direction in creating a more harmonious whole out of a mixed-up world. Religion, along with aiding our worship of God, helps to provide a basis for order in a society.

Nature—with its volcanoes, fires, earthquakes and especially its floods—seemed out of control, but it was not. "The idea of widespread human evil being punished by a global catastrophe is shared by many mythological traditions, including those of India, Native America, China and Aboriginal Australia. Usually, a few righteous people are saved from the devastation, and they repopulate the world, passing on their knowledge, skills and high moral standards," says the *Time-Life* book, **Titans & Olympians**.

Nature in a constant state of flux was simply adjusting itself. Humans did not understand its scientific cause and effect relationships.

Evil in Mirror Lake

The inspired authors of the Bible thought that God was dealing with both aspects of evil: nature and bad decisions. In reality, God is not controlling nature (Chapter III) nor bad decisions (Chapter IV), but God is here guiding and nurturing me by influencing my loving decisions (Chapter VI).

These biblical authors knew some things about the mystery of life, but not everything. God's ability to express is not limited, but our capacity to understand is. None of the divinely inspired authors of the Bible have solved the mystery of evil. How a good God can allow evil to happen. It is a matter of faith. We do have the rebellion of Lucifer and the fall of man.

If you insist on a literal interpretation of every story and event in the Bible, then you will believe that God directed people to massacre other people. (Did Hitler get his permission to massacre other people from the Bible?) Also, you will accept that in the Book of Job, God allowed Satan to kill Job's sons and daughters in a strong wind (Job 1:19). Some fundamentalists strongly believe that God did literally participate in these killings because they think that God told us so in these inspired writings. An inspired book is one with both God and a human as its author.

Scriptural inspiration means at least that God is the author, but not that God dictated each word—Hebrew or Greek. I feel inspired to write this book, but scriptural inspiration is more than that.

Scripture, or the Word of God, is one of the most precious gifts we have. When we proclaim it in our liturgy, it is God speaking to us in the NOW. As the archaeologist tried to extrapolate the meaning of my diary, so we need scholarship to help understand God's *diary* to us. This process is not easy. I must depend on experts to tell me what God has said.

The first reason I need experts is that I am not fluent in Hebrew nor Greek. These are the two languages that God used to inspire the writers of the Hebrew and Christian scriptures. And then there are the Oriental scriptures with the language of Sanskrit. All I have are English translations, which are not the inspired text of God. I am dependent on my human faith in human translators. Who selects the experts? God or me? How do I know if the designated expert is free of subjectivity, ego or ecclesiastical influences when making his translations or interpretations?

Second, I need an expert to help explain to me the mentality of the human inspired author. I need explanations of the metaphors and stories that they tell. What they mean to me today may not be what they meant in an ancient culture. I need help.

Evil and the Bible Interpretted

Take for example the "tree of knowledge of good and evil" which is a metaphor open to great misunderstanding. In one sense, I can interpret the story to make Eve out to be the champion of humanity because she made the costly sacrifice to attain the necessary knowledge—of good and evil. She sacrificed her innocence to become a free human person capable of guiding her life—to virtue or to vice. Usually, however, people interpret the story as an act of disobedience by a creature that wanted to be equal to the Uncreated Being. Or possibly the story tells of a creature who will not love without understanding.

Although this is what it seems to say, I disagree. I think the author (Yahwist) of the story intended to tell his people, and so me, that to seek all experiences in life is not good. I should shun some few, lest I die. Leopold and Loeb in the 1950s chose to kill a child in Chicago for the experience of doing a perfect crime. If only they had neither bragged nor dropped those unique eyeglasses… Or the two youths (they shall and should remain nameless as should have the first two so named), who killed their classmates and teacher in Columbine High School in Colorado (1999). Were they not willing to sacrifice all (suicide) for a brief moment of experiencing the deadly power of being in control and the center of the nation's attention?

A more tempting and likewise forbidden experience for most of us is the desire to know what it is like to be involved in an *affair*. The very word itself explains the desire for a forbidden experience. The author of the tree story was probably speaking to a congregation that half yearned to experience the pagan sexual religious rites of their Canaanite neighbors. I need to realize that there are some experiences on the tree of life that I would do better to avoid—especially the carnal knowledge of good and evil.

For example, a teenager wishes to know what the sexual experience is like. The teen has neither the mate nor the means to settle down. If he carries out this knowledge of sexuality, one of two results will follow: 1) The experience is good to great—then who would want to stop with just one experience?; 2) The experience is poor to bad—who needs that! My first experience should be the greatest so I should wait until I can do it right and often.

And then, another avenue is that private interpretation of the Bible is open to me. This was a key thesis of Martin Luther, the scripture professor. God is not limited to speaking to me through any written word. God also speaks to me in my heart.

My purpose in this chapter is not to discuss what the Bible says or does not say about evil—I obviously disagree with some interpretations. But, since many people use the Bible as a touchstone in coming

Evil in Mirror Lake

to their conclusions about the meaning of evil, I only wish to reflect on how we should go about interpreting or understanding the Bible with the help of scripture scholars. This exegesis or explanation of the words and experiences proclaimed in the Bible is an integral part of our Western religions.

I also have an eye on the Eastern religions. Just as Thomas Aquinas gleaned all that was true and useful from the pagan Aristotle, whom he turned into a sort of honorary practicing Catholic, so I wish to incorporate all that is true and beneficial from the Orient. God has always spoken to all cultures. Some cultures have listened better than others. Christianity during the Crusades and the Inquisition had at least one deaf ear. We integrate **evil** into all facets of **life,** (Mirror Lake) thus the title of this book. As I gaze at evil, I find it reflected in all facets of life, much as I see my own reflection as I look into the calm, clear waters of a lake—Mirror Lake.

I am speaking to anyone who has ever wondered why bad things happen to good people. Some people blame God for evil in their lives, and then abandon all religion. I never blame God for the evil in my life.

RELIGION HELPS OVERCOME EVIL

We need help not only in interpreting the Bible, but also in the intricate details of our relationship with God and with each other. We call this *religion,* which comes from the Latin word *relatio,* which means relation.

Religious faith aids us in the rearing and training of our children. Most parents and teachers are glad to have the help of religion. It counters the natural rebelliousness of youth with a moral code based on an omnipotent God watchful of every act, threatening eternal punishments, and offering eternal rewards as steps along the path to justice and love. Religion can be a *super* parent.

Sometimes religion can go too far. Samuel Butler describes this well in his semi-autobiographical, **The Way of All Flesh**. He relates how his pastor used religion to intimidate and terrify children. If I misbehave, "God can send a fit of paralysis and death to me as the Almighty did to old Mrs. Pontifex. Then whisk me off to the Judgment." Butler also argues, on the other hand, that I have an obligation to seek all permissible pleasure and avoid all pain that we can honorably avoid. I agree. Ernest, the hero in Butler's book, did not go the expected way— the way of all flesh. His life was not to be stuck in the same fate as his religious parents. He went beyond the norm and the predictable. Unfortunately for him this meant no religion.

Evil and the Bible Interpretted

Most people in authority, especially the government, are grateful for an educational process that would produce a public taught to accept as natural and inevitable the inequality of abilities, and thus of possessions. Being created equal is limited to giving everyone an equal opportunity to compete and obtain. Some competition among us seems to be necessary in order to bring out the best in some of us. If we understand equality correctly, it can lessen the chances of evil among us. Thus, religion has always been important to the government and to penitentiaries in helping people overcome moral evils.

Virtue is real only when practiced for its own sake. Virtue should spring from our experience. It should not be a means to an end. Also, remember that every virtue inclines toward stupidity, and every stupidity, toward virtue. "Stupid to the point of holiness," they say in Russia. True virtue is always in the middle. This is not to be confused with being lukewarm.

Religion also assists us to choose right from wrong, in helping us to choose right from wrong when it inculcates belief in future punishments and rewards. Religion has always appealed to our personal sense of dependence upon supersensual powers, and to the propensity of even the learned to ask for supernatural aid. The Church continues to offer a home to miracles, myths, mystery, music and art.

"The world is running mad with its notion that its evils are to be relieved by political changes, political remedies, political nostrums, whereas the great evils—civilization, bondage, misery—lie deep in the heart, and nothing but virtue and religion can remove them," as Henry Wordsworth said.

We need a word in support of *moccasin-walking*. Keeping one's own religion yet being open and appreciative of other beliefs and practices, is necessary for a world to live together successfully. Sometimes, cultures, not religions are fighting. In Northern Ireland, it is not Protestant vs. Catholic. They have not been fighting over religion, but over nationalities—English *versus* Irish. It is Arab *versus* Jews, not Islam *versus* Judaism. Sometimes, though, it is religion—Hindu *versus* Islam in India, or Christianity *versus* Islam in the Crusades.

We need religion to relate people to God and to each other. The character Heathcliff, in **Wuthering Heights** by Emily Bronte, returns to his childhood friends to work upon them his unimaginable revenge for slights felt in early life, and for a love lost because of miscommunication and sibling jealousy. If he had true religion in him, we would not have this classic fictional tale of woe. But as Cathy admits, "I am Heathcliff," so all of us have a bit of Heathcliff in us. Beware!

Coleridge ended his **Lay Sermons** by conceding to the theolo-

171

Evil in Mirror Lake

gians that no pure lay or secular wisdom can solve the problems of people; only a supernatural religion and a God-given moral code can check the inherent selfishness of people. He said that evil was so deeply inborn that human intelligence alone is inadequate for restoring health to the will. He called for a humble return to religion, and to full faith in Christ as God dying to redeem all people.

"Morality cannot be maintained without faith and religion," George Washington said in his Farewell Address. How right history has shown him to be in the city named for him. What would George say about children praying privately in public schools?

This is just to quote some famous names who were pro-religion. Of course, there are many famous names that are on the opposite side—religion is the opiate of the people, religion is only for the weak, all religious people are hypocrites, I can pray at home just as well, religion cures guilt.

Even Voltaire, that antireligious, Deistic believer, whose historical importance lies in his uncanny and unique knack of reflecting the concerns of the intelligent men of his times, says in his **Epistle to The Author of "The Three Impostors"**:

> *If God did not exist, it would be necessary to invent him;*
> *But all nature cries out to us that he does exist.*

Note how often they quote only the first of these two lines! Voltaire's most famous book is his satirical novel, **Candide** (1759). Unlike John Bunyan's **Pilgrim's Progress**, which puts off this earth for the glories of heaven, Candide wants to reach a heaven-on-earth. This fantastic story illustrates Voltaire's belief that unless I use my reason, the world is random and without a plan. There is no hidden pattern upon which to rely. His chief message is that religious speculation must give way to practical work—to "cultivate our garden." He understood God as Father and even built a church to God the Father in his town of Ferney—the only such named church in France. He dismissed Jesus as God, and apparently the Jesuits never introduced him to God the Holy Spirit. Beneath the power of his pen (the first bomb thrown at the aristocracy), lies a *lost and desperate soul*. Because of its mimicking of many religious Orders, this book was on the Catholic Index of Forbidden Books. The Catholic Church eliminated this Index after Vatican II.

Candide's teacher, Pangloss, assures him that he lives in "the best of all possible worlds." His reasoning was that "since everything is made for an end, everything is necessarily for the best end." Candide's

Evil and the Bible Interpretted

experiences assure him that "regrettable things happen in this world of ours"—evil. In the end, Voltaire teaches that we are incapable of understanding the evil in the world, and concludes that the fundamental aim in life is not happiness, but survival.

Probably the name most associated with *evil* and anti-religion is Niccolo Machiavelli, author of the infamous book, **The Prince** (1532). His subtle and ironic view of morality has made him both famous and execrated. Did he believe in evil? No! Although he had a vivid and poetic imagination, he was simply tough-minded. He chose pleasure and avoided pain. He saw that it was the possession of power rather than of the moral high ground that got results—at least in the short run. Machiavelli noted that his contemporary, Savanarola, steadfastly refused to incite the mob, when by rioting they might have saved him from being burnt as a heretic. Mostly, Machiavelli lacked a sense of God. That religion is often a delusion does not mean that it is *always* a delusion. The *all-powerful* God does not always see to it that good wins out over evil, so it seems at times. This has been my experience, and has been mystery, if not delusion, to most people. This is precisely the mystery we are attempting to solve.

In certain respects, Thucydides, the *historian's historian*, the author of **History of the Peloponnesian War** (Greek Civil War 5th Century B.C.E.), is the precursor of Machiavelli. The bleak message of his history is that people will always pursue the course of expedience rather than that of virtue. Thucydides, the admiral, failed to relieve the Athenian city of Amphipolis and so lost it to the Spartans. They then exiled him for twenty years from his city of Athens, during which time he wrote his history. This defeat of Athens by Sparta in this Second Peloponnesian War heralded the end of Greek civilization. The First Peloponnesian War (Greek Civil War) ended in a draw between Athens and the other Greek city-states led by Sparta. This first war concluded with the Thirty-Years Peace Treaty in 445 B.C.E.

It was Herodotus (4th century B.C.E.), the father of history, who wrote about the earlier war where the Greeks defeated Cyrus the Persian, who had a much greater force, in the famous Battle of Marathon in 490 B.C.E. We know his book simply as **History**, or better translated as *Researches*. Herodotus believed that a type of fate—of which humans have displayed only an occasional glimmer of understanding—rules human aspirations. My understanding is that this fate is a play between free will and God's plan for us. Religion helps in that direction.

Religion helps me to mold my future human direction in life away from moral evils or bad decisions. Of course, I always think my deci-

Evil in Mirror Lake

sions are *good* at the time I make them. I always think I am obtaining satisfaction or avoiding pain. It is only in hindsight that I and others see them as bad or evil. Religion helps me to see these moral evils beforehand.

Let us move on to look at life's experiences from that high precipice, from which we can plumb the depths of human encounters of good and evil mirrored in this lake of life. It is now high noon and the sun is piercing the depths of the churning lake. Every time the surface moves, it shifts its mirrors. At times deciding is hard—life and evil. I look around and do not see my shadow. How about some examples of people who have changed the world by their human decisions?

CHAPTER VIII

PIVOTAL HUMAN DECISIONS

"Whoever wants to be creative in evil or good,
He must first be an annihilator and destroyer of old truths."
Friedrich Nietzsche

"Strife is the creator of all great things [ideas]."
Heraclitus

"Any new thought always begins as a minority of one."
Anonymous

Having reached the peak and found a ledge to sit on, I begin to realize that thinking people do make a difference, for good or for evil. We need to think better than our teachers, as Plato improved upon Socrates, and Aristotle improved upon Plato. Let us accentuate the positive.

Several pivotal points in history come to mind. The plow brought food to the people (farms), instead of people to the food (hunting). From farms came cities where they could trade their food, the oldest city found being Hiiyiik, Turkey (C. 8000 B.C.E). Damascus is the oldest continuously inhabited city of the globe—it existed a millennium before Abraham was born—some 3000 B.C.E. Next came the act of writing, born in Sumer in Mesopotamia, for keeping financial accounts of business ventures between cities. The flow of ideas in writing followed. The wheel (3400 B.C.E.) transformed transportation, and eventually laid the foundation for the Industrial Revolution. The forging of iron instead of the weaker bronze changed warfare.

Many civilizations contributed to these pivotal, global changes. The Egyptians, the longest continuous civilization in history, taught writing by pictures. The Greeks taught city government, and furthered the world of thought. Next, the Romans gave engineering and the law

Evil in Mirror Lake

upon which to build an expanded society or empire.

In religion, the Hebrews taught there is but one God. Christianity is a heresy of Judaism. The Crusades taught the Europeans that their will was not always God's will, or at least not under God's control. Catholics came to know other ways, such as Islam, of relating to God and to each other. The Catholic way was no longer the only way. Protestantism is a heresy of Catholicism. These were pivotal decisions that changed the course of history.

Individuals likewise contributed to major changes: Gutenberg, in 1450, invented movable type. (The Chinese invented the printing press some 800 years before.) Cheaper books gave the wealthy a library to guide and stimulate their thinking. The Industrial Revolution allowed us to make ten pots for the price of one. Alexander Graham Bell's telephone expanded communications so it became instantaneous.

Albert Einstein is many peoples' Man of the Century. No one in the past century has had such a long-lasting or significant influence on the cause of human history and thought. He gave us the idea for the atomic bomb that finished, for the time being, the hot world wars previously engaged in. He used his Special Theory of Relativity to explain the relationship between energy and matter—($E=mc^2$).

Einstein showed that motion is always relative. A given speed depends on who measures it—from where to where—the change of position of one body in respect to another. In other words, movement becomes relative, and both depend on the particular frame of reference of the observer. If I am on the shore watching a ship moving north to south, and a man on the ship is walking south to north, how fast is the man walking—in reference to what is the question—of relativity. Lightspeed is the one measure in the universe that *is* constant and absolute. **(Special Relativity** (1905).

His **General Theory of Relativity** (1916) came next. Until then we had looked upon gravity as a force acting instantaneously. His solution tells why his theory of relativity is really a theory of gravity. Essentially what Einstein did, was to substitute *spacetime*, or space-time, for the previously separate notions of space *and* time. By this means he could cease to regard the ubiquitous gravity as force. Instead, he redefined it as a property of spacetime—which is curved because of it. Or, put another way, matter shapes the geometry of what is around it.

I mention these ideas because Einstein did not derive this theory by way of experimentation, but on grounds of symmetry and mathematical elegance. Though its proofs derive events from principles running counter to the accepted empirical methods of science, even so, this beautiful, intellectually satisfying general theory has so far with-

176

Pivotal Human Decisions

stood every test to its validity. It remains the closest approximation to ultimate truth yet devised or discovered, some say. "I think and think for months, for years," Einstein said, "Ninety-nine times the conclusion is false. The hundredth time I am right." I admire his courage and originality.

His theory showed how the nucleus of the atom could be separated or split thus releasing a tremendous amount of energy in a chain reaction called fusion. The idea that a body would increase in mass and decrease in length when it approached the speed of light, led Einstein to the conclusion that mass (m) and energy (E) are related—$E=mc^2$. With c representing the speed of light, cxc is obviously an enormous number. The symbol "c" comes from the Latin word *celeritas* which means *swiftness*, says David Bodanis in his understandable book, **$E=mc^2$**. So, even the partial conversion of a small amount of matter will release tremendous amounts of energy—thus we have the atomic bomb which he encouraged President Franklin Roosevelt to allow. Maybe what is more important, Einstein taught us that what we may observe is not always the way things really are.

A physical example of this is the St. Louis arch—the Gateway to the West. When I look at it, it always seems taller than it is wide. If I get a picture of it and use a ruler to measure it, its height and width are exactly the same. I do not believe it, and I measure it again. It is only with great difficulty that I finally do not believe my eyes. I need to be able to get beyond appearances.

The world today is, as ever, engaged in economic competition. Being computer literate is now the equivalent of reading and writing. If knowledge is power, then knowing the computer is the electronic key to it. The future belongs to the *techy-nerds* of today. (Computer knowledge is not to be confused with *playing* computer games.) Computers cannot correct incorrect input or poor logic. Too many high school graduates know a lot about computers but little else. Forty years ago they predicted that television would enable everyone to be well informed on a variety of topics, but now we use it primarily for sports, news and entertainment. Hopefully the computer will not head in the same direction. I am talking about individual pivotal decisions.

The new strata of society might be or is:

1) Techy-nerds (New Breed)   2) Wealthy old money (stagnating)
3) Middle class (shrinking)   4) The poor (frying hamburgers)

The good news is that a bright and hard-working youth can end in the top strata, but only if computer literate. The other good news is that

Evil in Mirror Lake

the middle class is shrinking into the wealthy and not into the poor class, according to *The Wall Street Journal*. The bad news is that not all of our schools are leading in that direction. Yet, the computer is just a tool. If I cannot think, I still may not get there.

We are entering a new epoch of communication. The first epoch was the oral or storytelling age. Next was the literary or book age. We have just entered the MTV age where audio and visual merge as never before. The church must also come to realize that the age of communication is in flux. Possibly, this is why the younger electronically weaned are not coming to the literary age church, as they did in past generations. Thomas Boomershine of Union Theological Seminary tells us this in his insightful book, **Story Journey—An invitation to the Gospel as Storytelling**.

Our free will not only directs our own lives to good or bad choices, but perhaps at times it can change the direction of history. Let us now look at the pivotal decisions people have made in the history of the Church.

Paul of Tarsus took the cosmopolitan, worldwide teachings of the itinerant rabbi, Jesus, and forced the church open to all and no longer to just an elite few—the Jews. Paul taught us in his letters that all (all races, all nations, both sexes, all ages) are now God's chosen.

Augustine of Hippo, a repentant fornicator and heretic, through his prolific and prophetic teachings, especially in his **Confessions** and **City of God**, led the church intellectually for a thousand or more years. After Jesus Christ and the Apostles, no human being influenced the course of Christianity more than he. His mighty presence managed to bridge the gap between pagan Rome and the Middle Ages.

Thomas Aquinas built an intellectual superstructure of faith based on the ideas of the pagan philosopher Aristotle, whereas Augustine had based everything on Paul and the gospels. Thomas' **Summa Theologicae** (often rendered **Summa Theologica**) defined Catholic church teaching for another 700 years, or until our time. He began it in 1266 and left it unfinished at his death. It is the crowning achievement of medieval theologies. However, one day at Mass shortly before his death he had an ecstasy or epiphany. Afterwards he said, "All that I have written seems to me like straw compared with what has now been revealed to me." He wrote not a word more and died soon afterward when a tree limb hit his forehead and knocked him off his horse. In only sixteen years, he wrote ninety-two works in all. In much of twentieth-century theology and even philosophy, his insights are still invaluable and widely discussed.

Martin Luther and John XXIII radically changed the direction of

Pivotal Human Decisions

the Christian church. I call this the fourth leg of the modern church, following Paul, Augustine, and Thomas. This fourth leg begins either with the Protestant Reformation or with Catholic Vatican II, though four hundred years separate these two entirely different historical events. The Reformation started the proliferation of Protestant churches, and the idea of the direct line to God being the ordinary way of contact. Catholic Vatican II opened the church window to new ideas—twenty-five new documents reappraising all areas of doctrine, except original sin which Vatican II never discussed but in passing.

Martin Luther, following John Wycliffe, William Tyndale, and Desiderius Erasmus, was chosen by fate, some say, to cause the emergence of Protestantism. In November 1517 Luther nailed his famous *Ninety-Five Theses* to the door of the Castle Church in Wittenberg. No man until the coming of Hitler had such charisma for the German people—one for good the other for evil.

Erasmus is also worth considering. He was born about 1466 in Rotterdam, the illegitimate son of a priest, a reluctant priest himself, persecuted by the church for his humanism, ever faithful to the church, a contemporary of the irascible Luther and the demonic Calvin. He was the heir apparent to Luther, but he remained faithful to the Catholic church. He foresaw the multiplication of Protestantism. He was also a friend of Sir Thomas Moore, to whom he dedicated his ironic book, **In Praise of Folly**. Erasmus was essentially an imaginative writer. His real subjects are human diversity and vitality as well as people's weaknesses. His book is the most famous of all examples of a sustained paradox. A paradox is a form of oxymoron (*pointedly foolish* in Greek)—an example of *folly*. We yoke two opposites together in hopes to display an unexpected truth which could not, less daringly, be reached. A present day example of this is a Yogi Berra Saying, "Nobody goes there anymore; it's too crowded!" Showing the nature of the relationship between seriousness and play, was Erasmus' greatest contribution to the understanding of self, and Yogi's.

These people and their ideas were instrumental in changing church and world history. I have just one example of an unmade decision that could have changed history. Not to choose is to choose. In 1260, two brothers, Messers Niccolo and Maffeo Polo, went on a business trip to what is today modern China where they supposedly became friends with the Great Khan, whose name was Kubilai. The Polo brothers so impressed the Khan with their Christian religion that he asked them upon their return to his empire, the largest that ever was, to bring back one hundred Catholic scholars to instruct his Court. If their religion made sense, he promised to convert his whole country to Christianity.

Evil in Mirror Lake

Upon their return to Italy, they found the Holy See vacant, and the papacy remained so for three years. When Gregory X (1271-1276) was elected Pope, the Polo brothers got an audience with him. Instead of one hundred, he sent two scholars who eventually deserted before arriving at the Khan's Court. What might have been? Niccolo's son tells us this in **The Travels of Marco Polo**.

Some people say that Marco Polo fabricated his story from accounts received at the trading ports of China. They say that a Khan would never so trust an outsider. If this is true, it is the greatest hoax since the love letters of Abélard and Héloïse.

As an aside, Peter Abélard was a charismatic philosophical and theological teacher, who was made a canon of Notre Dame in 1115. He fell in love with the beautiful and learned Héloïse, niece of Canon Fulbert, and seduced her. She became great with child, and her uncle castrated Abélard. The only honorable thing to do, then, was for Abélard to go to the monastery, and Héloïse to go to the convent. From there she penned her three *Letters*, which have kept their place among the great love letters of the world. Will Durant, the noted historian, says these letters are hoaxes.

Pivotal human decisions can also be lived in great literature which creates an accurate, vivid milieu from which the reader can emerge feeling he or she has lived the adventure. Sir Walter Scott was the inventor of the historical fiction novel. In **The Lady of the Lake**, Ellen Douglas (the lady of the lake) eases the reunion of two cultures in collision—the wild Celtic Highlanders, loyal only to their chieftain, and the peaceful, agrarian Saxon Lowlanders, devoted to following their King. This romantic metrical poem guides us through a maze of emotions, creating sympathy and understanding for both sides. We can never underestimate the importance of any single person's decisions.

One person, seen by more people than anyone else in all of history, is John Paul II, Karol Wojtyla. As G. K. Chesterton wrote of Thomas More, "If there had not been that particular man at that particular moment, the whole of history would have been different." Like Thomas More, John Paul II is above all things historic: He represented at once a type, a turning point, and an ultimate destiny—heaven.

George Weigel speaks thus of John Paul II in **Witness to Hope: The Biography of Pope John Paul II** (1999). "John Paul has demonstrated that culture, not politics or economics, is the engine of history. In his view, as an extension of John XXIII, everything Vatican II did, revolved around two great themes—that Christ, the redeemer of the world, reveals the astonishing truth about the human condition and our final destiny. The other is that self-giving love is the path along which

Pivotal Human Decisions

human freedom finds its fulfillment in human flourishing." This last truth sounds very Buddhistic as well as Christian. Or as Faust said, "In the beginning was the deed." Surprisingly, Friedrich Nietzsche also claims that **culture** is what matters most in any civilization. He states this in his **Twilight of the Idols**, "What the Germans Lack #4."

Another example of how I choose to look at something and its dire consequences, is the case of Karl Marx, the German economist who fled to England. He was a constant visitor to the British Museum's reading room where he read all the classics as well as all the English labor reports. He also read that "ownership is theft" according to the French socialist and anarchist Pierre Joseph Proudhon in his then famous 1840 book, **What is Property?** Proudhon, a fiery reformer, denounces private property as an institution which perpetuates inequality and injustice. Marx failed to see a win-win situation between labor and management.

As Marx painstakingly wrote his brilliant analysis of the relationship of labor and management in his now famous, **Das Kapital**, he refused to allow the capitalist any monetary return on their invested capital. He erroneously claimed that all of the capitalist's profits came from the surplus labor of the working person. Marx failed to see that besides making some industrialists quite wealthy, capitalism also gave sustenance to the otherwise unemployed peasants and others. The injustice, to cite one, was that laborers were put to work twelve plus hours per day, including workers ten years of age or less.

He likewise failed to acknowledge the value of being able to purchase mass-produced products at a much lower price. His one-sided view of the "exploitation of the worker" led to his *dialectical materialism* which was expressed in his and Friedrich Engels' **Communist Manifesto**.

This manifesto (Ch II) calls for the "abolition of private property," and (Ch IV) "They openly declare that they can attain their ends only by the forceable overthrow of all existing social conditions." This world famous document ends with the ringing, "Let the ruling classes tremble at a Communist revolution. The proletarians have nothing to lose but their chains. They have the world to win. Working men of all countries, unite!"

The following famous statement (1845) contains the essence of Marxism taken from his writings, "The philosophers have only interpreted the world in various ways, the point is to change it." According to Marx, the Heaven of the Christians will exist here, on earth, in properly concrete terms that will make all speculation of the hereafter absurd and unnecessary. This Heaven is communism on earth, which is

Evil in Mirror Lake

inevitable in any case. However, that communism is inevitable does not mean that we should not hurry it along with violence as the *Manifesto* exhorts.

Marx did not quite deny the existence of God, but he did argue against the idea of the Christian God as anything more than a necessary, albeit temporary, phenomenon. The goal, Marx continues, is to replace man's love of God with man's love of Man. Why not both?, I ask. Marxist-Leninism became the first secular religion. However, this theory does not give a sufficient value to the inner lives of individuals.

Leo XIII and his groundbreaking (1891) encyclical, *Rerum Novarum* (On the Condition of Human Labor), supported Marx. Leo XIII wrote that we should allow workers to organize and form labor unions, and we should give them a wage sufficient to allow the thrifty to work toward owning land.

"The evil in capitalism is the capital," wrote Marx. He, like the old Church, saw it as evil to make money from money. What the capitalist is doing, he maintains, is stealing from the workers what they create by their labor. He calls profits unpaid labor.

However, not even good wages and fine working conditions would have been enough for Marx, because his hatred of the upper class or bourgeois was so great. The workers should own and control the factory. It took over seventy years of communism to show the world that it simply does not work. What works in overcoming the evils of capitalism (market economy) is morality (enforced by the state).

Instead of Communism, Alfred Emanuel Smith, the red-headed Catholic Governor of New York, when he confronted the inhumane conditions in New York City, said, "The only cure for the evil of democracy is more democracy." I hope that today Russia and others believe this.

Marx departed from Adam Smith, who a hundred years before, in 1776, said in his masterpiece, **An Inquiry Into the Nature and Causes of the Wealth of Nations**, "Wages, profit, and rent, are the three original sources of all revenue as well as all exchangeable value." His greatest claim to originality lies in his emphasis on the division of labor into many steps in the creation of wealth. He was somewhat over-optimistic about the free market, if only because the market has never really been as free as he imagined. He even says that selfishness operates to the good of all—management is forced to produce goods (*good*: so the term) that people like at a price they are willing to pay. The free market ultimately sets the sale price of anything which supply and demand govern. He called the process natural liberty. The cost of production does not set prices. Profits are the result of management's direction of

Pivotal Human Decisions

labor. Profits have no relation to how much effort anyone puts into his enterprise. "The increase of revenue and stock is the increase of national wealth," concludes Dr. Smith, the Scotsman, an apostle of economic freedom.

Marx quotes Smith's **Wealth of Nations** thirty-nine times in his **Das Kapital**, mostly in footnotes which the reader must not skip. In fact **Das Kapital** is 35 percent footnotes, all of which are indispensable. Adam Smith delineated the cause of social unrest. Karl Marx gave us his solutions. Ideas grow out of ideas, and ideas can grow into an empire—good or evil. All new ideas begin as a minority of one.

(It took me sixty hours to read **Wealth of Nations**!) Why would I spend sixty hours reading a book? This is more than a week's work. Where is the payoff? If I were an English teacher, I could consider it part of my work. But I am not, and in this case I am not even an economist. The answer must lie in the pure enjoyment of reading it, not in any utilitarian gain.

Reading, as life itself, can use dancing as a metaphor. The purpose of dancing is not to get to the other side of the floor. Walking does that better. The motive for dancing is in the movement itself, which would also make it a suitable metaphor for the existentialists.

"Information is endlessly available to us; where shall wisdom be found?" is the crucial question. Harold Bloom instructs us to read for the purest of all reasons: to discover and augment the self. He says this in **How to Read and *Why***.

In reading any book, I need to be enjoying the present chapter so much that I want the book (the music) never to end. This is an essential ingredient for making it to my list of the 101 greatest books. When this does happen to me, like a pause between dances, I put down the book at the end of each chapter, and I reflect on what just happened to me. Maybe this is the Irish in me, but I am equally proud of my German half (Stroer) which compels me to finish what I have started, no matter what. Sometimes this perseverance pays off. It did not with Lawrence Sterne's **The Life and Opinions of Tristram Shandy**. This is a digression; I must get back to evil.

Chinese communists, by the millions during China's disastrous *Great Proletarian Cultural Revolution,* carried and read the **Little Red Book** whose more accurate title was **Quotations From Chairman Mao Tse-tung** (Zedong, 1966). The five billion button-badges made for this new secular religion had all the authority that the Bible has for an enthusiastic evangelical today. Again it is practical, common sense ideas, even aphorisms, that rule the world. " Be resourceful, look at all sides of a problem, test ideas by experiment, and work hard for the common

Evil in Mirror Lake

good." Mao, one of only three peasants in China's long history that ever rose to supreme power, tortured and executed more people than Alexander the Great, and enough to make the holocaust look like a weekend riot.

Mao's Communism or Marxism is more in line with the thinking of the later Trotsky or Rose Luxembourg than that of Lenin or Stalin. It is also almost the only case of a genuine populism gaining control of a country for communism—and a large country at that. Mao organized the people of the district of Hunan—first those of his own village—into a powerful force. This highly pragmatic strategy was a main influence on Fidel Castro who in 1959 was able to take over Cuba. Attention to it also enabled the Vietnamese, Laotian, and Cambodian communists to take over their countries. Mao ruled a quarter of the world's population for a quarter of a century. He was probably more of an anarchist (mob rule) than a Marxist.

China's Great Leap Forward (1958) for increased steel production, together with The Red Guards (1960) leading a populist revolution against the current communist state, turned the country into an experiment in anarchism—brutal mob rule. This rule by the mob is why the new leaders arrested the Gang of Four, tried and convicted them after Mao's death in 1976. All of this should be a clear warning to those attracted to utopian ideas.

Some people today consider capitalism also an evil. These people are usually, but not always, religious types or professors—people who live in libraries and think. Thought alone is not enough. Life also needs experiences. The experience of communism lived is what eventually caused its downfall—not its theory.

John Paul II, a great fighter against communism, does not totally embrace capitalism. The capitalistic way of living works only when infused by a great deal of morality. The *maximization of profits* leads to the other extreme. Such extreme is not a win-win situation for both capitalists and workers. Greediness is still rampant today.

Today's greatest advocate of Christian capitalism is Robert A. Sirico, the priest founder of **The Acton Institute**. They named this institute after Lord John Acton, the 19th-Century English Catholic historian, who upheld the liberty to "do our duty unhindered by the state (and) by society," as the highest human value. "In the economic realm, that cashes out as unbridled capitalism," comments *Our Sunday Visitor* (12-5-99) which did a favorable article on the Institute. Sirico's Institute is for the study of religion and liberty. He insists that good capitalism must be permeated with good moral values.

The great opportunity of living in America is that anyone who can

Pivotal Human Decisions

save some extra money, then, can become a capitalist. If I cannot save money, I can never become a capitalist. Smart people not only work hard, but also have their hard earned money working for them. Happy are the people who learn to live beneath their means. Happy are they who embrace the simple lifestyle and live the win-win philosophy.

I need to be constantly adjusting my thinking and so my decision making process. "Every thought which genius and piety threw into the world," Emerson said, "altered the world." My choices, just like the people mentioned here, lead me and the world to good or evil.

I have been mentioning great people of history: Gutenberg, Bell, Einstein, Paul, Augustine, Aquinas, Luther, John XXIII, Erasmus, Marco, John Paul II, Marx, and Mao. Now I would like to talk about you and me—ordinary people who sometimes make an extraordinary decision—for good or for evil.

AMERICA UNDER TERRORIST ATTACK!

Individuals can act to change the course of history. Their decisions can be pivotal – for good or for evil. On September 11, 2001, terrorists identified as fundamental, religious fanatics attacked the World Trade Center and the Pentagon, slaughtering thousands of innocents. These maniacal terrorists, often identified as religious zealots, are said to have been devoutly religious, and did the unthinkable in the name of God. The terrorists became militant extremists; yet, God permitted it!

Evil happens when individuals make bad decisions for whatever reasons, even in the name of God. Why did God not interfere with the terrorists' slaughter of thousands of innocents? Why did God not interfere with their terrible plans of contemplated colossal massacre? Why did God not cause them to fail? Did God bless these terrorists and religious enthusiasts with success in their brilliantly executed plans of turning passenger airlines, loaded with maximum fuel and innocent passengers, into Kamikaze bombers? Why did God not bless America on this day?

Usually, we think of God as encouraging us to do good things and the Devil encouraging us to do evil things. However, getting the voices mixed up is always possible. Sometimes we are tricked by our own weaknesses or even by the Devil himself into thinking that some action is good when it is surely evil. The fact that terrorists have continued their evil actions for years and decades underscores their intellectual inability to correctly interpret their religion. The terrorists do not understand who God is. The terrorists' anger, coupled with a sense of hopelessness, gives rise to the inability to distinguish between good

Evil in Mirror Lake

and evil voices.

The terrorists' frustration is the engine that ratchets up the evil voice. The terrorists' reliance upon false and misconstrued theology gives rise to a mislaid rationalization that directs their intellect. Subsequently, idealism propels the terrorist's will, which will always seek what it perceives as good.

The terrorists' sense of hopelessness stems from thinking that there is no other way for a David to slay the giant Goliath. September 11th was such a day, David *versus* Goliath. Nevertheless, the voices of the terrorists' consciences, prompting them to do good *versus* evil clearly got mixed up. The result? Suicide and the taking of over six thousand innocent lives. Terrorists did an appalling deed, presumably in the name of Allah.

These catastrophic events demonstrate just how crucially important it is to have the correct understanding of who God is and what God's will is in our lives. It is precisely our understanding of God's love for us and creation, which protects us from the thought of suicide or the taking of innocent life. In fact, the Koran strictly forbids suicide and the killing of innocent people.

How important then is a religion of compassion! How essential is the correct understanding of God's will for us!

We live in consistent and constant danger of blundering into an evil deed. Sometimes, we intentionally choose to do evil. But, why does a good God not stop us? The only answer: We have free will. God will not interfere with our decisions, except by way of persuasion and at times through the prayerful intercession of others to God. Yet, God's persuasion can be very powerful for good, because the God of freedom allows us to choose good or evil. Without freedom, there could be no love between God and the human race.

Consider the acts of heroism performed by those in the New York twin towers by the firemen and policemen who risked, and in many cases lost, their lives in an effort to save others.

> *And I will carry this: It is the police shield of a man*
> *named George Howard, who died at the World Trade*
> *Center trying to save others. It was given to me by his*
> *mom, Arlene, as a proud memorial to her son. This is my*
> *reminder of lives that ended, and a task that does not end.*
>
> Pres. Bush's address to a joint session of Congress and the
> American people, September 20, 2001

These human acts of love could not be performed out of love if it

186

Pivotal Human Decisions

were not for our God-given gift of free will.

We have all taken time to think on these events, and in the morning we have been able to see more clearly.

DREAMS AND DAYDREAMS

Dreams are the windows to the character of my soul. I use my dreams as a trip wire to guide me concerning where I need to repair and build my character so that I will not act out undesirably. My dreams can tell me where my weaknesses in character are lest I do evil deeds. Dreams are the most intimate form of relationship I have with myself.

Joseph Campbell suggests that we have certain feelings and orientations hidden away in our genes. Aristotle advocates that our intellect was born a *tabla rasa*. Campbell is a soul pantheist who neither believes in a personal God nor holds that life has a purpose. A soul pantheist believes not only that all matter is God but also that this matter is informed with a soul. All of this is God. He calls to mind how most of us enjoy sitting around a campfire. This lived experience recalls millions of our ancestors who spent almost one-third of their lives in this fireside situation, and somehow have passed this experience on to us. Campbell's thought is something akin to *mind is mingled with all nature*. In this respect he is a panpsychist, as was Spinoza, that God-intoxicated man. A panpsychist believes that we are all part of the one world spirit. Unlike Arthur Schopenhauer and Carl Gustav Jung, who would agree with Campbell, I believe that we inherit some things through our genes, but our intellect comes to us blank, *tabla rasa*, as Aristotle taught.

Panpsychism is not found in most dictionaries. It is a spiritual step above being a pantheist in that one also believes that a spirit is part of the material things of existence. A panpsychist calls both elements together—uncreated God. I call matter a created participation in the uncreated spirit, God. God continues to live in all created matter.

The Swiss Jung, at first a collaborator with Freud and later a dissenter postulated an entity that he called the *collective unconscious*—a deeper layer of the mind that lies beneath the merely personal. I say that I simply inherit this culture as part of the society into which I am born. Subsequently, I absorb my tribe's unconscious into my personal unconscious. On the other hand, he may have this collective unconscious confused with the Holy Spirit. Jung's most influential book was **Psychological Types** (1921) in which he gave us for the first time the distinction between an extrovert and an introvert.

Shortly after our parents conceive us, we begin feeling and hearing

Evil in Mirror Lake

even in the womb. Before and after birth, all of the senses begin recording our reality. Nothing of this is ever lost. It is like a tape and video recorder running constantly, storing everything in our passive intellect.

When we wish to remember something, having an imaginative picture is necessary for us. We base our imagination in a physical organ of the body composed of nerve endings and brain cells. These change or deteriorate, and thus we forget. Nevertheless, we never lose the experience or knowledge. From time to time reviewing things is necessary for us. Usually, when we relearn something, it comes back to us more easily.

When we dream, all these experiences bypass our consciousness and float directly into our dream world. Everything we dream about, we have already experienced in some way at some time. We may rearrange things in our dreams as to place and time so that we do not recognize them.

When it comes to our dreams, no logical connection or union of events exists. Nothing in it is a sign of anything else (the Bible notwithstanding) unless I, or my culture, have preprogrammed something to be a sign, e.g., a snake to be a symbol of sex. Freud comes to this same conclusion "that no special symbolizing activity of the mind in the formation of dreams need be assumed; that, on the contrary, the dream uses such symbolizations as are to be found ready-made in unconscious thought, because of their dramatic fitness, and particularly because of their exemption from the (dream) censor." Again, "a good part of this symbolism, moreover, is possessed by the dream in common with legends and popular customs." We have archetypes of dreams which mean that we all have dreams with common symbols.

What is crucial in my dream is my behavior because dreams are windows to my self. "Dreams are the touchstones of our character," said Henry David Thoreau. Dr. Marie Mahoney insists that the unconscious launches a dream to *wake up* the dreamer to some aspect of his or her conscious life or personal attitude. If in my dreams, I do something immoral or evil, like stealing, let this be a warning that I have not yet developed my desires, decisions, virtue or character so that I would never steal—shoplift.

As Heraclitus said, "A man's character is his fate." According to Joseph Campbell, "Our life evokes our character." Marcus Aurelius in his 167 AD **Meditations** said, "Such as are your habitual thoughts, so will be your character." The Guatemalans say something like this, "Se hace el camino caminando" or "a path is made by walking." This theory seems to hold up during hypnosis. In a hypnotic state, the hypnotist

Pivotal Human Decisions

cannot induce me to do anything against my moral character.

> *Sow a thought, and you reap an act;*
> *Sow an act, and you reap a habit;*
> *Sow a habit, and you reap a character;*
> *Sow a character, and you reap a destiny.*

Samuel Smiles

Nietzsche, in one long sentence, calls for character, "What is essential 'in heaven and on earth' seems to be, to say it once more, that there should be *obedience* over a long period of time and in a *single* direction: given that, something always develops, and has developed, for whose sake it is worthwhile to live on earth; for example, virtue, art, music, dance, reason, spirituality—something transfiguring, subtle, mad, and divine" (**Beyond Good and Evil** *Natural History of Morals* #188).

From the beginning of time dreams have fascinated people, and so it is understandable that dreams may have portrayed important religious events. Sirach 34:2 says, "Like a man who catches at shadows or chases wind is the one who believes in dreams." Nevertheless, he also says in Sirach 34:6, "Unless it be a vision specially sent by the Most High, fix not your heart on it."

One of the most popular dream interpretations in the Bible, is Joseph interpreting the dream of the Pharaoh. A possible explanation is that the Pharaoh had learned that the history of Egypt was replete with feasts and famines. He was subconsciously worried about this but not conscious of it. Joseph, a wise man, simply made the subconscious, conscious.

God, though, does not speak to me in my dreams, but I speak to myself in my dreams from the depths of my character. Dreams do not foretell the future. They tell me what I have deep down in my subconscious. They somewhat accurately predict what my character will have me do in future situations. Some people, though, follow John Hume who defined virtue as "every quality of the mind that is useful or agreeable to the person himself or to others." This leads to situation ethics and *Slick Willies*. This is what led President Nixon's press secretary, Ron Ziegler, to say at one point, "All previous statements concerning Watergate are now non-operative!" Such statements display a lack of consistent character. The question is whether we want consistent character or only what is politically correct at the time.

Aristotle treats dreams as an object of psychology in his book, **Concerning Dreams and Their Interpretation**. He did not consider

Evil in Mirror Lake

the dream a product of the dreaming mind, but a Divine Inspiration, as did most of the authors of sacred scripture. In the Bible, the angel Gabriel came to Joseph in a dream and told him to take Jesus and Mary to Egypt. Today, most authors look to the real world as the source of dream material. Some like L. Strumpell in **Nature and Origin of Dreams**, has dreams turn their back on the world of waking consciousness. Others like P. Haffner in **Schlafen und Traumen** state that the dream is the continuation of the waking state. So, is there a connection between the dreaming and the waking state?

Most everyone agrees that the material composing the elements of the dream, in some way, originates in experience. The soul or mind is like a constantly running video and sound recorder. We store up both the most insignificant to the most traumatic experiences in our memories. We conjure up dreams from some type of stimuli—objective, subjective, organic or physical. Thus, we have the saying: *Dreams come from the stomach.*

Dreams are difficult to remember because they usually lack sense and order. They usually crumble the very next moment. Upon awakening, we experience the in-rushing sensory world, and only a few dreams can withstand this onslaught. They fade before the impressions of the new day, like the glow of stars before the sunlight. Another factor in forgetting our dreams is that most of us usually take little interest in them.

The stuff of dreams is all of our experience. The distinguishing mark of dreams is the absence of time and space. This is why we often do not recognize the picture in our dreams. They are composites, and as we will see, not very important in themselves. The dream pictures are incoherent stage-settings for the performance of my character. According to Hegel the dream lacks all objectivity and comprehensible connection. Dreams nevertheless, are so real to us that they are confused with reality, whereas, daydreaming never is.

Also, dreams seem strange because our feelings about things in the waking state are separated from the pictures in our dream state. These feelings, or psychic value of the pictures, are left to float about in the mind dependent upon their own resources. Our dream characters can independently pick up these feelings and act them out in our dream.

When I fall asleep, the trap door to my passive intellect, which my ego guards during my conscious hours, drops open. Anything in my passive intellect, or subconscious, can now float out and can connect, however it wants. This is why Radestock says, "It seems indeed impossible to recognize in this absurd action any firm law. Having withdrawn itself from the strict police of the rational will guiding the wak-

Pivotal Human Decisions

ing presentation of life, and of the attention, the dream whirls every-thing about kaleidoscopically in mad play."

This is where my character takes a stance. Schopenhauer assures us that in the dream every person acts and talks according to his char-acter. With this I agree when it comes to my person. When it comes to other people acting in my dreams, they too must be the product of my subconscious. From where else could this material possibly come?

Regarding the other characters in our dreams, I once dreamed that the Pretty Lady of our diocesan youth group was on a balcony at a hotel talking down to the teenagers mingling below. All dreams seem like they are in the present tense. Everyone below is dressed formally for a banquet, but she is wearing short shorts with legs that would not quit. As usual, I am standing on the side—just an observer. Then the Director appears, and he becomes obviously angry. He comes over to speak to someone in authority who is standing close to me. That is when the inappropriateness of the Pretty Lady dawns on me. I over-hear the Director angrily complaining that the color of her shorts does not match her top.

Who could make up these two characters? It must be I. It was my dream. It probably says more about me than the simple fact that I am not very color coordinated. Some may see sexual repression. Many of our dreams are comical, as well as revelations of character.

A lady dreams about an intruder with rape on his mind who climbs through her window. The woman screams out, "What are you going to do to me?" The man replies, "I don't know yet, ma'am—it's **your** dream!" This is from the Dalai Lama's book, **Sleeping, Dreaming, and Dying**.

On the other hand people like Jessen say, "Nor does one become better or more virtuous in the dream; on the contrary, it seems that conscience is silent in the dream, since one feels no compassion and can commit the worst crimes, such as theft, murder, and assassination, with perfect indifference and without subsequent remorse."

If this is true in my dreams, I should take heed for that may be exactly what I may then do in the waking state when my ego lets down the trap door. About an action that can have no place in my mind, I say with truth, "I never would have dreamt of such a thing." A familiar proverb says, "Tell me for a time your dreams, and I will tell you what you are within."

Hildebrandt observes that the dream at times allows me to glance into the deep and innermost recesses of my being that is in general closed to me in my waking state. Immanuel Kant, in his **Anthropol-ogy**, says that my dream exists to lay bare for me my hidden disposi-

191

Evil in Mirror Lake

tions and to reveal not what I am to myself, but what I might have been if I had a different education. Radestock says the dream often reveals to me what I do not wish to admit to myself, and so I unjustly condemn my dream as untrue of myself.

Dream theories abound: sensory impressions cause dreams of the preceding day that have not attained sufficient recognition by the dreamer. Dreams are the fulfillment of a wish. Dreams are emanations of thoughts nipped in the bud. Dreams, which possess healing and un-burdening properties, guard the mind from over-straining; they cleanse the mind. Dreams come from the psychic energy accumulated through the day by inhibition or suppression. Dreams contain a symbolizing fantastic activity as its central force. Lastly, absurd combinations of ideas and weakness of judgment are the main characteristics of the dream, and of insanity.

The secret of understanding the proper approach to dreams is bal-ance. Our intelligence, at times, needs to let its guard down. It does not seem beneficial to the creative work of the mind if intelligence in-spects too closely the ideas pouring into our imagination. My creative mind needs to withdraw my *intelligence watchers* from the gates to let ideas rush in pall-mall. It is only then that we look over critically and examine the great heap. My intelligence cannot judge all things if it does not hold them long enough to see them in relation to each other. What my mind or soul or intellect or will does in my dreams is all of the above. This is why I say, "Let me sleep on it before I decide." In the morning, my mind thinks more clearly, and makes better decisions.

The most famous dream interpreter is Sigmund Freud. In his **The Interpretation of Dreams** (1900), he explains what dreams mean to me in my waking state. Dreams have fascinated people throughout the ages. This fascination comes from the unexplainability of most of my dreams. Freud thinks symbolism is one key to explaining my dreams. Freud points out both the superficial and manifest content of dreams, and the latent or hidden meaning of dreams. The dreaming processes are all very complicated. I condense and transfigure characters, I cen-sor all, I misplace the feelings, I abate time and place, I am fulfilling some infantile wish, and yet the psyche makes my dream have some semblance of sense.

My unconscious mind acts like a continuously running video re-corder, containing everything ever seen, heard, touched, tasted, or smelled. In my conscious state, I need my imagination to remember everything of the past. My imagination depends upon physical brain cells that deteriorate. The contents of my passive intellect or subcon-scious are spiritual, so they stay with me forever, even through trauma

Pivotal Human Decisions

and Alzheimer's. I think about elderly people talking about youthful experiences long forgotten to consciousness.

Freud says that I have a dream censor. When I sleep, the dream censor also dozes a little, and the trap door to my unconscious opens and out pours all my experiences. In fact, the more these experiences lie incomplete, or worse, repressed, the greater the psychic force needed to help them escape. If they get past my dream censor, they become part of my dream in my mind.

My dream censor has a last chance to keep me from seeing the dream by causing me not to remember the dream in my conscious state. The motive power for my dream wish comes from my unconscious.

Freud introduced the preconscious where I store my impressions of the previous day or two. These impressions eventually pass into my unconscious. For anything ever to get out of my unconscious, something, even very insignificant in my preconscious, must trigger its activation and pull it into my dream world. We sometimes call this preconscious the subconscious.

I am fulfilling some wish, mostly infantile, in this and all my dreams. For me, everything I do in waking life is similarly wish fulfilling. After I have done something and someone asks, "Why?": I can always answer, "At the time I thought it was a good thing to do." Why can I always truthfully say this? Because I am always doing what I wish to do to ultimately make me happy or to avoid pain. This is also true in all my dreams.

Sigmund Freud emphasizes that I must recognize the dream as the fulfillment of a wish. What does the goose dream of? Answer: Of corn! Again, "I should never have fancied that in my wildest dream," I exclaim when I surpass my expectations in reality. According to Freud, the fulfillment of a wish, if not obvious in a dream, is nevertheless always there in its latent or hidden content. His rules of evidence for proving this would never pass the scrutiny of a Sherlock Holmes. He substitutes people, censors out significant incidents, changes times, and he even says that at times someone's wish fulfillment can be to prove Freud wrong in his wish fulfillment theory. Freud always had an interpretation.

This dream, as reported to Freud by Mr. B, can describe the difference between the manifest dream and the latent dream. Mr. B's manifest dream was that he and a friend were hauling wet cement on the floor of his automobile. Somehow a door came ajar and they were trying to stop the seepage of cement out of the door. Because of the rocks in the cement, they could not get the car door closed.

The manifest part of this dream is nonsense. Freud translates the

193

Evil in Mirror Lake

latent part as follows: Mr. B. likes his friend's wife. Though they have never been intimate, he has had dreams of making love to her. He was at their home the night before. The wet cement is his semen that he is trying to keep in check. (His dream censor objects to making this manifest.) The door becoming ajar is a slight misstep with the Mrs., and he is trying to rectify this. I say all of this psychic detective work is not the point, especially when Freud adds in compression and displacement to the interpretation.

What is important in the dream is for Mr. B. to recognize how he acted in his dream. He is trying hard with his friend to rectify the mishap. He is frustrated but keeps his cool and does not blame his friend or anyone else for the problem. Finally, he is wondering why he is doing such a stupid thing as trying to transport wet cement in an automobile. In fact, this is an accurate picture of Mr. B. But I say, "So what!" What I do in my dreams, to fulfill my wish, is the practical question. Mr. B. is trying in his dream to correct a bad relationship with a friend's wife before it becomes worse.

I find it more useful to consider that dreams are the windows to the character of my soul. It is what I do in my dreams that is important for me to notice. Fortunately, for this I do not need to pay an analyst, I just wake up and remember what I did in my dream. Then I decide if I like what I have seen, or if I wish to change my character before it is too late and I act out badly in my waking state.

"...in all of us, even in good men, there is a lawless wild-beast nature, which peers out in sleep," Plato said in **The Republic IX**. If you seldom ever remember your dreams, it is usually a good sign that your inner self is in harmony with your conscious self.

The human individual, according to Freud, has a vitalistic driving force called the *libido*. It is that primitive part of people called the *id* that holds only murderous, incestuous, adulterous, and always selfish impulses. Parents mitigate this unconscious force, as do the police, the authorities, teachers, who help us to form the *superego,* whose function is to cause us to seek to slake our need for gratification by socially acceptable means. We sometimes call this conscience, although Freud would never call it a God-given conscience, since he considered God an illusion. The *ego*, then, is the self of which we are all immediately aware, and is an uneasy compromise between the *id* and the *superego*. Dreams are the stage upon which the *id* and the *superego* have, so far unconsciously, worked out their tension. Dreams are some pictures of our unconscious *ego*. "We have met the enemy, and he is us," Pogo.

Freud's interpretation of dreams reminds me of psychics who would like to tell my future. They take a few things from my life and

Pivotal Human Decisions

spin a yarn about it. They make a story fit and they expand on it. Analysts and psychics, they are first cousins. This Darwinian pessimist did give us a valid insight into the waking of our psyche—his model of the human mind upon which he based his psychoanalysis as a treatment for neurosis. Freud revolutionized the way I look at myself, or refuse to look at myself. His *worldview* of the human mind has made a great book, if not an easy read.

Daydreams also can help me lead my character away from evil. They have the advantage of being half-conscious so I can direct them to a desired end. As a youth, my teachers told me not to waste my time daydreaming but to get my work done. A person without a dream is a person without ambition. Daydreaming can take me down the road to success by visualizing not only the desired results but also the perceived problems along the way. On the other hand, my uncontrolled daydreaming could make me into a victim of advertising, which business people design to mesmerize my desires—the modern American mantra of feel, want, need, and then buy.

Thomas Aquinas said the future belongs to the youth because their exuberant vision of the future is so vivid that they rush in before realizing all of the pitfalls. Once involved, youth struggle through to the end. Older people, when presented with a new project, let the vivid problems of experiences eclipse the force of their future vision. They give up before they start. Of course, youth and "older people" has little to do with chronological age.

Daydreams can also keep us from doing something bad. If I daydream about becoming a drug kingpin, and direct my daydreaming to a probable natural life term in prison, then I may decide to abandon that dream since I came to a conclusion in my daydreaming that crime does not pay. For an understanding of how to use your daydreams and how they mingle with your night dreams, see **Daydreaming** (1997) by F. Diane Barth.

Dreams and daydreams are part of our life for a purpose. I believe the reason relates to our character and our future. The way we daydream deals with the way we feel about ourselves and about the rest of reality. The message contained in the title of the book, **Mind As Healer, Mind As Slayer,** says it quite well. This author, Kenneth R. Pelletier, delineates the relationship between mind-related stress and four major types of illnesses: cardiovascular disease, cancer, arthritis, and respiratory disease. So our daydreaming can lead to health or illness, good or evil.

Andrew Greeley, in **The Religious Imagination**, speaks of the power of imagination to animate, vitalize, and thus transform knowl-

195

Evil in Mirror Lake

edge. Contending that the Holy Spirit works through imagination, Greeley defends the centrality or importance of symbols or sacraments in religious life. The transcendent power of imagination allows me to project an image of God as a dynamic movement of the Holy Spirit— God on the move. This image influences all people to do good and to avoid making bad decisions, which in hindsight we will call evil.

I myself feel a great need to change my image of God. My image used to be a fatherly figure sitting on a throne judging me. I have moved to my good friend Jesus walking with me, but I need to go further. I need to encompass the Holy Spirit as God pouring out love into me and into creation. Although I know that God lives within me, I still picture God as too separate from me. I am finding it hard to come up with a better symbol. In the Hebrew Testament we read about God leading the Chosen People as a pillar of fire by night and a cloud by day. I like the cloud but it is too far above me. Bring it down in the form of fog or mist or haze, and I have my image of the Holy Spirit among us. The fog is in me and I am in the fog. I can see a little ahead, but not too far. It is mysterious, I know some things, others are simply shadows—like God. A good symbol of God must be life giving—mist causes life to grow. Consider the Emerald Isle. My best symbol so far for the Holy Spirit is the God of Haze. (It just happens to be a play on my name.)

Daydreams can help me create my character while dreams tell me what my character presently is. My character, whether good or evil, is an integral part of my immortal soul. How important is my soul? Standing on the ledge of the peak, viewing the depth of the lake, I now look to the next frontier—my inner life. I feel all alone, but not quite.

CHAPTER IX

MY IMMORTAL SOUL

After a battle, the mighty Napoleon found one of his favorite lieutenants lying dead on the ground. Little blood was evident. He ordered his adjutant to stand the dead lieutenant up against the wall. The startled adjutant did so, and when he let go of the corpse, it fell back to the ground. Napoleon ordered the adjutant to repeat the process; the result was the same. Napoleon rode off, shaking his head, and said that something on the inside of his dead friend must be missing. That something was his soul—source of his life.

Standing on the edge of the ledge, I can almost see the still water running deep. It becomes a metaphor of my inner life. The soul, by definition, is the *source of life*. It is there at the first moment of life. In plants and animals, the soul's power is totally dependent upon its material body. When the body decays and ceases to function, its soul also ceases to exist for it has nothing to function through. These souls in plants and animals are as mortal, it seems, as are their bodies. Yet, many people, and not just children, will argue with me that their cats and dogs will live on in heaven. I do not argue back. Though we have a lot in common with the rest of creation, when I begin to equate animals and even insects with humans, I devalue humans.

Besides my senses and locomotive powers, I, as a rational animal have the powers both to think and to choose, which I call intellect and will. These powers, to think and to choose, must be more than just material—the souls of plants and animals are more than just material—the rocks are just material. That which encompasses more than just material I, in general call spiritual. The spiritual, which can think and choose, can continue to exist and function after the body has undergone death and decay, I hope. Therefore, Christians and others like to believe that human souls are immortal. I also like to believe that Social Security checks will be there for me at the end of employment. These beliefs matter to my present well being.

Evil in Mirror Lake

Death is the separation of the body and soul. Body or matter cannot explain this presence of consciousness within me. I look to my feelings (which come from the instincts to survive, procreate, associate) and my consciousness (which could be the product of a larger, very complex biological brain) to tell me that this world is more than birth, procreation, and death. I have a purpose, a destiny, and I am immortal. I seek more than an experience of being alive, as important as that may be. I seek a fuller expression and experience of aliveness. This is why some say that all paths in life are the same, and none more meaningful than others. What matters, then, is to choose the one with the most heart. "Don't die with your music still in you," says Wayne W. Dyer, author of **Wisdom of the Ages**.

John Keats expresses this aliveness in his poem *Endymion*:

> *But this is human life: the war, the deeds,*
> *The disappointment, the anxiety,*
> *Imagination's struggles, far and high,*
> *All human; bearing in themselves this good,*
> *That they are still the air, the subtle food,*
> ***To make us feel existence**, and to show*
> *How quiet death is. Where soil is men grow,*
> *Whether to weeds or flowers; but for me,*
> *There is no depth to strike in: I can see*
> *Naught earthly worth my compassing; so stand*
> *Upon a misty, jutting head of land . . .*
> *Alone? No, no.* **(Emphasis added)**

William Wordsworth criticized this poem as a kind of hymn to earth, "a pretty piece of paganism." I think and choose, and I plot my own eternal destiny in life. My life experiences must be more than what I perceive on a purely physical plane, as alive as these experiences may make me feel. My consciousness, if not my reason, tells me most assuredly that part of me is immortal, amid the impermanence of life. At the very least, I can relate to Henry James who in his last year, while collapsing from a stroke, thought he heard a voice, not his own, saying, "So here it is at last, the *distinguished* thing." It is life after death that makes sense of this world.

But who knows for sure? None of us have any personal experience of deceased people living after we carry them to the cemetery. Even the resurrection of Jesus we know only through the witness of other humans—Mary Magdalen first, then the women and finally the apostles.

In all areas of my life I strive to make sense of events, changes,

My Immortal Soul

losses, luck, love, computers—why should my life in the universe be the exception? "Although the universe is under no obligation to make sense, students in pursuit of the Ph.D. are." —Robert P. Kirshner says with tongue in cheek.

"Why is it that everything is always changing?" said Andy Rooney, whining. This was the original philosophical question asked by the pre-Plato thinkers of ancient Greece beginning with Thales. An over-simplified description is that Plato gave us to understand *Being*, and Aristotle gave us *Becoming*. At any rate this is how life is. Time and circumstances change everything, and time is always changing. Nothing, nothing at all (possibly save God), has any lasting character.

Before the Greeks, the Chinese gave us one of the earliest efforts of the human mind to find its place in the universe. An unknown author gave us the **I Ching** (c. 1500 B.C.E.), whose true origins remain shrouded in mystery. The usual title translation is **Book of Changes**. Though the book's ideas are used for divination and at times meditation, its followers claim a meaningful coincidence between the throw of the coins (or yarrow stalks) and the simultaneous play between the *yin* and *yang* of the universe. The Greek pre-Socratic philosopher Heraclitus would have called it an *unapparent connection*. But it is all based on being in touch with a reality that is always changing. Some people call this instinct or luck.

I am ever in transit. The Buddha said:

This existence of ours is as transient as autumn clouds.
To watch the birth and death of beings is like looking at
the movements of a dance.
A lifetime is like a flash of lightning in the sky,
Rushing by, like a torrent down a steep mountain.

Yeats, the Irish poet, invites me to look within, "Man needs reckless courage to descend into the abyss of himself." It is this primal energy deep within my soul with which I need to make friends. This inner friendship with myself gives me the courage to utter *No Fear*, a now popular phrase that recurs 366 times in the Bible. We frequently find this friendship with ourselves in out-of-the-way places. Many have found it in silence and solitude, or when fishing. "It is in the unexpected or neglected place that I find the lobster," a Boston fisherman once told me.

Ezra Pound said something similar about beauty, "Beauty likes to keep away from the public glare." It likes to find a neglected or abandoned place. Within my soul is deep beauty. Beauty is not cos-

Evil in Mirror Lake

metic perfection, but is the illumination of my soul—my life—my immortal life.

If I expect to find nothing of value within myself, I will find emptiness, loneliness and desperation. Loneliness is epidemic, as Henry David Thoreau said in **Walden, or, Life in the Woods** (1854). This imaginative and detailed account serves as a blueprint for simple, frugal living. To achieve true freedom, I must cast off material encumbrances. Only then I can find my inner spiritual instinct that will reveal my Divine Calling. "Most people live lives of quiet desperation," Thoreau assures me. It is the worldly necessity of making a living, of working for a paycheck, that inevitably overshadows the creative parts of people, the things people really want to do. Thoreau thought it possible to live within a natural environment. He also thought that it was "the unquestionable ability of man to elevate his life by conscious endeavor." In a vital sense, perception is reality. My focus is my reality.

Meister Eckhart, a great Middle Age's mystic, wonderfully expresses this idea, "Thoughts are our inner senses." I need to learn the unique language of my own soul. I relate to my inner world through my thoughts. If I have only borrowed thoughts (like too many borrowed quotes), I am missing the unique language of my own soul.

Dostoyevsky said that many of us live our lives without finding us within ourselves. If I am afraid of solitude, I am afraid of my inner self. So, I turn on the radio/TV, or make sure I have something/anything to entertain/distract me.

Driving alone in my car becomes a religious moment for me. Here I can exchange thoughts and form a friendship with myself and God. Only after an hour of this, will I permit the car radio its time. As I travel deep into my soul, I find no simple, singular self. "All man's miseries derive from not being able to sit quietly in a room alone," said Blaise Pascal (1623-1662). Pascal also said, "The eternal silence of these infinite spaces terrifies me." Probably this is why I sometimes find it so difficult to do my meditation.

One thing I do find there is my conscience. Thoreau's other influential book, or an essay (initially a lecture), was **Civil Disobedience** (1849). It remains the classic defense of conscience against unjust law. Mahatma Gandhi and Martin Luther King Jr. both took it as a model. Thoreau was not an anarchist, but he wanted governments to be invisible—the least amount of government interference as possible. He drew from many philosophies and beliefs, but we note him for his "quizzical nudgings toward truths." This quirky Harvard graduate, along with Francis of Assisi, is the most admired and least imitated of the greats.

My higher and lower natures, at times, conflict with each other. It

My Immortal Soul

is important that I do not become divided. These opposing forces, the dark side and the light side, in my nature are not enemies but different sides of my one being. I know enough about how I am different; I need to learn how I am the same. Just as I cannot live without my body; I cannot die without my soul. Dying is the separation of body and soul. Without a soul, I could not go through this process of separation.

Once I develop a new sense of the wonderful complexity of my inner soul, I begin to lose fear. When I lose my separateness from the Holy Spirit, and become one with all, I lose all fear. Fear leads to anger, anger leads to hate, and hate leads to suffering. This is like Yoda's advice to young Luke Skywalker—suffering, born of anger and hate, imposes itself upon others and myself. Misery loves company. If on the other hand I turn my cheek, I short-circuit this process. It is startling how desperately I held onto what made me miserable. It was the fear of the unknown, including the unknown God. Often I was destructively addicted to the negative.

Rainer, a German poet, says that difficulty is one of the greatest friends of the soul. I can befriend the negative if I recognize that it is not necessarily destructive. A negative experience contains essential energy that I need and would be hard pressed to find elsewhere. John O'Donahue in **Anam Cara** puts these contradictory forces into symmetry:

> *This is where art can be so illuminating. Art is full of*
> *intimations of the negative in ways that allow you to*
> *participate imaginatively in their possibility. The*
> *experience of art can help you build a creative friendship*
> *with the negative. When you stand before a painting by*
> *Kandinsky, you enter the church of color where the liturgy*
> *of contradiction is fluent and glorious. When you listen to*
> *Martha Argerich play Rachmaninov's Piano Concerto No.*
> *3 in D Minor, Op. 30, you experience the liberation of*
> *contradictory forces that at every point threaten and test*
> *the magnificent symmetry of form that holds them.*

(Rachmaninov wrote this music despite or because of it, while in an insane asylum.)

I must take the rough timbers of my life and construct a temple, not a tavern. To live the unlived life is one of the greatest sins along with all those evil things I do. One of the most sacred duties of my destiny is the duty to be myself. When I come to accept and even like to be with

Evil in Mirror Lake

myself, I learn not to be afraid of my nature which includes my upcoming death. Then I stand on my own ground, and I am no longer in the politics of fashioning my *persona* to please the expectations of others. I put aside the need to hammer second-hand thoughts into myself, so I would fit in. I am my own person, and I am happy with that person. I should strive to appreciate my own *persona*—and forget what the tribe thinks of me. Yet, I must keep the tribe thinking that I am one of them. When I publicly dissociate myself from the tribe, my ego gets involved, and I get separated. I wish to remain one with all, yet live my own life.

To get to this appreciation of myself, some significant other must also think that I am a worthwhile unique person. For me this perception began to grow because my parents affirmed me. If my parents did not do their part, then there might have been someone else who would have valued me—such as a girl/boy friend, a mentor, a psychologist, etc. When I finally caught onto the possibility to experience such recognition and appreciation of my inner self, I was within reach of the fulfillment of what life has to offer—to love and to be loved. George Sand penned it succinctly, "There is only one happiness in life, to love and be loved."

Sometimes I can understand something best by recognizing what it is not. Read **The Great Gatsby**, a human drama set in New York City and Long Island in 1922, probably F. Scott Fitzgerald's best novel. In Tom and Daisy, he creates "two careless people [who] smash up things and then retreat back into their money... and let other people clean up the mess..." On the other hand, Gatsby, who deals in stolen bonds, is larger than life. He is a hopeless and hopeful *great romantic* who represents the worldly ambition in all of us. He believes in seizing whatever and whomever he dreams of, no matter the human cost. Although it is a romantic story about men and women, it is not a drama of *to love and to be loved*.

What about the advanced form of *homo erectus* named after the town in Germany where the first remains were found—the Neanderthals? They walked erect, had big brains, wore clothes, engaged in warfare, used tools, and buried their dead. Does this latter practice mean that they believed in an after-life? After a long and widespread success, however, they failed as a sub-species for reasons still unexplained. They—unlike us *homo sapiens*—were not in the end to be the inheritors of the earth. But, what about eternity? Did they have immortal souls? Facing my own death has brought an immense freedom and peace to my life. This facing death was not a particular experience, but a simple awareness of unfinished business—like making my will. I think of the saint who when asked what he would do if he knew that he

My Immortal Soul

would die tomorrow, answered "the same as I am doing today." I also think of the joke about the Irish priest who heard that Jesus was coming to visit his parish. He cabled Rome asking what to do. The telegram came back: "Look busy!"

Facing death has made me aware of the urgency of the time that I have. I must not waste it excessively on either the past or the future. So many people, as Patrick Kavanagh puts it, "are preparing for life rather than living it." I can say the same for regretting life.

I try to live about 80 percent of my life in the present moment. The present is the only time that exists. The past is about 10 percent important to me. Past circumstances do not make a person, they reveal him. It gives me my history, my roots. I can also learn from it, but I can never change it. Sometimes I replay the past as I would replay a taped Notre Dame football game—continually hoping that this time they will call a different play and win. Also, the future deserves 10 percent of my attention. I need to make some plans, even if tentative. I need a vision of where I am going and how I want to get there. I have but one journey through life—only one chance, that I am positive of, for my immortal soul.

This is why I have already created my pine coffin. My carpenter, Tom Loos, did such an artistic job, I put it in my living room to replace the coffee table. The kids have dubbed it my coffin table. On Halloween I open it and let those, who wish, lie in it—a little like a dry run. I look upon death as the doorway to immense possibilities. Throughout life, I (body and soul) have journeyed with my eternal Other in great satisfaction and happiness. I (immortal soul) expect the same on the other side—after I have wrapped up my mortality.

When I imagine myself in my mother's womb and someone coming to tell me that they are about to expel me and cut my chord, pushing me through a narrow passage, finally dropping me out into vacant open light, I imagine the same kind of fear as I have associated with dying. From within the womb, being born would seem like a death. My problem is that I can see only from one side—envisioning my inevitable, expectant death. Ludwig Wittgenstein summed this up when he said, "Death is not an experience in one's life." Death is about a rebirth. Life is not ended, only changed.

Wittgenstein proposed a critical method of linguistic analysis as the solution to most philosophic problems, which were the result, he argued, not of difficulty or inadequate knowledge but of the systematic misuse of language by philosophers. "Philosophy," he said, "is a battle against the bewitchment of our intelligence by means of language." He was the primary influence on the development of Logical Positivism.

Evil in Mirror Lake

In his **Philosophical Investigations**, he developed the idea of meaning not as a connection between thought and reality, but as a *language game*. A meaningful statement is a correct deployment of words according to the rules of a particular language. Words then masquerade as ordinary descriptions. This is an intellectual description of a lie. Meaning ought to be a connection between thought and reality.

My parents sent me into this world to live to the full everything that love awakens within me, and everything that comes toward me. This is the Divine Gamble being played out by myself. This is why God does not interfere with either my free will or nature. I still feel privileged to have time to create the me I wish to be. I know my calling is different from any other's. Irenaeus, a wonderful philosopher and theologian in the second century, summed it up with, "The glory of God is the human person fully alive." In our day it sounds like Fr. John Powell, S.J.. Also, as Stanislavsky, the Russian dramatist and thinker, said, "the longest and most exciting journey is the journey inwards."

John Henry Newman, the English Catholic cardinal, summed this up beautifully when he said, "To grow is to change and to be perfect is to have changed often." In the Book of Revelation, God said, "The world of the past has gone... Behold I am making all creation new."

Faith redeems me from the greatest curse of all—to be meaningless in a meaningless world. The purpose of all great religions has been to fight a certain weariness and heaviness grown at times to epidemic proportions. Since Copernicus, humanity's existence appears more arbitrary, beggarly, and dispensable in the *visible* order of things. We are no longer the centers of the universe, as we once thought. I am a microbe on a speck of dust. Sadly, the faith in the dignity and uniqueness of people, in their irreplaceability in the great chain of being, seems a relic. People have become an animal, literally and without reservation or qualification. To many, the idea that we are, *children of God*, seems a relic of the past.

Some people agree with the bumper sticker that says, "Life is a..., and then you die." I do not agree; no matter how hard life is, I have a purpose, a destiny. I have an immortal soul. My actions count for something. I am important. I am finding more of me all the time. I will live forever. *"Vivo yo!"* I love and people love me and, most comfortingly, God loves me. God is in me and I am in God. If logic tells me that life is a meaningless accident, then I will not give up on life, I will give up on logic.

I listen to my feelings that tell me that life cannot possibly be meaningless, and all reality still make sense. What makes sense of life, besides eternity, is the experience of something more than the struggle

My Immortal Soul

for bodily comforts in satisfying the imagined needs of my ego. That something, is the experience of being personally involved in co-creating with divinity the kingdom of justice and peace here on earth. "Follow your bliss," as Joseph Campbell said. A state of uninhibited and unimaginable joy awaits me—both here and in the hereafter.

For a more classical understanding of feelings or sentiment, consult Vilfredo Pareto's **The Mind and Society** (1916). His main points are that people live according to what he called *sentiment*, but they pretend to live according to *reason*. Freudian in spirit, Pareto studies the nonlogical actions of people and states that these actions provide the foundation of the social system—sociology. Society's foundation arises from people's sentiments. We generally do what we feel like doing.

Most people agree with Pascal's *wager* that if one were a betting person, one would be wise to believe—since in the end the believer would be losing nothing if proven wrong. He would go into nothingness and not hell. On the other hand, the unbeliever would lose everything if proven wrong. Another way of saying this is that the believer sacrifices a finite amount of pleasure in this life for infinite pleasure/ reward in the next, while the non believer evokes infinite loss and pain in the next life *versus* finite pleasure in this life.

Those who do not believe in the immortality of the soul, such as the Buddhists, may say that I invent a happy and personal afterlife to alleviate the drudgery of the NOW. Just to *make believe* would never do. Both sides of the immortality question do admit that blessed are those who do believe in the immortality of the human soul, rather than in the proposition that we live on only in other people's memories. It would be even worse to believe that we are simply a piece of yeast living off other people as Mr. Wolf believed in Jack London's great book, **Sea Wolf**.

This materialistic, atheistic philosophy dates back to Epicurus (341-270 B.C.E.) and his major work, **On Nature**, but very little of it has survived. We do have the poem, **On the Nature of Reality** (c. 55 B.C.E.) by Lucretius. Both taught that the world consists of an infinite number of indivisible atoms and an infinite void in which they move at a velocity faster than that of light. I need to regard everything in my experience as the result of a collision of atoms. The soul itself consists of very fine atoms, and at death it will dissolve. There is no afterlife. In place of the search for truth, Epicureanism puts friendship or peace of mind as the goal of life. After finishing his poem, Lucretius committed suicide. In his writings he was anxious to prove that death is the end of personality, but there is nothing in his poem about what we call, vari-

205

Evil in Mirror Lake

ously—the soul, spirit or essence. Today I see this Epicurean philosophy advertised on billboards.

A division has always existed between those of us who treasure religious belief as our final support in a world that otherwise for us would be unintelligible, meaningless, and tragic, and those who have come to think of religion and immortality as fruitless superstition. Religion, with its calling for good over evil, is definitely a help to me as I struggle along between life's two immensities after birth and before death. It reminds me of Tibet's famous poet saint, Milarepa, who said, "My religion is to live—and die—without regret." I do not want to die wondering if my life has been wrong. Where does all this lead? Dante would have us believe...

HEAVEN, HELL OR PURGATORY

Religion leads into eternity. If the human soul lives beyond death, then there is every reason to suppose that the soul, being a spirit, survives forever. My soul, through its free will, forms relationships. In my final fundamental option before death, if I opt to relate to God as a significant Other in a loving, dependent, meaningful relationship, then I will be forever in union with God and share eternal life. This will be my heaven.

HEAVEN

What is heaven like? I imagine that it will be all that would make me happy—and more. When children ask me if they can have all the cake and ice cream they want when they go to heaven, I always say, "Yes." Nevertheless, I know that heaven will be much better—as Paul said, "Eye hath not seen… " This is also true with adults. I know nothing of the details of heaven. Happiness covers it all. As Horatio says in **Hamlet**, "there is more in heaven and earth than is dreamed of in mere philosophy."

Have you ever seen two long separated lovers meet at the airport? They run into each other's arms with reckless abandon and frequently shed tears of joy. Most of these people will later say that, at that instant, time for them stood still. Heaven is something like that, but even better. It is more than an eternal embrace with a lover. As a Hindu Upanishad says, "When before the beauty of a sunset or of a mountain you pause and exclaim, *Ah*, you are participating in divinity." This is also the Fifth Insight in **The Celestine Prophecy**.

Heathcliff in **Wuthering Heights** says, "What do they know of

My Immortal Soul

heaven or hell who know nothing of life." Eternity is like life, but more so.

Time is so relative. Jack Buck, the Hall of Fame sports announcer for St. Louis, tells the story about when he was on vacation visiting a small village in Ireland. Early one morning he went to Paddy's Pub to get the newspaper. Paddy asks him if he wishes today's or yesterday's paper. Jack responds, "Today's." Paddy informs him, "Then you'll have to come back tomorrow." For some, time is timeless.

I must always remember my own little manner of thinking. When a larger experience of God approaches as a greater experience than I have ever anticipated, I must not take flight from it by clinging to the old image in my mind, since I am not here to preserve my faith, but to perfect it. This is what the psychologist Maslow called *peak experiences*, and what James Joyce called *epiphanies*. These are esthetic arrests caused by the rhythm of beauty which stills the heart. Beauty is a picture, formally organized and interesting, which has wholeness, harmony and radiance. Thomas Aquinas defined beauty as something that has "unity, balance and splendor of form."

HELL

On the other hand, if at the end of my earthly time I opt that I do not need God in my life then I will go my way and God can go another way. That separation would be my hell forever. I use the phrase *be my hell* as a state of being rather than a place of torture. Jesus describes hell in the New Testament as an eternally burning city dump, something like the one outside Jerusalem, Gehenna (Matt. 10:28). Think of the worst death imaginable (for me it would be burning to death or drowning), and hell is much worse than that. It is living forever without that for whom I was born, namely God. It is a true love wrongly cast aside. It is hell!

When talking about angels and devils, I explained earlier that they cannot change their decisions once they have made up their minds since they cannot receive any new information upon which to base a change in decision. It is the same for me after death. After the separation of my soul from my body, I will no longer have operating bodily senses to bring me new information upon which to base a change in my ultimate decision. I will choose the same forever.

The traditional image of God casting me into hell fire and damning me is not accurate. "If there is one thing more certain than another it is that we shall all appear before the Judgment Seat of Christ, and that the wicked will be consumed in a lake of everlasting fire. Doubt this, Mrs.

207

Evil in Mirror Lake

Thompson, and you are lost," says Parson Theobald, in **The Way of All Flesh** by Samuel Butler.

Most of us, following the imagery of the Bible (Matt. 25:31-46), or James Joyce's description in his book **A Portrait of the Artist as a Young Man**, see ourselves coming before God the Father at the end of our lives for judgment. The devil is the District Attorney or Great Recorder making us out to be as bad as we really are. Our guardian angel or Defense Attorney recalls all of our good deeds. God listens and then pronounces judgment, "Go into the everlasting fire prepared for you and the devil," or "Come, ye blessed, into my kingdom where I have a mansion prepared for you." This is not an accurate picture because it puts the onus of judging on God. It is accurate, however, in saying that a separation of the good and the evil will exist at the end of time. God does not judge me, as much as I judge myself.

I have made up a different image of my judgment day. "All things are metaphors," as Goethe said, so I add another. Suppose that I am living in a world filled with darkness. When death comes, God turns on the eternal light switch. If I have developed the power of sight, then I can see God in all glory. No judgment is necessary. I have either the power to see, or no power to see. The power to see is my relationship with God. I help create this relationship, and not God alone. God's hand of friendship is always extended in my direction. Whether I accept it or not is my decision, not God's judgment. As I see it, God still extends the hand of friendship, not only to the devils, but also to all of the damned humans. It is not that God is judgmental and unforgiving. It is that I am ever unchanging after death.

All metaphors or similes falter in that some aspects of the comparisons do not match. This eyesight simile limps in that we do not usually think about being able to make or strengthen our eyesight. However, some doctors do give eye exercises for strengthening, and we can do bad things to weaken our eyesight. To carry this simile a step further, I believe that just as we have different degrees or strengths in relationships so some people have different eye strengths. I can have 20/20 vision and others 20/40.

Some years ago, my niece Mona, in the sixth grade, was found to need eyeglasses. When she received them, she sat near her picture window at home, and with amazement and joy she described to us all that she could now see across the street. Before getting glasses, she had less than 20/20 vision, but she had been perfectly happy with her nearsightedness. We will all enjoy different degrees of relationships with God, and so happiness will vary for each of us. However, we will all be ecstatically happy in our loving relationship with God, whatever it is.

208

My Immortal Soul

When that eternal light switch is flipped on, I picture myself in a most beautiful room with a ceiling by Michelangelo, walls by Raphael, and furniture by Chippendale. Depending on the quality of my eyesight, I can appreciate all of the detailed beauty that is there. Whatever I do see will be perfect for me. The stronger my relationship is with God, the greater my happiness. The sharper I can see God with all of the exquisite details, the greater my happiness will be. Yet I will be perfectly happy no matter what.

Although Faust had sinned, he had struggled toward growth, knowledge, and transcendence. The seraphic angels, snatching and bearing Faust's immortal part—his soul—to heaven, acclaim:

> *Who e'er aspiring, struggles on,*
> *For him there is salvation.* (L 11936)

All people are called to exist and struggle within a constant state of *becoming*—a lifelong striving toward greater realms of knowledge, choices and emotions. If I stay true to this call, even when I stumble into excesses and error, I will not go unrewarded by God. In fact, the devil's role is to blind me to this end. But when I overcome myself, I achieve my true destiny—heaven.

In reverse, the same seems true about being unhappy in hell. According to Dante, hell is in varying degrees, but maybe everyone there is totally unhappy. The Great Beyond is an unqualified mystery, or misery, that is just not up to words, not even poetry. The experience of God, and much more the idea of heaven or hell, is beyond description.

C. S. Lewis gives this description in **The Great Divorce**:

> *All answers deceive. If you put the question (whether, as*
> *Paul seems to say, that all men will be saved) from within*
> *time and are asking about possibility, the answer is*
> *certain. The choice of ways is before you. Neither is*
> *closed. Any man may choose eternal death. But if you are*
> *trying to leap on into eternity, if you are trying to see the*
> *final state of all things as it will be when there are no*
> *more possibilities left, but only the Real, then you ask*
> *what cannot be answered to mortal ears. Time is the very*
> *lens through which you see—small and clear, as men*
> *through the wrong end of a telescope, something that*
> *would otherwise be too big for you to see at all.*

On the other hand, I disagree with Piet Schoonenberg's point in an

Evil in Mirror Lake

essay entitled, *I Believe in Eternal Life*:

*A certain growth also remains possible in the final
fulfillment. Otherwise, we would perhaps cease to be human.
Just as life constantly rediscovers itself from the past into the
future, so we shall constantly rediscover our past and present
in and from God in new and surprising ways.*

This suggests change that calls for time. Thomas Aquinas assures us that in eternity no time exists. My life on earth is a one-shot complete experience. **Now** is my only time. Schoonenberg's quote sounds like purgatory… which calls for change… which calls for time.

"Put bluntly, it couldn't possibly be in anyone's long-term best interest to be eternally damned," says C. Stephen Layman in, **Faith Has Its Reasons**, "so a loving God wouldn't damn anyone eternally. It would be more loving to annihilate people than to make them miserable for all eternity." Hell, then, would be the ultimate extinguishing of all evil— even the people who have done the evil.

I think this is a good example of how logic can lead astray. Layman has not distributed his middle term, or his premise is not valid. This is like stating that no one would prefer a natural life sentence without a possibility of parole instead of a death sentence. Ask the people on Death Row! Nowhere does the Christian God mention annihilation. As I have said elsewhere, God forever extends the hand of friendship to all damned people. These damned people just do not want this loving, dependent relationship. God does not damn anyone to hell. People choose it—forever.

PURGATORY

Yet, there may be another place. Some people, such as Catholics, believe in purgatory, a place where after death you will purge your smaller sins away. This is like the Elysian Fields of Dante. Purgatory is like having a cataract operation so I can see more clearly again. Interestingly, the Jews also believe in a type of purgatory. If I do not make it immediately to heaven, I go to purgatory for a time. No one, though, goes to hell, says my Rabbi friend.

I like to think of purgatory in terms of drug or alcohol withdrawal. It is one thing to say and mean that I will never again use drugs or alcohol. It is quite another thing for my body to go through the withdrawal. Withdrawal is like purgatory. I will pay a price (withdrawal) for past decisions, but the future looks bright. All of us who go to pur-

My Immortal Soul

gatory will eventually get to heaven.

Some of us, in our final option for God, continue to attach ourselves to persons, places, or things in a way that is not in harmony with God's plan for us. Withdrawing from these illicit, somewhat sinful attachments, is purgatory. Again, it is not God punishing us for our past sins, any more than a friend is punishing his comrade as he goes through withdrawal with him. It is just part of the nature of a friend, like Jesus, to go through withdrawal with me. Happy is the person who has such a friend in this and the next life.

Meanwhile... let us move to that yonder plateau for that perspective of life in time and space. There, I hope to discern clearly my solution to the problem of evil before leaving Mirror Lake.

CHAPTER X

MY SOLUTION TO THE PROBLEM OF EVIL

In 1960, I was in the seminary during the Third Arab-Israeli War (Palestinian-Israeli Conflict). The evening news showed a Jewish mother hurling herself on the flag-draped coffin of her dead soldier son, and screaming in Hebrew, the question, "Why?" At the dawn of the 21st century, we are still asking, "Why?" for similar incidents.

I have approached my solution to the problem of evil in life by penetrating the depths of my experiences—in Mirror Lake. The existence of evil has for a long time been a problem for philosophers and theologians. For most of us, it has also long been a personal one. The problem is our belief that God is both all-good and all-powerful. This generates the incongruity that the all-loving God is responsible for evil.

Having traversed through the forest of past opinions, and having answered some questions, I am now peering down into the lake of knowledge of good and evil. The Spirit rises and tells me that the solution to this problem of evil is to understand that God has chosen not to be all-powerful in all situations. Yes, the all-powerful God can choose not to be all-powerful in nature and free choices. We must look deep into the blue waters to fathom this part of the mystery. We must also be willing to risk that our past beliefs were not totally correct. Christian theologies need to be re-analyzed, occasionally.

In modern times, Søren Kierkegaard in his **Idea (Concept) of Dread** (1844) and Jean-Paul Sartre in **Being and Nothingness** (1943) discuss the problem of evil in terms of dread, forlornness, despair and the absurd. Yet, the age-old chant is ever before us, "From where comes evil and why?" Sartre wanted the individual's life to mean something in what he took to be a godless world. He called this "being in freedom and with meaning." This would give you authenticity. That is about as absurd as my castrated cat, Tonto, protecting his territory and not knowing why!

My Solution to the Problem of Evil

This conflict between evil and our idea of a God-driven world led to the philosophical term—the absurd. We can trace the roots of this term to an early church Father, Tertullian (160?-230). He argued that the surest sign of the truth of Christianity was its absurdity. He said that an almighty God becoming a man and dying for humans is so irrational that it could not be a made-up story. It must be true, he said.

Kierkegaard, the Danish theologian, satirist, philosopher and an archenemy of Hegel, re-emphasized the absurdity of Christianity. He offers that rational *proofs* are blocks, not aids to faith. "A faith that required proofs is no faith at all," he contends. The choice for Christianity must be a *leap of faith* for which there are no strictly rational criteria. Kierkegaard turned respectable theologies upon their head by insisting that subjectivity be the only sort of truth worth knowing. This is also called relativism.

Either/Or is Kierkegaard's most influential book. Either reality is an intense and absolute subjectivity, or reality is a false and dingy objectivity that is not even objectivity at all. He is fascinating because he knows so much about the inner life, the stream-of-consciousness. He emphasizes inwardness. Too much subjectivity, though, causes the loss of faith. Faith collapsed because objective reality collapsed. We need both subjective reality (res rationes) and objective reality (res reales). And both realities need to jibe. We represent him sometimes as the essence of individualist Protestantism, yet he challenged the good faith of his state-sanctioned Lutheran church.

Jean-Paul Sartre completely secularized the idea of absurdity as a basis for his Existentialism. This notion puts people in an irrational world in which they must create their own purposes through a series of choices for which there are no guiding criteria. Existentialists claim that to accept criteria is to surrender the distinguishing feature of being human. This idea condemns people to be free, but for no known purpose. Sartre calls this the irresolvable paradox of human existence.

I plan to show how I can support faith with reason, while allowing faith to be separate from reason. Faith gives me my defining purpose for being created free—to love and to be loved. This purpose is not absurd.

My friend Donald Winston sums up the traditional answer to evil:

> *The reason I do not agree with the explanation of evil*
> *arising solely from nature and bad decisions is because I*
> *understand God to be responsible for evil's existence.*
> *Both Scripture and Church teaching tell us that nothing*
> *happens in our lives by chance and that God created evil.*

213

Evil in Mirror Lake

*Good and evil go hand in hand. We cannot have one
without the other on this earth. I empathize with people
who are hurt by seemingly senseless violence, but I
believe that what does not kill us makes us stronger when
we are focused on God and not on ourselves. The problem
with pain is that it makes us focus on ourselves. I would
counsel people to focus on God, to unburden themselves
to God, to vent their anger toward God so they can
receive the gifts and strength God is holding out to them. I
believe this because I have lived it. Evil has good results
when we let go of the pain.*

One advantage of this theology is that injured people have someone to blame for any predicament—God. A person has a boxcar job (a
job paying $100,000 a year). He loses his job because of poor perfor-
mance. How much easier it is to say, "This is God's will for me," than
to say, "Man, I messed up!" Adam blamed Eve, and Eve, the snake. In
the end both blamed God. And we are still doing it.

What if the person does die of this God-inflicted (permitted) evil.
No stepping stone to making that person greater is then possible. On
the other end, can a person do something so horrendous that God would
issue the death penalty? Overlooking the Hebrew Testament and some
noxious actions of past popes, the present Vicar of Christ is campaign-
ing against the death penalty—in all cases.

I feel that my solution solves most of these problems. The problem
is this: Where is God in my evil situation? If I can legitimately remove
God as the cause of the evil, I have eliminated the God problem—God
causing or permitting evil. This problem of evil, again, needs to be
broken down into moral evil and physical evil. I have come to see that
my relationship with God is a loving, dependent one. It is much like
children relating to their parents—when I say "No" to God—my heavenly parent—moral evil enters my life. Evil also comes into my life
from nature when it impedes my happy living—by causing terrible
things. Evil does not come from God, as Job suggested; nor does it
come from the devil, as we often presume. However, both God and the
devil do play a big part in influencing my decisions. It is bad decisions
and nature which bring evil into my world.

At this time, a shadow approaching from the west, interrupts my
thoughts. The setting sun is to its back, and so I am having a hard time
recognizing the form. Whether shade or a real man I am not sure. It is
not a ghost, for it casts a shadow. Suddenly, the shadow takes shape.
The shadow-walker is Joseph! Joseph was the young man who was

My Solution to the Problem of Evil

with Tom when he drowned, in the poem I recited at the beginning of Chapter I. We have not spoken in years. He had gone his way and I had gone mine, but I have never forgotten him. It is strange that he should show up right now. He is very happy to find me, and we begin to reminisce. We start with the drowning tragedy. I had been there at the drowning also. He is still shaking his fist at God; however, he does not seem very happy with his stance.

Almost like Jesus walking with the two disciples on the way to Emmaus (Luke 24: 13-35), beginning with Genesis and all the prophets and sages, I interpret for Joseph every passage of Scripture and great literature which refers to evil. He presses me to go on. So I explain to him the ideas which we have just covered in the first nine chapters of this book.

Joseph is a great listener. "One seeks a midwife for his thoughts… This is the origin of a good conversation." (Nietzsche **Evil** #136). He asks a few pertinent questions as I am speaking, but he never interrupts my train of thought. He does not seek his time to explain his views on evil. When I bring him up to this stage in the book, I try the Ted Koppel effect. Ted, of *Nightline*, is the greatest at retelling someone else's points of view, and then the other person saying in effect, "Yes, that is very much my stand." So often people repeat to me their version of what I have just said, and I do not recognize my ideas.

So I say, "Joseph, what have I been trying to say? What are the causes of all evil in our world?" Joseph responds, "**Your solution to the problem of evil has helped me to understand that all evil comes from nature, from my bad decisions, or from other people's bad decisions toward me.** This frees me from the grief of wondering why God would do bad things to me, especially if I do not think I deserve it. Now I understand why Tom drowned. We swam out too far after a mother told us not to do so. God had nothing to do with it, but God is much easier to blame than myself."

I asked Joseph if he had now resolved his anger with God. After a brief hesitation, he answered in a voice that was audible only with eyes. He sighed a "Yes," releasing in that one instant the years of angry resentment he had felt toward his Creator. Anger, a passion, can be changed by how I think. I continue thinking aloud since Joseph is now conscious of all I am saying. Lying beyond this immediate problem of evil is the ultimate problem of God's responsibility, first for making people intelligent and free-willed, and second, for unleashing the powers of nature. We will see that God gambled to give us free will so that we would be free to choose to love. God's choice to create people intelligent and free was a good one, because more love than

215

Evil in Mirror Lake

evil exists in the world.

God's decision to allow nature to operate freely was a good choice. I can then use my intelligence and love to understand and thus to overcome the situational evils of nature. **My life is all about using both my free will (choices) and my intelligence (knowledge) as well as my energy and matter to create myself into a loving and intelligent human being, working with reality (nature) and with the Spirit (a partner).** These forty-two words sum up my whole thesis.

This threefold analysis dates from the Stoics who divided their philosophy into three parts: *physics* to deal with the universe and its laws (nature), *logic* to distinguish true from false statements (intellect), and *ethics* which takes from these two disciplines its determination on how to act (free will).

It is time for a look at skepticism. I have been skeptical of all the previous solutions to the problem of evil—should people not be skeptical about mine? On the other hand, unexamined answers are not worth holding, except tentatively. The father of skepticism was Pyrrho (365-275 B.C.E.). His theories were explained by Sextus Empiricus (c. 150-210 A.D.) by way of his **Outlines of Pyrrhonism**. In the wake of the vainglorious, if well-educated thug, Alexander the Great, Pyrrho went to India where he picked up ideas from *magi* (wise men), particularly among the practitioners of Buddhism. Like the Stoics and the Epicureans, his goal was tranquility of mind. Did Jesus not likewise say, "My peace I give you?" Maybe the goal is to avoid striving for what Keats called "irritable reaching after fact and reason." This causes anxiety. Yet, nothing new comes to mind if not preceded by doubt. Pyrrho recommended "passive conformity accompanied by inner suspension of judgment in all matters outside commonsense experience." Just because I cannot be certain about all things, does not mean that I cannot be certain about some ideas, beyond commonsense. Most of life's choices, including ideas, come down to percentages. It is a big difference if I can be 95 percent certain as opposed to only 15 percent certain. I grab the best answer I can get at the time, and then wait until I recognize a better answer later. This is good skepticism.

My solution to the problem of evil starts with my idea of a not-all-powerful God as a hypothesis. We must ask whether this idea or hypothesis adequately explains the good and the bad of reality as we know it. To understand fully where evil comes from, we need to understand all of its dimensions. Our trip around the lake has already explored life: **Nature** (on its own), **Miracles** (only for the bystanders), **Free Will** (exactly that), **Influences** (powerful), **Prayer** (conversation with God), **Jesus** (like us), **The Bible** (words vs. meaning), **Religion** (a help),

216

My Solution to the Problem of Evil

Pivotal Decisions (ours included), **Dreams** (windows to the character of our soul), **Daydreams** (guards or guides to our future), **My Soul** (immortal), yet our day's tour around the lake is not completed. Later we will explore the possibilities in **time** and **space** for **people**.

A few questions yet remain. Did God really give us total control over our free will? Is nature left to operate on its own? If we have free will from God, and God will not interfere with nature, why is God not responsible for what happens? **The crux of my view is understanding the self-imposed limits of God's power.** Joseph is all ears.

THE ALL-POWERFUL GOD REVISITED

There is a basic need to understand God as all-powerful. My friend Father Henry Ray Engelhart states it vividly.

> *To understand what it means to be a sinner is to believe implicitly in God as <u>ALMIGHTY</u>; to make the Lord anything less is to throw the sinner into despair. Once his awareness of sin begins, the bigger the sin, the more he needs to know the LORD is almighty. It is on that quality that the sinner dares to repent & to hope. To diminish that to any degree is to destroy the one finger hold on life. The sinner says: I can only take the risk, I can only turn if & IF God is almighty, ...nothing less can save me. This is the fact that comes with the Babylonian captivity... this is the belief that created the Creation story... "And He said: `Let there be light'" The ONE who is almighty creates something out of nothing... Many of us depend totally on His Almighty power each & every moment. Take that away & suicide casualties will make the plague & the 1918 flu look like whooping cough.*

God is all-powerful because this Supreme Being created all things in nature and can control nature if the Omnipotent so chooses. Yet, God may choose freely to avoid changing the laws of nature and human free will to suit a particular event. This does not make God less than all-powerful, just selective in the use of this power. This may seem like begging the question by saying it is true because I say it is true. In fact, I use this idea of a not-all-powerful God as a working hypothesis to see if it helps me to explain my experiences of life, and of evil in particular. Theologies should follow life. Some conclusions come from reason, and some from intuition.

Evil in Mirror Lake

Dostoyevsky, in explaining his first important novel **Crime and Punishment**, describes this superb work by expressing his fascinated horror at a mind that allows reason and willpower alone to be one's guide. Reason gone astray without compassion can seat itself above good and evil.

This is partly what happened to Naziism (and certainly terrorism) and many other *isms* throughout the centuries. See Nietzsche's *Natural History of Morals* in **Beyond Good and Evil** #203 for the basis of the German *superman* and a Hitler-like commander. Either FDR or Hitler—the two runners-up for *TIME's* Man of the Century award—would have been Nietzsche's first choice. Yet, he did not like democracy—he called it the herd mentality. Likewise, he would not have liked Hitler for he, too, was part of the herd—even though its head. Nietzsche, above all else, admired the person who could walk or better run against the herd—someone like himself.

Why study such a person? It is ideas that form culture, and culture runs the world. Was it 20 million or 40 million people who died because of the culture of Naziism? Bad culture must always be straightened out by better ideas. Nietzsche believed that the all-powerful God, if indeed there is one, was not doing a good enough job of making a great world. The alternative was that **man** was to accomplish this through his *will to power*—forget intuition, forget feelings. He saw no middle ground. I have that middle ground—people do the work, and God advises—I am here to do Thy will. Amen.

Nietzsche provided neither positive doctrines nor answers, and even made a fetish out of so doing, or not doing. Nevertheless, he has gradually emerged as an outstanding critic of the modern age. He has flashing insights, sudden illuminations that still intrigue me. He is not a joy to read in English. The vocabulary is too abstract and the continuity is sometimes menacingly absent because a verbal nuance suggests so much. He is much loved in his homeland probably because in German he comes across as acute, witty and passionate. I read him because I found, among other things, that his understanding of evil was faulty, thus leading to some of his big problems with Christianity. Besides, I always like to know what my opponents are thinking.

Someone told me—I know not whether it is true or not—that the second most seen person on cable TV is Adolf Hitler. The first is Lucille Ball. The two youths at Columbine High School apparently bought into Hitler's vision of how to solve life's personal problems. Hitler began his rise to power by mesmerizing the dirty brown shirts, the dregs of German society at the time. Later, of course, he betrayed them to the army; in one bloody evening the army massacred them all.

My Solution to the Problem of Evil

Even his suicide seems to radiate glory to some misfits. "If you can understand people like that, then we would have to worry about you," said J. Edgar Hoover.

Some people are calling for the punishment of the Columbine youths' parents. Ultimately, the only power parents have over their children is the power of persuasion. We can point our children in the right direction, but we cannot be with them 24-7. However, we can inspect their rooms. Their parents, teachers and friends failed to lead the children to a better vision of life. God also failed in persuading the teens to listen. The two youths killed someone who believed in God. They failed to get to know God.

When we begin our reasoning process, we always begin with certain basic principles, from which conclusions follow. In discussing evil, I can begin with my experiences or with what the Bible says. Jerry Bridges, a minister in the Protestant Fundamentalist group called the Navigators, builds his evangelical book, **Trusting God**, upon scripture: "Our trust in God must be based, not on someone else's experience, but upon what God has told us about Himself in His Word." He ignores the fact that the words recorded in the Bible are the results of someone's experiences. How could they have been anything else?

"How sin and evil ultimately respond to God's glory is a mystery, but it is a truth affirmed throughout Scripture," Bridges says. After all, evidence does suggest that people develop perspective and character through difficulties. That is not so mysterious. If you lock your faith on these passages, and believe in the literal word of the Bible, you will have problems justifying some atrocious doings—God allowing Satan to kill children.

I, too, believe that God can be trusted—trusted to be with me through it all, advising me how to respond to the evils that come to me, either from nature or other people's bad decisions. I just disagree that these evils also come from the all-powerful and all-loving God—even if God is so powerful that the Almighty can bring good out of evil. I simply believe that God has freely withheld power over nature and our free choices. It is interesting how Bridges admits that God's sovereignty does not eliminate my free will, though I cannot do anything without God's willing it. He calls this conflict a mystery—the exact mystery that I am attempting to explain.

Another place where tension exists, is between the two poles of tradition and progress. Although this ironically is what gives a culture both its identity and its life, it pulls its members, sometimes tragically, in opposite directions.

A *coming of age*, introspective novel which considers the dishar-

219

Evil in Mirror Lake

mony that may exist between traditional religious values and modern scholarship is **The Chosen** by Chaim Potok (1967). This book describes both the great depth and sorrowful shallowness of human relationships. Reuven Malter, the fifteen-year-old Jewish narrator, becomes friends with Danny Saunders, a Hasidic Jew, after almost losing his eyesight in a baseball game accident. The fathers of both are rabbis—one liberal and the other orthodox. The boys work out the conflict into a synthesis—of sorts. At least, each side ends up understanding the other side.

"Why doesn't it say in the Bible that God has freely given up power over nature and our free choices?" some people ask me. Others remind me of all the power that God seemingly gave to Moses. Maybe somehow we have lost some words of God. Jesus said he told us everything his Father sent him to tell us. Maybe it is between the lines. No, Jesus also said that he would send the Holy Spirit to teach us all things. The Spirit works slowly and through other people in our lives. We are still forming syntheses. Maybe this is it, maybe not.

The theological position that I suggest is between Deism and the Hebrew theistic theology. It does include a belief in the God-Man Jesus as my Lord and Savior. I call it **deistic theistic**. Theism says that God is interested in the world. Deism says that God does not run nature. God does not run us nor the natural world. Yet, God and the communion of saints are intimately involved in all of our lives, calling us to build the Kingdom of Jesus, influencing all of our free decisions, as we live in a nature-driven world. God does run my life, but only if I permit it. This is my theodicy, my understanding of God—Good and Evil. It is a personal deism that involves the God-Man Jesus. I call my theology **Deistic-Theistic Christian**.

In using this working hypothesis of a voluntarily not-all-powerful God, I enjoy knowing that even God cannot be a contradiction, only a paradox—a seeming contradiction. Despite what I do know about God, I must recognize that I am a creature in time and space and God transcends time and space. Some truths are beyond my capability to know.

A basic principle in all of philosophy is the Principle of Contradiction—a thing cannot both **be** and **not be** simultaneously (and in the same way). Plato states this in his **The Republic IV**, "The same thing clearly cannot act or be acted upon in the same part or in relation to the same thing at the same time in contrary ways; and therefore whenever the contradiction occurs in things apparently the same, we know that they are really not the same, but different."

This also applies to God. Even God cannot make me **free** and **not free** simultaneously and in the same way. Sometimes logicians call

220

My Solution to the Problem of Evil

this *logically impossible* or *a logically contradictory state of affairs.* God cannot make a square circle, neither can God make a boulder so heavy that even God cannot carry it. These are intrinsic contradictions. My ability to utter nonsense does not limit God's omnipotence.

God has created me free-willed, and I have sinned—chosen to assert myself against the unity and love that unite all things in the One. If I can stop something from happening, and do not, I am responsible. All theodicies (from two Greek words meaning God and justice) acknowledge explicitly or implicitly God's ultimate responsibility for the existence of moral evil since God created me free. This is why most moralists hold God responsible for moral evils.

Nevertheless, since God gave me free will, God can no longer be responsible for the results of my individual decisions. God, though, is still responsible for the overall first decision to create each of us free willed. Nevertheless, this Divine Gamble is paying off with more love than evil, I say. Let us now consider whether God made a good decision in creating us free.

God's purpose for me is not that I become a perfect robot, doing exactly what nature or God programmed me to do and no more. Like in **Stepford Wives,** Ira Levin depicts substitute wives created by their scientist husbands as replacements. The Stepford wives do exactly as their husbands wish—cook, clean, and provide sex.

Rather, my purpose in life is to confront the uniqueness of my person and my calling. I need to forge my *persona* into a being who is redeemed and destined to live forever in union with the Divine Other. In short, God fashioned me out of love to do a specific job. This call is personal, unique, and it varies at different stages of my growth. It is the call that Jesus was always responding to as he sought throughout his life to do his Father's will.

Sometimes I say that of all the possible worlds, this is not the best. I say that, because what I would prefer is for my world to be problem free. However, that would only make me innocent and untried, like a little child. But, God wants me to become a virtuous adult, meeting the problems of life head on, and dealing with them courageously. In the process I may become knowledgeable and virtuous. This is why the all-good and all-powerful God created me rational and free, and does not interfere with my freedom even in my perceived emergencies.

"Struggle is in the nature of being human. People spend their whole lives trying to avoid problems. To have a conflict-free life is contrary to our nature," says my lawyer friend. Of course, lawyers thrive on conflict. No conflict means no work. No pain, no gain. No earth, no heaven.

Evil in Mirror Lake

Life is difficult. This is a great truth, one of the greatest truths. It is a great truth because once we indeed see this truth, we transcend it. Once we truly know that life is difficult—once we truly understand and accept it—then life is no longer difficult. Because once it is accepted, the fact that life is difficult no longer matters.

M. Scott Peck thus opened his celebrated book, **The Road Less Traveled** (1978). Discipline is the key theme: Delaying Gratification, Accepting Responsibility, Dedication to Truth, and Balancing Life. Love provided the motivation, but it is not a feeling; it entails action. Love is not passive dependency, nor is it self-sacrifice. It involves being with someone—empathy and active listening. Scott concludes, "nurture ourselves and others without a primary concern of finding reward, then we will have become loveable, and the reward of being loved, which we have not sought, will find us, so it is with human love and so it is with God's love."

Empathy begins with active listening. I have noticed when someone comes to me in emotional pain, they repeat the same story over and over. This venting is like an ointment soothing the wounded soul. Just as a burn cannot be healed with one application of a salve, they cannot be soothed with one telling of their story. I must listen to it again and again. I feel like interrupting and telling the story myself, I have heard it so often. But that would be like putting sand in their ointment. I must stay out of their stories, no matter how well I have them memorized. The listening is the healing ointment for their suffering.

Nietzsche says, "The discipline of suffering, of *great* suffering—do you not know that only *this* discipline has created all enhancements of man so far? That tension of the soul in unhappiness cultivates its strength, it shudders face to face with great ruin, causing inventiveness and courage in enduring, persevering, interpreting, and exploiting suffering, and whatever has been granted to it of profundity, secret, mask, spirit, cunning, greatness—was it not granted to it through the discipline of great suffering?" (**Beyond Good and Evil** #225).

Nietzsche attacks the problem of evil head on in his **Genealogy of Morals** (#6&7), "Without cruelty there is no festival: thus the longest and most ancient part of human history teaches—and in punishment there is so much that is festive!" Maybe this is why there was such a festive crowd at the execution of John Wayne Gacy, the mass murderer of Chicago.

Consider Don Quixote at the court of the Duchess. How uncom-

My Solution to the Problem of Evil

fortable I feel at the torment caused him, but his contemporaries read it with the clearest conscience in the world as the most cheerful of books. Quixote, despite his misconceptions, devotes himself to high ideals. In a world filled with scheming and base people, he sometimes seems to be the only sane man in an insane society. We see this crude, slapstick humor, today, as a warm, human tale, depicting the conflict between noble idealism and brute, unfeeling practicality. We now perceive the foolish knight, once seen as the butt of all the other characters' jokes, as a symbol of noble though impractical idealism.

Let me share a whole paragraph of Nietzsche with you. Reading it is difficult, and you may skip it until the second time you read this book, but it points out his misunderstanding of from where evil comes. I wish I could have had a conversation with him before he went insane. It is from his **Genealogy of Morals** #7.

> *What really arouses indignation against suffering is not suffering as such but the senselessness of suffering; but neither for the Christian, who has interpreted a whole mysterious machinery of salvation into suffering, nor for the naive man of more ancient times, who understood all suffering in relation to the spectator of it or the causer of it, was there any such thing as **senseless** suffering. So as to abolish hidden, undetected, unwitnessed suffering from the world and honestly to deny it, one was in the past virtually compelled to invent gods and genii of all the heights and depths, in short something that roams even in secret, hidden places, sees even in the dark, and will not easily let an interesting painful spectacle pass unnoticed. For it was with the aid of such inventions that life then knew how to work the trick which it has always known how to work, that of justifying itself, of justifying its "evil." Nowadays it might require other auxiliary inventions (for example, life as a riddle, life as an epistemological problem). "Every evil the sight of which edifies a god is justified"; thus spoke the primitive logic of feeling—and was it, indeed, only primitive? The gods conceived of as the friends of **cruel** spectacles—oh how profoundly this ancient idea still permeates our European humanity! Merely consult Calvin and Luther. It is certain, at any rate, that the **Greeks** still knew of no tastier spice to offer their gods to season their happiness than the pleasures of cruelty. With what eyes do you think Homer*

Evil in Mirror Lake

*made his gods look down upon the destinies of men? What
was at bottom the ultimate meaning of Trojan Wars and
other such tragic terrors? There can be no doubt
whatever: they were intended as **festival plays** for the
gods; and, insofar as the poet is in these matters of a
more "godlike" disposition than other men, no doubt also
as festival plays for the poets.*

A great tendency for humans is to make their gods into their own image and likeness, instead of vice versa. After all, I do not know God personally, just through the effects of God—and there are many terrible effects in our world. Some of those effects are teenagers who like to destroy the city park, and not just on Halloween. Some few choose to leave their mark in bloodstained classrooms, as in Columbine High. High School bullies beware! Treat all the "creeps" nice! In trying to explain the origin of this dark side in human nature, the ancients have turned to the gods. My solution is quite different.

Once upon a time, a scientist had manipulated nature to where he was about to develop a new species of butterfly. It was at the stage of extracting itself from its cocoon. The butterfly could not get its second wing free. The struggle went on and on. Just as it seemed that the butterfly had lost all strength, the scientist intervened with a scalpel, cutting loose the cocoon. At first there was great joy, but soon it became evident that this butterfly would never fly. It did not have enough strength. It needed more strength that would have come from more struggle to free itself. All-good and all-powerful naturalists (like God) will not interfere with life in the wild. Yes, evil can strengthen us.

This world is the best possible world if what I am looking for is to become a free and loving person, conquering the problems of nature, while constructing Thy Kingdom of justice, love and peace. This world then is a logical necessity in that God is both available, and yet gives me a free rein to co-create a small part of the kingdom.

Homer understood this in his **Odyssey** seven hundred years before Christ. As Odysseus languishes in the caverns of the wooded island of Calypso with Nausikaa, this nymph-goddess, along with her playmates, entertains and entraps him, refusing to allow him to leave their inexhaustible pleasures. "I also want this," says modern man. "I feel God or nature should make these pleasures available to me also." Nietzsche cautions us, "One should part from life as Odysseus parted from Nausikaa—blessing it rather than in love with it." (The Greek Odysseus, according to the Roman tradition, is Ulysses.)

In **The Divine Comedy,** Dante has Ulysses say to his crew a short

My Solution to the Problem of Evil

and effective speech to get them to leave this island with him, "Consider your origin; ye were not made to live as brutes, but to pursue virtue and knowledge." (Canto XXVI # 112)

On the other hand, one meaning of the Greek word *Odysseus* is *to make trouble*. What our lives are all about, is to overcome trouble in a loving way as we travel our personal odyssey. Odysseus broke away from this island of Calypso, and fought his way back home to Ithaca where Penelope, his ever-faithful wife, and Telemachus, his needy son, awaited him. My life is a journey or pilgrimage on which I meet the problems of nature and people head on, struggling to create a me that I wish to live with eternally. This earthy life is neither home nor haven for me.

From almost the beginning of recorded history, thinkers have looked upon God as a being in total control of all that has happened, at times to the exclusion of free will. This relieves me, the individual, from taking responsibility for any bad decisions. The Bible personifies Adam and Eve in me. "The devil made me do it," ought to be "the devil has influenced me to do it." "It was not my choice," should be, "I made a bad decision." Certainly not, "It's God's will."

In 458 B.C.E., Aeschylus described his all-powerful and most-high god as the Great Accomplisher in his Greek play, **The Oresteia**. It was a different time, but the same all-powerful image of God, called Zeus. Jupiter is the name in Roman tradition.

> *Ah woe, ah Zeus! From Zeus all things befall—*
> *Zeus the high cause and finisher of all! —*
> *Lord of our mortal state, by him are willed*
> *All things, by him fulfilled!*
>
> (Translated by E. D. A. Morshead)

Then again, Virgil in his **Aeneid**, about the time of Christ, explains the burning of the ships. Virgil's understanding from 2000 years ago is probably not useful to minds who have passed through theology, philosophy, psychology, and personal experiences. These new minds view the universe a bit more precisely and less mythological. Nevertheless, a bit of them is still in us:

> *The pious hero (Aeneas) rends his robe, and throws*
> *To heaven his hands, and, with his hands, his vows.*
> *"O Jove! (he cried) if prayers can yet have place;*
> *If thou abhorr'st not all the Dardan race;*
> *If any spark of pity still remain;*

Evil in Mirror Lake

If gods are gods, and not invoked in vain;
Yet spare the relics of the Trojan train!
Yet from the flames our burning vessels free!
Or let thy fury fall alone on me:
At this devoted head thy thunder throw,
And send the willing sacrifice below."

Scarce had he said, when southern storms arise:
From pole to pole the forky lightning flies:
Loud rattling shakes the mountains and the plain:
Heaven bellies downward, and descends in rain:
Whole sheets of water from the clouds are sent,
Which, hissing through the planks, the flames prevent,
And stop the fiery pest. Four ships alone
Burn to the waist, and for the fleet atone.

(Translated by John Dryden)

Likewise, many prayers today begin, "O God, almighty and all-powerful..." I do not suggest we change our prayers, but we do need to adjust our thinking. While praying to God, who is almighty, I must realize that God will never take away my free will and rarely changes nature. "In essence, God has purposely become weak so that we may become strong. Why God chooses to be weak vis-a-vis the creation, is Her secret," says Andrew M. Greeley in private correspondence, "but I much prefer to place the mystery on the weakness of God than in God's lack of concern. When the little child cries, God weeps."

Thomas Lynch, a Funeral Director, wrote the book, **The Undertaking: Life Studies from the Dismal Trade**. He refers to the night a family from his town was traveling through Kentucky on their way to the purported apparition site in Conyers, GA. Some boys heaved a stolen cemetery stone from an overpass sending it crashing into the family's van, killing their daughter. "If it's God's will, shame on God is what I say. If not, then shame on God. It sounds the same. I keep shaking a fist at the Almighty asking, *Where were you on the morning of the thirteenth?* The alibi changes every day."

We all yearn for control over our lives—or at least the illusion of control. Give me life and let me run it. Control is extremely powerful stuff. Power can protect our car or health, keep us alert in the face of danger and energizes the mind. Religious and scientific beliefs, visions of things unseen, world views, all offer the feeling of control, an indispensable fuel for the physiological powerhouse of life. If we seek power over our lives, should not our God seek even more such power? Who

My Solution to the Problem of Evil

holds the levers with which to manipulate an invisible world?

Especially have the Irish had this pounded into them. According to **The Irish in America** (1997) edited by Michael Coffey, the Famine Irish, who immigrated by the millions between 1840 and 1850, believed that their suffering was a judgment from on high. "The poor people should not be deprived of knowing that they are suffering from an affliction of God's providence," was the analysis that Charles Trevelyan, who was in charge of Britain's relief operation, hoped the Irish Catholic clergy would communicate to their hungry and dying congregations. To this very day when a tragedy is recalled in a second generation Irish gathering, someone is bound to say, "Of course, it was God's will."

The *harmony of the universe* theory and the *there-is-no-evil* theory of the Buddhists may please the imagination of a speculative person who sits in ease and security in his living room. Nevertheless, crush him with the reeking pain of a split finger or the death of his child, and he will not want to hear about the harmony of everything. Some things impede my happy living, and someone or something causes these evils. I want to know the who and what of it. Damn these evils! Where is God in this situation?

First, God is present to me as, "Emmanuel—God is with us." I am never alone in my plight with an evil situation. Second, God talks to me, giving me good advice. This can come through my conscience or through others. God is there like a good friend, not as the omnipotent creator.

God, like a good and wise parent, knows that it is not always best to step in and straighten out all of a child's problems, even if it were possible. This choice, not to intervene, is a type of noble restraint. Perhaps, it is best if God can help me solve my own problems of evil. Either I can rectify my previous bad decisions and learn from them, or I can know how best to respond to evil decisions inflicted upon me by others. God is not going to, nor should God, solve all my problems for me.

It is imperative that I not return evil for evil. It is even better if I know how to spot the possibility of evil coming, so I can choose to avoid it. Ultimately, I need to keep in mind that what I want most from my enemies is to turn them into my friends. This, too, takes a type of noble weakness—choices, which often require immense strength of will. God, who loves the just and unjust alike, will teach me how to be godlike in my plight of evil happenings. This is the *weak* role that God plays in my encounters with evil situations.

"If Heaven strikes me through my children (for my sin),"

Evil in Mirror Lake

Stendhal in **The Red and The Black** has the sinner say, "it is in vain that I should try to live only to love you (God), and not to see that it is my sin that is killing them (my children); I could not survive such a punishment."

"Terrible experiences pose the riddle—whether the person who has them is not terrible?" probes Nietzsche in his **Beyond Good and Evil**, *Epigrams and Interludes* #89. My answer is, sometimes *yes* and sometimes *no*, about whether a person with terrible experiences is himself or herself so responsible. And again Nietzsche says, "One is best punished for one's virtues" (#132). My evil can come from either myself or others or from nature.

Another title of Nietzsche's book could be, **Beyond Right and Wrong**, and my answer to this supposed question of what is beyond—is **love**! Nietzsche's idea of greatness is not love but single-mindedness—passion. In his words, "I need to be *overrich in will*" (#212). From this comes his *will to power*. Most people's great substitute for love is not hate nor apathy, but power—over employees, over employers, over spouses, over children, over parents, etc. Nietzsche wants to get **beyond** what is **right** (good) or **wrong** (evil). He is not interested in any moral code imposed upon him by anyone. He is interested in using his power to be all that he wants to be, period.

In public life, both bureaucrats and public servants serve me, but there is a difference. The bureaucrat goes home at the end of the day feeling good that he or she has followed all of the rules and regulations of the department. The public servant goes home at the end of the day feeling good that she or he has helped people. Love or caring goes beyond what is right and wrong. Remember Scrooge.

Usually the best way to help people is to follow the rules. Rules are the distillation of the wisdom of the past. Adherence to the rules is usually the best way to help people. But are they always? Does the end ever justify the means, or never? Paul says "No." Joseph Fletcher, in **Situation Ethics**, says "Yes." What was the meaning about Jesus' story of the Good Samaritan?

Back to the role of the all-powerful God—Giovanni Boccaccio in **Decameron**, a book of stories, repeatedly tells us of preordained events: "This Cisti was a man of exceedingly lofty spirit, and yet Fortune made him a baker," and "Since God has ordained that I should tell the first of our stories today," and finally, "the gods... control us... by a process of eternal and infallible logic." This type of thinking makes all things, the good, the bad, the ugly, come from God or Fortune. The mad, or delusional, Don Quixote de la Mancha, the Knight of the Sad Continence, explains or preaches to himself and to

My Solution to the Problem of Evil

his ever faithful squire, Sancho Panza, the all-pervasive and all-powerful role of God in their lives:

But, anyhow, get on your ass, good Sancho, and follow me. For God, the provider of all things, cannot let us want, especially as we are engaged in His service, since He does not fail the gnats of the air, the worms in the ground, nor the tadpoles in the water, and He is so merciful that He makes the sun rise on the good and the bad, and rains on the just and the unjust.

Your worship, said Sancho, would make a better preacher than a knight errant.

I can never explain away evil because evil exists, as suffering or misfortune—terrible things happen. However, I can explain from where evil comes. Physical evils all come from physical or scientific causes and effects. Moral evils come from bad moral decisions. They do not come directly from the all-powerful God, nor from the devil, though both invoke powerful influences.

If it is physical evil, such as a volcano or tornado or cancer, I scientifically look for its physical cause, and then seek to rectify or to adjust to it. If it is moral evil, such as murder or theft or rape, how can such evils be prevented? I compassionately look for alternative influences on free will and try to defeat them in the future with positive motives and God's grace for making loving decisions.

Ultimately, free choice is exactly that. It is beyond my ability to control others' use of it. The reason for this Divine Gamble is that only as a free person can I freely choose to make loving choices. God gambled that more good than evil would come from this choice. Unlike the dinosaurs, God gave to me this godlike power to choose: evil or good. I live in a proving ground where I choose to do things, either God's way or my way. However, it is not that God is putting me to the test as in the book of **Job**. Life itself is the proving ground.

Take two examples of the all-powerful God not interfering with physical evils or nature. First, a good young boy, Joseph, had decided to swim out too far into the lake with his best friend, Tom. As previously mentioned in my poem, *A Double Tragedy*, they did not make it back to shore. When they dragged the boys out of the lake, Joseph was okay but Tom was blue. All the way to the hospital Joseph prayed, begging God not to let Tom die; but Tom did die. My friend, Joseph, then shook his fist at God and said, "I have been a good boy all of my

Evil in Mirror Lake

life. When I really needed you, God, you let me down. I do not need you anymore in my life." The young boy walked away from God, because he misunderstood God's role in nature, and did not want to take responsibility for having swum out too far.

The other story is about me fixing my mother's kitchen sink on a holiday. While taking off an old part, I stripped the threads. In trying to screw the nut back on, I could not get the threads to catch. I began to pray. Then I realized that my prayers were asking God to come and bend the threads straight, and God was not going to do that. I took the part off, sat at the table and prayed, 'God, I need your help. It is very important that I get this sink fixed tonight.' After a minute or so, an inspiration (Holy Spirit?) suggested that I go downstairs, put the bolt in the vise, and use the hacksaw to cut off the edge where the damaged threads were. It worked. That is how God answered my prayer. If prayer is talking to God, then intuition is listening to God. If I listen, God will suggest good decisions for me. God will not bend threads for me. Nor will God stop the dying process caused by drowning.

God's purpose for me is not that my life should be a bowl of cherries with no problems or evils of nature confronting me. God's purpose for me: use your intelligence and free choice, Leo, with my help and direction, to live in the nature I, the Almighty, has fashioned—and so I am holy. If I say "Yes" to God, I am in a relationship with my heavenly Father. God's role is not to intervene with a miracle to save me from some problem or physical evil. It is not my role to be so rescued from such pain.

To get the sense of how I, as a human, should live my life as an adventure or pilgrimage, I reread **The Life and Strange Surprising Adventures of Robinson Crusoe** (1719). Daniel Defoe, the author of this first successful realistic modern novel, depicts the power of the average person to triumph over his environment. This triumph rests not only in survival but also in the ability to organize, invent, create and maintain a viable structure for life even in the most hostile and unlikely circumstances. This book is a testament to my human qualities of endurance, integrity and ingenuity. Defoe also incorporates into his novel many of his own beliefs in Divine Providence and the importance of faith in the all-powerful God. All of our lives are meant to be such a pilgrimage, such a test, in this—our Earth school.

Moll Flanders, also by Defoe, similarly describes triumph over adversity. Both of the main characters in Defoe's books overcome problems and bad luck and survive an environment that is both hostile and friendless.

After the Bible, Defoe was the first to abandon the Greek notion

My Solution to the Problem of Evil

that all fiction is a form of lying. We can see the stories in the Bible as serving the same purpose. As Defoe put it, writing fiction is after all in large part a matter of "telling lies like truth." The other day a friend of mine told me a funny story about another friend. At the end we both said, "Even if the story is not true, it is true." Defoe used the story to teach a lesson or moral message. My favorite prayer of Moll Flanders is, "Give me not poverty lest I steal."

We shun difficulty as a disturbance, but disorder can be a great source of creativity. Paul Valery, a French poet and critic of the early nineteen hundreds, says, "A difficulty is a light, an insurmountable difficulty is a sun." I can choose to perceive an evil of nature as a sun. The problem is that I want everything preshaped for me, but my call in life is to co-create with the Creator—using my free will in cooperation with God's direction. Difficult moments are our opportunities.

Blaise Pascal, reminds me that in a difficult time, I should always keep something beautiful in my heart. Perhaps, it is beauty that in the end will save me from evil, or at least lead me to love—which will then save me.

Friedrich Nietzsche also debunks the notion that the ideal life should be one that is care free. **Beyond Good and Evil**.

> In all the countries of Europe, and in America, too, there now is something that abuses this name [free spirit]: a very narrow, imprisoned, chained type of spirits who want just about the opposite of what accords with our intentions and instincts—not to speak of the fact that regarding the **new** philosophers who are coming up they must assuredly be closed windows and bolted doors. They belong briefly and sadly, among the **levelers**—these falsely so called "free spirits"—being eloquent and prolifically scribbling slave of the democratic taste and its "modern ideas"; they are all human beings without solitude, without their own solitude, clumsy good fellow whom one should not deny either courage or respectable decency—only they are unfree and ridiculously superficial, above all in their basic inclination to find in the forms of the old society as it has existed so far just about the cause of **all** human misery and failure—which is a way of standing truth happily upon her head! What they would like to strive for with all their powers is the universal green-pasture happiness of the herd, with security, lack of danger, comfort, and an easier life for

Evil in Mirror Lake

*everyone; the two songs and doctrines which they repeat
most often are "equality of rights" and "sympathy for all
that suffers"—and suffering itself they take as something
that must be **abolished**.*

This is akin to my idea of people wanting the world to be a *bowl of
cherries*. Nietzsche continues with an opposite view. (These two quotations are found in the chapter on *The Free Spirit* #44.)

*We opposite men, having opened our eyes and conscience
to the question where and how the plant "man" has so far
grown most vigorously to a height—we think that this has
happened every time under the opposite conditions, that
to this end the dangerousness of his situation must first
grow to the point of enormity, his power of invention and
simulation (his "spirit") had to develop under prolonged
pressure and constraint into refinement and audacity, his
life-will had to be enhanced into an unconditional power-
will. We think that hardness, forcefulness, slavery, danger
in the alley and the heart, life in hiding, stoicism, the art
of experiment and devilry of every kind, that everything
evil, terrible, tyrannical in man, everything in him that is
kin to beasts of prey and serpents, serves the enhancement
of the species "man" as much as its opposite does.*
(Translated from the German by Walter Kaufmann.)

Nietzsche is one of the most influential thinkers of modern times,
but we virtually ignored him until almost the end of this last century.
Having gone mad during his last eleven years, he never knew that he
had become so famous. His most influential and popular book is the
prose poem **Thus Spake Zarathustra** (1883-1885)—a literary-philo-
sophical experiment. The book has no bearing whatever on the Zoroastrian religion. He had become enamored with the philosophy and
the writings of the pessimistic Schopenhauer whom he tried to repu-
diate in his first book, **The Birth of Tragedy** (1872). The kernel of
Nietzsche's philosophy is that truth is only in the mind—apparent
perspectivism—or truth is only truth from a particular perspective.
This is affirming the truth in the mind, but denying the truth in outside
reality—truth outside the mind. His books could have used a good editor, but they are still a mine of ideas. His most novel ideas are: Death
of God, Superman, and Eternal Recurrence.

The Death of God simply means he diagnosed the old Christian

My Solution to the Problem of Evil

God as dead. He looked at the world and the all-powerful God in charge, and declared this Christian idea of God dead—not that God is really dead.

Supermen, better called Overmen—nothing like the Nazis or the *blonde beast*— were people who could think for themselves. He would have approved of people who march to their own drummer—like Dietrich Bonhoeffer's **The Cost of Discipleship**. Although Adolf Hitler kept a bust of Nietzsche, he barely read him. He gave his works to his friend Mussolini who never read them. Nietzsche was betrayed by his Nazi sister, Elizabeth, who unscrupulously resorted to forgery and selective quotations to make him look like a Nazi, after his insanity and death.

Eternal Recurrence of the same, an old Stoic idea, is what happens to people who fail to overcome their deficiencies, and transcend the tired values of their time, and cease to conform for the sake of conforming. They are bound to repeat the past with its same problems.

I should look upon myself as a problem solver. (Business consultants love to find businesses that are in trouble.) Similarly, life's problems become opportunities to create my soul. The world gives me opportunities for growth. In fact, this type of world goes beyond helping me eradicate my evil faults. Life points me toward maturing myself in the love of God and of others. I use this good world as a kind of boot camp that challenges me to develop my character—the essence of me! Yet, if I am only a problem solver, I would be of limited use to a person seeking intimacy.

Other people look at the world differently. "If I were granted omnipotence, and millions of years to experiment in, I should not think Man much to boast of as a final result of all my efforts," Bertrand Russell, the over-intelligent cynic, wrote.

"Has creation a final purpose at all," the German philosopher Friedrich Schelling asked, "and if so why is it not attained immediately, why does perfection not exist from the beginning?" If the almighty, perfect God made me in the Divine Image and likeness, why am I not now perfect?

The answer given by others is that what seems like chaos can conceal design. In a created universe, God should betray no trace of the Omnipotent Presence, since to do so would be to rob the created forces—me—of my independence. This would turn me from the active pursuit of answers to being a mere supplicant of God. And so it is in nature: God's language is mostly silence. As with the suffering Job, God weakly restrains the devil from pressing me beyond my capacities. Martin Luther says as much in his book, **Evil: A Historical and**

233

Evil in Mirror Lake

Theological Perspective. The fundamental problem of evil is not merely ignorance (a defect of the intellect) but sin (a defect of the will). "I resist in my will," Luther said, "the dependence that God calls forth from me. Like my ancestors, I emulate their destructive independence. Like Job, I must accept my dependence upon a Creator whose ways are not always my ways, and are often beyond my comprehension."

As Henri Blocher puts it, "Evil is not there to be understood, but to be fought." We are called not just to read books and think, but also to do God's will in spite of evil. This is holiness. God is with me and gives me good and loving advice, much as a good and loving parent. God's care for me is personal as mine is in return. God works in me by pointing to open doors. God speaks to me through the church community, through events, through others, and through my own interactive heart. God's access to me has no limits. I also speak to myself, and the devil may enter through my imagination. I have feelings with which I must contend. After listening to all such experiences, I must discern what God is encouraging me to do, and go for it.

Most people believe in the spiritual, although it cannot be seen. I exempt some extreme materialists, yet they believe in gravity, the magnetic field, and maybe even love. However, materialists usually believe that love is just a case of chemical reactions.

To some extent, people are saying the old truths of my youth in a new language. Carlos Castaneda, in **The Power of Silence**, talks about the spirit of all knowledge. We need to allow the spirit to change our assemblage points so we can have a heightened awareness of our energy fields which will lead us to its silent knowledge (intuition). What all of this means to me is that the Holy Spirit knows everything and lives in me—I am the temple of the Holy Spirit. I can focus my attention on many things—assemblage points—or on a single event. Being focused on a point of heightened awareness, starts my ability to absorb intuitive knowledge.

It is like eating at a dining room table. Judy is focused on what the decor is, Bob on how much the table cost, Elizabeth on the health quality of the food, Bill on the interpersonal relationships that are going on. Leo is absorbed with what everyone else is thinking of him. These are five different assemblage points or focuses. The most common and difficult to break are the mirrors of self-reflection (meism). "It is extremely powerful and lets its victims go only after a ferocious struggle," says Castaneda.

Another analogy of Castaneda's thought is that in my side control room, I have an infinite number of TV screens. They are all simultaneously putting out their energies (images). The spirit decides to which

My Solution to the Problem of Evil

TV channel I am tuned. Eventually, I may choose to become a partner with this *spirit* in determining to which energy field inside me I should be tuned into at any particular moment. This is the point when I truly become free—and, I hope, for a purpose, even an eternal one.

Castaneda, however, only concentrates on the present moment, and many of his stories smack of science fiction or fantasy. Believing that a man once rose from the dead is easier for me. Carlos Castaneda has become a Godfather of the New Age Movement, according to the *Los Angeles Times Book Review*. His intent is not to call me to a life of great sacrifice, but rather how to be my great self—how my being relates to the Great Being, the (Holy) Spirit. This relationship leads me to a sense of power, but not to egotistical striving. Castaneda says that my relationship with God will unlock my uniqueness. My ego is meant, he continues, to serve me, not vice versa. Yet, I need my ego to get the job done. I experience the world of the ego, verses the world of the spirit.

Through the power of silence, I need to collaborate with the Organizing Spirit to refocus on the many other channels of energy inside myself besides the ego channel. Ego can stand for **E**arth **G**uide **O**nly— where I separate myself from the rest of existence, and place my value in only the material things of my life. The power of positive thinking is the opposite of this. I allow myself to get beyond myself, and my previous limiting views, and to tap into the Eternal Energy that directs all of existence. When I get tapped into this Mystical Awareness, all reality connects with me, "Branches in a tree are never foolish enough to fight among themselves," is an old Native American saying.

Castaneda pushes this power of the inner life to the extent that he can say, "There is no witchcraft, **no evil**, no devil. There is only perception." By means of words, he can gloss over real evils. Your head creates your world. Change your map! After all, my dad had taught me years ago that it is all, *mind over matter*—but is it totally so? What about the holocaust? This was evil despite what anyone's mind says. I could not perceive it to be anything less.

After the *Age of Reason* which followed the *Age of Faith*, Rousseau taught us to value intuition. Castaneda says that *silent knowledge* or **intuition** comes first. Some people in their concern for survival over the environment developed their reason along with their intuition. The beauty is that we, today, have both paragons—reason and intuition—at our disposal.

Oui-Gon in the first *Star Wars* prequel, *The Phantom Menace*, says, "Your focus is your reality." He later tells young Anakin, "Concentrate on the moment. Feel, don't think. Use your instincts." No wonder he

Evil in Mirror Lake

went to the dark side. We must use both our thinking and our feeling to succeed. I remember, in my opening story, how my intuition warned me not to try to kiss Susie Johnson, when I was a teenager. I felt she was setting me up for a put down, so I refused to try.

If I could make that choice again, I would make it differently. When I have a choice to do or not to do something, and both options seem evenly balanced, I now would choose to do rather than not to do. The reason is that if I choose not to do, I will never know how the decision to do would have turned out.

For example, my decision not to try to kiss Susie has left me wondering *what if*. If I had tried and Susie had wanted to kiss and to be kissed, then I might have lived happily ever after, at least for a month or two. On the other hand, if she were setting me up, the only downside would have been my bruised ego. The upside might have been much higher than the risked downside. In retrospect, I wish I had tried.

This is also a good example for how my practical intellect made the final decision in determining for me the best choice at the moment to gain pleasure and more importantly to avoid pain. My will, though, in the process directed my intellect to consider more the defense of my ego than to consider my own intention. There may have been something in my self image that I was unwilling to risk, like the pain of rejection. Still, I am not certain that behind that particular impulse of my will, there was not a deeper, though yet unconscious, sense of another purpose or path for my life.

This is about as far as I can probe into my own nature and the nature of God. I do not want to seem to lose sight of the fact that God is ever mystery. Mystery is not the act of not knowing something; that is ignorance. Mystery is knowing something yet acknowledging that I do not know everything about it. The church is a mystery; I cannot define it, only describe it. Theology, though, is faith seeking understanding, so said the early Christian theologian, John Chrysostom.

Remembering *The Ultimate Principle* is always good, "By definition, when you are investigating the unknown, you do not know what you will find." Knowing that I do not know all the answers, but am in search of those answers, that is what we describe as being in the state of grace (sanctifying grace or God living in us). It is in the searching that I find God's life in me.

A young virgin named Mary received a call from God to do a certain job in life. After a few questions she said, "Behold the maidservant of the Lord." Remember, she could have said, "No!" There may have been others before her who did say, "No." The rich young man said, "No" to Jesus' invitation to come and follow him.

236

My Solution to the Problem of Evil

Another story is about Jesus' friend, Judas. Jesus had both dipped his hand in the dish with Judas and ultimately greeted him with a kiss, hoping to influence him from his betrayal. God forced neither Mary nor Judas. The history of salvation would be different if either had done differently. That, though, is a different mystery—one of God's foreknowledge versus my free will.

After admitting that the all-powerful God has freely given up control over free will and nature, I ask myself if this was a good decision by the Almighty. I can easily see its necessity if I am to be truly free to love—the Divine Gamble. Now I ask what about not interfering with nature.

If the governor can commute a death sentence, but chooses not to, then to some extent he or she is responsible for that person's death. If God can divert hurricane Mitch from the Honduran coast (1998) and does not, then God is responsible to a certain degree for the deaths of many innocent people, including many children. Although the hurricane may make the fishing better, is this necessary to keep nature in harmony with itself? If the possibility of a Divine Intervention is possible, "Why not?" This is the crux of the mystery of physical evils.

Should God intervene, and if so, when? And when not? As I picture the explosions in the universe from the possible Big Bang, through the supernova's exploding, to the Earth's collision with that rock which led to the extinction of the dinosaurs, to our ancestors' arrival, I see no physical evils and so no need of any interventions. The problem arises only when nature conflicts with the happy living of individuals, especially me.

If happy living is God's ultimate goal for people, I would call for a Divine Intervention, and regularly. However, if God's goal for people is character building, then physical evils and the suffering they cause are no problem. They are just stepping stones to greatness. Even death is no problem: call it an unusually, very large stepping stone.

Life is a pilgrimage and our number of years spent on earth has no significance in eternity. It is about equivalent to winning an Olympic Gold Medal for the Fifty-Yard Dash or the Hundred-Yard Dash. The Gold Medals (character) are the same for both races. What counts is that I finish the race of life with good character. Suddenly it all fits together and makes sense. At least I think so.

I need to distinguish my character ethic from my personality ethic. The cult of personality teaches that success is a function of *persona*, of public images, of positive attitudes and behaviors, human relations skills and techniques. This attitude prevails today, and does give temporary success. The proponents of character building, on the other hand, be-

Evil in Mirror Lake

lieve that there are basic principles of effective living, and that people can only experience true success and enduring happiness by integrating these principles into their lives.

Stephen R. Covey tells us to *see* the world through this character paradigm in his book, **The Seven Habits of Highly Effective People**. These are the habits: Be Proactive (Initiative), Begin With the End in Mind (Creativity), Put First Things First (Productivity), Think Win/ Win (Interdependence), Seek First to Understand, Then to Be Understood (Empathy), Synergize (Valuing Differences), Sharpen the Saw (Consistency). These are the practical steps to what I call character— being a loving, caring person.

My beliefs have delivered me from both a meaningless world and a meaningless life. But my recently reunited friend Joseph, asks that I discuss further the question of suffering: "Is suffering itself not meaningless? Suffering is an evil, so how can it have any good purpose? Having suffered under the lash of cruelty is bad enough, but it is insulting to be placated by soft assurances of its unreality. I know evil is a co-fundamental reality with goodness. Both are necessary to make a person possible. How does the Fundamental Person or Originator (God) fit into all of this?"

Today, most religious people cling to the notion that God is all-powerful and does not give up any use of this power for any reason. Accordingly, God is responsible for all that happens, including the presence of evil deeds in the world. Thus, God is responsible for permitting the bad things that happen to good people. People justify their belief in God's omnipotence by stating that the Almighty can bring good out of any evil deed.

Many times the Bible assures me that this God who loves me also sends me evil: Lamentations 3:37-42; Isaiah 45:6-7; Deuteronomy 32:39; Amos 3:6. This is certainly the picture of an all-powerful God.

Personally, I have difficulty accepting the view that God "creates" evil as well as good because it lacks proportion. I understand that the evil is always looked upon as medicinal and not punitive. Did not my father love me when he punished me for wrong doings? He did, but his chastisement was always in proportion to my evil. Nevertheless, the problem is that the all-powerful God's punishments, at times, seem **unjust** because there is no **proportion** between the evil suffered and the good gained. This is the problem of evil. Some people have given up on the all-powerful God because of this disproportion, and others simply call it a mystery. Why would God love me and yet mistreat me? This is more than a word problem.

The holocaust is a good example. A group of rabbis found God

My Solution to the Problem of Evil

guilty of injustice in a famous trial because their suffering was nowhere proportionate to any evil the Jews may have committed, or any good to come from it. The Jews usually say that God slept during the holocaust.

Many great books in history have exploited this dilemma of disproportionality. Dostoyevsky has Ivan Karamazov decry that Richard somehow makes up for his unjust execution by receiving the faith (the whole truth), and as if *going to the Lord* makes it all worthwhile! His Salvation is not *worth the price* of an unjust execution, says Ivan. The two are not proportionate.

Part of the disproportional problem arises from the fact that God's Divine Justice is being examined according to the terms of human justice. However, even if I were to accept the possibility that evil and good are usually proportionately dispensed by God, then evil and suffering become shrouded in mystery because there is no clear answer to why a good God would at times permit such disproportionate evils as holocausts and unjust executions to occur. Thus, the problem of disproportionality remains.

The problem, rather, the mystery of evil and suffering, is rooted in the belief that God is all-powerful and does not give up any of this power for any reason. But, we know that God gives up some of this power by creating us with a free will. So, while God may be all-powerful, we know that there is a limit to the exercise of God's power. Now, if we see this limit as applying to nature as well as people's free choices, then we solve the mystery of evil and suffering.

God loves. **All evil comes from our freely made choices and our interaction with nature.** Because of the enormity of God's love for us, God, on the rare occasion, causes a miracle to occur, which intervenes in nature's normal course for the sake of the bystander. Likewise, because God is ever-present and loving, our lives are forever to be persuaded toward making loving (that is selfless) decisions.

Of course, this is human justice looking at Divine Justice. Since we must give God the benefit of the doubt, we end by saying, "Evil and suffering are a mystery." But if we remove God as the One in charge of nature and people's free choices, we solve the mystery.

All evil—terrible things—come from nature which God freely supports with his will but chooses to let act according to its own somehow established laws, and also evil comes from our free choices which God freely chooses to maintain but not to interfere with, except through persuasion.

"If God created nature, then God created evil and suffering in our lives," someone objected. "Thus, God is still the responsible party. And,

Evil in Mirror Lake

the mystery remains. Why would God love us and yet subject us to such suffering?" he concludes.

God did create nature, yet nature operates according to its own laws. Remember nature is neutral, not malicious, never evil in itself. Nature causes physical evils (death etc.) only when in contact with people who then become hurt. My challenge from God is to use my intelligence to understand nature and so learn to live in harmony with her. God creates the nature that causes the hurricane, but not the terribleness that can come from people choosing to be at the wrong place at the wrong time. Thus, God does not cause the evil, just the nature. This makes God pre-responsible for the evil, but not its cause. We can also be responsible for the evil if we choose to ignore the signs of impending natural disasters. The ultimate reason for physical evils or terrible things is to test my reactions to them. Life is a proving ground for my character. My character is instrumental in determining my eternity. This is why we were created in the image and likeness of God.

Likewise, I, as well as nature, come from God. God lets me act according to my own free will and freely made choices, choosing not to interfere except through persuasion. End of mystery for me. I suffer because of nature and bad choices made by others and myself. This suffering helps create my character. Let us put this theory to the test.

God, who is all-loving, permits evil to befall us because God exercises power as the God of Love and not as the Almighty Manager of our lives and the world. Yes, God created nature, and creates us as part of it, but our free will wrests creation (us and nature) from being God's responsibility and assumes it as our own. Many parents have seen this occur with their children. One day they are dependent, helpless creatures, and the next day they are persons in their own right who have wrested responsibility for their lives away from their parents. We are responsible for evil. God, however, is always present with unending selfless love that can bring good out of evil, and, just as importantly, give meaning to our suffering.

Evil and suffering are always going to be with us as long as we remain imperfect; that is, as long as we fail to return God's love as wholly and endlessly as God gives it. We are, as the saying goes, our own worst enemies. We end up suffering because evil has befallen us— whether from our freely made choices, choices made by others, or our interaction with nature. Sometimes, we try to love, but we end up sorrowful when we find the love was selfishly given and/or selfishly received. Whatever the crisis, we will at some point wonder: "Am I a meaningless person in a meaningless world?" Or, we could ask, "What's the point?" or "Where's the meaning, the purpose in life?" Evil, and

240

My Solution to the Problem of Evil

the suffering it causes, always leads us to question the value of our life and where we are going. Just as God's power is an ever-present gift of love, God's love helps to fill the vacuum of meaning caused by crises of evil and suffering.

MEANINGFUL SUFFERING

In addition to showing that suffering does not come directly from God, I now ask, "Is suffering salvific?" or "Does suffering contribute to my salvation?" This is a different kind of question than asking where suffering originates. Suffering causes pain, but that pain may or may not have meaning attached to it. I wish to make a distinction between purely physical pain—including mental suffering—and meaningful suffering. Obviously, suffering can help me to develop my character or soul, but suffering does not always accomplish that.

Suffering in and of itself contributes nothing to my salvation. Love is the only contributing factor to my salvation. Nevertheless, a connection does exist. Suffering or pain makes it more difficult for me to love. So, if I love even when faced with pain and suffering, my love is strengthened because of the difficulties I endure. This is why we love firefighters so much.

Christian soteriology is the theology of salvation. It asks the question of whether suffering contributes to my salvation. John Paul II addresses this in his Apostolic Letter, **Salvifici Doloris** (1984), in which he says:

> Salvation means liberation from evil, and for this reason
> it is closely bound up with the problem of suffering.
> According to the words spoken to Nicodemus, God gives
> His Son to "the world" to free men from evil, which bears
> within itself the definitive and absolute perspective on
> suffering. At the same time, the very **word** "gives"
> ("gave") indicates that this liberation must be achieved
> by the only-begotten Son through His own suffering. And
> in this, love is manifested, the infinite love both of that
> only-begotten Son and of the Father who for this reason
> "gives" His Son. This is love for man, love for the
> "world": it is salvific love.

Salvific or saving love goes beyond the limits of justice. God's love is in the dimension of redemption or damnation. If accepted we are saved; if rejected we are damned. John Paul II also says, "These

Evil in Mirror Lake

transcendental roots of evil are grounded in sin and death: for they are at the basis of the loss of eternal life."

The roots of evil are grounded in sin (our bad free choices) and in death (nature). The only-begotten Son conquers sin (by His obedience or good choices) and death (by His resurrection). And so I "should not perish, but have eternal life," as said Jesus. As a result, Christ's salvific or saving work of love through suffering gives me hope of eternal life. He is the light of my salvation.

"Precisely by means of this suffering... of His cross," John Paul II says, "He (Jesus) must strike at the roots of evil, planted in the history of man and in human souls." It was precisely through Christ's saying "Yes" to God's call which redeemed me. Nevertheless, this "Yes" also involved suffering and the cross. Christ is united with His Father in this love, and as the Father so freely gave His Son to me, Christ's love extends to all. And for this reason Paul wrote of Christ, "He loved me and gave Himself for me."

John Paul II continues,

> *In His suffering, sins are canceled out precisely because He alone as the only-begotten Son could take them upon Himself, accept them **with that love for the Father which overcomes** the evil of every sin; in a certain sense He annihilates this evil in the spiritual space of the relationship between God and humanity, and fills this space with good.*

Human suffering reached its climax in the passion of Christ on the cross because both he and we have linked it to love. When I love, I act to help my beloved no matter what suffering it may cost me. Christ's suffering is salvific because He was doing the will of His Father (preaching the Good News). It was not because he was suffering (an evil perpetrated upon Him by His enemies, not by God).

John Paul II next moves into the question of our sharing in the sufferings of Christ. "Christ achieved the Redemption completely and to the very limit, but at the same time He did not bring it to a close," the Pope admits. He is reflecting what Paul said, "Now I rejoice in my sufferings for your sake, and in my flesh I complete what is lacking in Christ's afflictions for the sake of His Body, that is, the Church." (Col. 1: 24)

It is our love, when we are sometimes burdened with suffering, that is co-redemptive with the love of Christ. We need more love in our lives. We do not necessarily need more suffering. But when suffering

242

My Solution to the Problem of Evil

does come as a result of our love, or from nature, it intensifies our love as we remain steadfast, no matter what the cross or cost to me may be, as Christ did.

Only my faith, and not the reasonableness of justice, can give me this vision. And, what a powerful vision it is—my love and suffering are meaningful. In some mysterious way, love, at times intensified by suffering, builds up the Body of Christ—His Church. Love does this by bonding me with another individual and with God.

We usually equate love with God, and evil with the devil. I must resist this apparent dichotomy. Suffering or evil comes only from nature or bad decisions—decisions influenced by both God and the devil. We must see this suffering as a stepping stone to greater love. No suffering will derail my love of God or other people, I hope. In the end it is my love, and not just my suffering, that builds up the Church.

Not only have I escaped a meaningless life in a meaningless world, but now even my sufferings (an evil), because of my love, have value and so have meaning. The Pope's Apostolic Letter is worth reading. I simply substitute his emphasis on *suffering* as something good in itself, with *to love,* which suffering will hopefully intensify. Also, I substitute nature for his emphasis on death, which is a part of nature.

In order for suffering, as opposed to simple pain, to be salvific and redemptive and meaningful, I need to endure it with love for the sake of helping someone else. What if I accidentally hit my thumb with a hammer? Then, I need to "offer up the pain" and not let it get in the way of my being a loving person.

John Paul II says, "At one and the same time Christ has taught man to do good **by** his suffering and to do good to those who suffer. In this double aspect He has completely revealed the meaning of suffering." I say—change the words **"by"** his suffering to **"despite"** his suffering. And it becomes, "Christ has taught man to do good **despite** his suffering." Love and suffering are meant to be sides of the same coin—just as Christ taught us by his love and suffering.

Many people have grappled with the problem of human suffering. Instead of trying to make suffering salvific, or worse finding a justification for misery, or even trying to solve the mystery, some have simply tried to eliminate suffering by attacking its causes. Karl Marx addressed, in **Das Kapital** (1867), this mystery of misery. In writing about "the stock of human happiness," he quotes the Church of England parson, The Reverend J. Townsend, as saying, "The Poor Law tends to destroy the harmony and order of that system which God and Nature have established in the world." The Poor Law was England's first welfare system.

243

Evil in Mirror Lake

Regarding the antagonism of capitalist production as a general natural law of social wealth, Marx also quotes the Venetian monk, Ortes, one of the greatest writers of the eighteenth century. Ortes says, "In the economy of a nation, advantages and evils always balance one another; the abundance of wealth with some people, is always equal to the want of it with others; the great riches of a small number are always accompanied by the absolute privation of the first necessaries of life for many others."

"If the Venetian monk found in the fatal destiny that which makes misery eternal–the *raison d'etre* of Christian charity, celibacy, monasteries, and holy houses," Marx responds, then "the Protestant prebendary (a clergyman on salary) finds in it (misery) a pretext for condemning the Poor Law which have (given) the poor a right to a miserable public relief." Marx could have, but did not, quote Jesus who said, "And the poor you will always have with you."

No wonder Marx, *The Moor* as his six children called him, was so anti-religious. His Jewish father had converted to Protestantism and had him baptized Christian. Marx's answer to the misery of the working or non-working poor in England was to eliminate the misery, especially economic misery caused by the Industrial Revolution—not to find justification for it, as many in the church did.

The old theologians thought that God would harmonize the world. Marx thought that nature, through a social dialectic (thesis, and antithesis and synthesis) would evolve society into justice. For Marx, the ultimate historical synthesis will be a perfectly just and egalitarian society, where everyone works *according to his ability* and receives *according to his needs*, but where the state itself finally *withers away*. Today, communism as a theory is withering away, but pain is still with its adherents. The state is not withering. All the money goes to the military which is part of the state.

Communism is a noble attempt to alleviate misery and suffering. After all, religious orders of priests, brothers and nuns share all in common which succeeds because of their intense love of God. This dialectical materialism of communism simply turns out to be an ineffective solution.

John Steinbeck tried to reform unbridled capitalism from the inside. As a portrait of the Joad family being destroyed by nature, mechanization, greed, and changing times, Steinbeck's **Grapes of Wrath** is a powerful, though sometimes sentimental, indictment of our capitalist economy. I cannot always control nature, and, similarly, I cannot control other people's decisions, especially those of large corporations, that affect me. Nevertheless, Steinbeck's book promotes an optimism—

My Solution to the Problem of Evil

a-milk-of-human-kindness theme is depicted in a journey from drought and despair that ends in water and hope.

Understanding evil and misery is not the same as counseling suffering people. My mentors taught me to counsel people who are grieving the loss of life by loving them where they are—in pain. I must comfort them. However, I cannot soften the truth of reality (and of God) by telling them half-truths. Often, it is what I, as a chaplain, say to a grieving person that she remembers the most. So, I must direct her to our loving Father's arms, and bless God's holy name. But what is the truth?

Some people would attempt to console hurting people with the truth that Jesus suffered no less from the Father's will, but even more. Maybe even the Father suffered when he gave us His only son to suffer and die for us. None of us has spent forty days alone in a desert without so much as a water bottle or compass and survived. We have not been betrayed and handed over for crucifixion. Nor have we prayed so earnestly that we sweated blood. Jesus did all those things, though, because he trusted God's will would not destroy him, but would strengthen and enliven him, prepare him for all that God had in store for him. This is useful—trust in Goodness. Translated into practical psychology, this means to let go of existential anxiety—which is automatic and even instinctive—and realize that our problems are only relatively important.

God challenges me, too, to accept whatever pain I must endure so that I can participate in the fullness of God's glory. I know that Jesus loved me to the point of tears, such as when his friend Lazarus died. How is God revealed then in the life of a grieving person? It is by submitting to God's will and by blessing God our Father in all things. This is the traditional counseling.

Some would say that the path to union with God is narrow. Therefore, I must guard against my natural tendency to please myself. I must be on watch for every temptation that would turn me away from God, however imperceptibly it may be affecting me. Grief is an excellent opportunity to turn to God because it is with this one act of my will— submitting to God's authority over me—by which I allow the Holy Spirit to flood my being with graces. This type of thinking can be found in, **The Knowledge and Love of Our Lord Jesus Christ**, by Jean Baptiste Saint-Jure, S.J., (1588-1657), a favorite book of the Curé of Ars—the patron saint of country pastors.

After this type of theological counseling, most people remain angry with the providential God in charge of life. Often, more than one occurrence or situation causes the anger. After this, they need healing

Evil in Mirror Lake

for past hurts as well. Such a person's journey back to God will undoubtedly take more time, and the counseling will be much more involved than offering him/her a few theological declaratives. Often, what they are working through requires an extensive reconstruction of their psyche and self-esteem. So, helping people with past hurts or with grief, requires expertise beyond the reach of theological explanations.

Helping people who are so angry with God, requires training in the social sciences—psychology, victimology and addictions. Community support and prayer also may be useful.

My counseling takes a different path: tell me what you are sad about (an evil) and I will help you see that this pain came from nature, from your bad decision or from someone else's bad decision toward you. It did not come from God. Nevertheless, God is present for you, to help you love despite the pain.

This perspective will not, of course, remove the physical pain a person may have to endure, nor grief from a great loss, nor anger and subsequent depression from a blow to one's self esteem. Toward a person having such pain, I would continue to offer my support and help to relieve it as much as I could. However, this perspective helps me shift from blaming God or anyone else to taming the sense of loss and pain which I naturally share with the aggrieved person. This outlook makes life a challenge to me and not a pity. I need to learn how to turn negatives into positives.

Another attitude is to thank and bless God for all things—both the good and evil that happens to me. If I can avoid thinking that God did this evil to me, and trust that God is on my side, then this understanding and attitude about evil will enable me to make it through the bad times. The evil will lead to an enhanced life if I adopt this attitude or posture.

Barney Visser writes a therapeutic book about the death of his son entitled, **Chad**. He tells how to live through tragedy and go on with living. The bottom line of his book is this: Sometimes life hurts. But it is going to be okay, because God is with us! We need to know how to accept disappointment and go on. His teenage son, Chad, died of a stroke. "Evil pertains to man in its turn; pain is neither always to be avoided, nor is pleasure always pursued," as Cicero said long ago.

It becomes much more difficult when your child dies of an addiction. An addiction is where I cannot get enough of what I do not want. The will becomes twisted—I see evil as good. Someone has to break into my cycle and shake me loose. And yet, I am always free. God loves me. If I can just see that love, then the darkness of evil and suffering becomes properly lit.

246

My Solution to the Problem of Evil

The all-powerful God has freely chosen to limit Divine Power when it comes to nature and free will. "And that, Joseph is the essence of my solution to the problem of evil."

As evening approaches and darkness comes Joseph and I behold a lush green valley in the distance. As we turn now from Mirror Lake, taking with us the wisdom it revealed, we find ourselves drawn towards the beauty of the valley.

CHAPTER XI

PEOPLE, SPACE AND TIME

Time
Is Too Slow
For **People** Who Wait In **Space**,
Too Swift
For Those Who Fear,
Too Long
For People Who Grieve,
Too Short
For Those Who Rejoice,
But For People Who Love
Time Is Not.

adaptation from Abbey Press, St. Meinard, Indiana

I lie down in the cool grass, push back my sombrero, smooth out my three inch long eyebrows, and invite Joseph to gaze with me into space. After some time, I wonder how **people** may fill all available **space,** given enough **time**. I am confronting my future. I live in a sacramental universe; I see God active in all things: in the time of history, in the creation of the cosmos, in ritual, myth, words and, especially, in people fashioned in the Divine Image and likeness. I do not want to be a postage stamp without glue. I want my world, indeed my universe, to hang together. Our last chapter will reflect on the role of evil regarding people in space and during time.

This chapter is meant to reflect on the two great mysteries of existence—God and nature. Both are mysteries—one we can see, at least in part, the other we can only see by effects. Nature is both extremely large and extremely small—beyond our present comprehension. We shall find that both mysteries are one and the same—$E=mc^2$.

People, Space and Time

PEOPLE

People, although they are drawn toward evil, are becoming better at living millennium by millennium. Tuesday, October 26, 1999, U.N. demographers determined that the world's population hit six billion. This was a doubling of the Earth's inhabitants in less than forty years. Adam Smith said in his **Wealth of Nations** (Bk. I Ch VIII), "In Great Britain and most other European countries, they are not supposed to double (their population) in less than five hundred years."

After another 100 million years, we will have learned to harness or tame our love for each other—much like nature has already harnessed the care of females for their children. Temporary setbacks, like a mother on crack cocaine, are still among us. Our living in harmony with nature and avoiding bad decisions, however, are in sight.

In looking at people's future victory over bad things in nature, we may find that the more we know about nature (disease and disaster), the more we can avoid its horrible effects (physical evils). Fewer cases of polio are found today because we better understand the laws of nature, not because we prayed polio away, though we did pray for guidance. It was the invention of the electron microscope that led to the lifesaving vaccines by Salk and Sabin.

The more I know, the more I will know what I do not know. May the wisdom of Confucius always be with me, "To know that we know what we know, and that we do not know what we do not know, that is true knowledge." Confucius felt that the individual is the hub of the universe, and the *flowering of the individual* is the ultimate aim in life. As I cultivate harmony within myself, I bring peace, not evil, everywhere.

As far as bad and selfish decisions (moral evils) are concerned, I suggest that the human race did not experience **the fall**, but instead **the rise**. The Yahwist tells me the Garden of Eden story. Sitting under his favorite shade tree, he was trying to make sense out of our common experience. "Life was ahead of theologies," as Ralph Waldo Emerson, the early eighteen-hundred preacher and essayist said. The Yahwist realized that each of us humans has a higher loving nature and a lower selfish nature. The Yahwist had no way of knowing about evolution so he elected to explain this internal conflict by **the fall**.

"Man must liberate himself because man is a microcosm, and there is in him Pharaoh and Egypt; he is enslaving himself," wrote the Jewish philosopher Martin Buber (1878-1965). Buber's most influential book, **I and Thou** (1923), saw life as essentially a form of dialogue. The other kind of dialogue is the I-It of everyday life. This is the spiri-

249

Evil in Mirror Lake

tual-material battle—a secular expression of Gnosticism. According to the Kantian Buber, I cannot know God as an objective entity. On the other hand, science cannot explain the fact of creation, and science blandly ignores the existence of the mysterious inner life which forms the background of everyday existence. Thus he wrote, "The religious essence of every religion is found in the certainty that the meaning of existence is open and accessible in the actual lived concrete, not above the struggle with reality but in it. A human being can enter an I-Thou type of relationship even with a dog or a meadow." *Listening* and *receiving* is an essential part of the I-Thou relationship. For him, this is how I become fully human with my spiritual germinating my material.

Joseph Conrad in **Heart of Darkness** explores the world of evil civilizations, greedy corporations and selfish people, which, of course, does not include all civilizations, all corporations, nor all people. This is the original world in which sin is commonplace and into which each of us is born—original sin. We must somehow rise from this darkness of our lower nature to be a light of Divine Love. My life may be the only Bible another person ever reads.

I wonder if my lower nature is not from the animal in me, and my higher nature from God, but then both natures are from God. With this holistic view, I will be rising to unknown heights by being a loving, dependent creature trying to fill the universe of space with an intelligent and caring community. When that time happens, it will validate Teilhard de Chardin's prediction in his **Divine Milieu**: "When we learn to harness or channel the energies of love, we will have discovered fire for the second time."

Some fundamentalists look at the world from the Biblical Exodus event and see slavery, evil, repression, and injustice, with God gradually drawing out order, freedom, goodness, and justice. They see the forthcoming good and give God credit for this.

I look at the same world and assume that all things should be good and in perfect order. When I find evil, physical or moral, I ask, "Where did this evil come from?" Now I know; it came from nature and people's bad decisions. I need to work from this basis. I need to understand and live with nature. I need to make loving decisions. Eventually, I will rise to this altruism. So, instead of looking at the fall of people—original sin—I can concentrate on **the rise** of rational, loving people.

At first we had only the Law with which to help overcome our lower nature, but it was insufficient. Christian people found no way to stand forward as righteous. It takes both that touch of the perfect soul (God) and our cooperation. At times, this will involve the predicted cross and eventual resurrection as we trek, arm in arm, with God through

People, Space and Time

time and space. Our dark side, though, is ever before us, lurking for an expression.

Immanuel Kant reflected:

> *How did the "radical evil in human nature" begin? Not through "original sin"; surely of all the explanations of the spread and propagation of this evil through all members and generations of our race, the most inept is that which describes it as descending to us as an inheritance from our first parents. Probably the "evil" propensities were strongly rooted in man by their necessity to his survival in primitive conditions; only in civilization—in organized society—do they become vices; and there they require not suppression but control. "Natural inclinations,"* **considered in themselves,** *are* **good,** *that is, not a matter for reproach; and not only is it futile to want to exterminate them, but to do so would be harmful and blameworthy. Rather let them be tamed, and instead of clashing with one another they can be brought into that harmony in a wholeness which is called happiness.*

George A. Maloney describes original sin in terms of alienation in his **Mysticism and The New Age**:

> *The Book of Genesis gives us an account of the reality of sin that first entered into the human race when man freely broke the social oneness that he was meant to enjoy with God and other human beings. Original sin is more than the first, personal sin of the first human being, that is then juridically imputed to every human being thereafter born. It is the first sin and each personal sin of every human being that has ever lived, including you and me. But it adds to itself a oneness that we all share with an alienated human community. We are all united in our broken condition and alienated from God and from each other and from the material cosmos.*

Al Hulsbosch describes the power of original sin in his New Age book, **God's Creation**:

> *Sin has taken root in the human community, in order to*

Evil in Mirror Lake

rule over it as a tyrannizing power. Whoever is born into
this community is irrevocably delivered to this power.

From the beginning of human time, people have wrestled with this tyrannizing power toward evil. Shakespeare understood this permanent power of evil when he had Anthony in **Julius Caesar** begin his funeral oration with these famous lines:

Friends, Romans, countrymen, lend me your ears;
I come to bury Caesar, not to praise him.
The evil that men do lives after them.
The good is oft interred with their bones;
So let it be with Caesar.

Evil does seem to have an institutional existence unto itself—slavery, apartheid, prejudice, mafia, drug trade, street gangs, maximization of profits, the tobacco industry. When some individuals leave the group, there always seems to be enough people to replace them. I contend that these organizations in themselves are not evil. It is just that many people are willing and able to step in and do evil things. When this source of evil-doing people dries up—or goes to prison—organizations committed to doing evil will cease to exist.

Conversely, the sacred book of Exodus, in the Ten Commandments, tells us in Ch 19 v 5 and 6: "For I, the Lord, your God, am a jealous God, inflicting punishment for their fathers' wickedness on the children of those who hate me, down to the third and fourth generation; but bestowing mercy down to the thousandth generation, on the children of those who love me and keep my commandments." This means that goodness is more powerful than evil in humans. It may also mean that wicked families kill off themselves since goodness lasts a thousand generations whereas evil only three or four generations.

The appetites, instincts, drives, and energies that bring satisfaction to other animals are not enough to bring peace to the self-aware human creature, says Gabriel Daly in **Creation and Redemption**. Their animal characteristics remain in the human being alongside the newly developed awareness of right and wrong. These primal emotions can destroy us and our relationships if we do not name them and come to terms with them. However, Daly insists that they are also the raw material of virtue. I can understand original sin in terms of discrepancy between the information coming to us from our genetic inheritance as opposed to our culture.

Reptiles came out of the sea some three hundred million years ago

252

People, Space and Time

and hobbled inland with a *reptilian brain*. As these creatures evolved into groups for both survival and procreation, they developed an additional *mammalian brain*. We humans have since wrapped these two brains with our *primate brain*. The *Homo erectus* came walking along about four to six million years ago, according to the empirical proof offered in a study by **National Geographic**. Homo Sapiens, the thinking, free-willed man, inherited the earth only about 35,000 years ago. Some say 200,000 years ago (**Prehistory and the First Civilizations**). Chris Stringer and Robin McKie speculate a breeding population back then of 300,000 in their book, **African Exodus: The Origin of Modern Humanity**. We humans are very late in time and small in space, and yet we are the children of God. Though we are microbes on this speck of dust, we will inherit the kingdom of God. We are more than the current stage in the evolutionary chain.

The theory of evolution, proposed in 1858 by Charles Darwin (and independently by A.R. Wallace), is the notion that species change by a gradual process of natural selection. We also know this process as *survival of the fittest*—a term he most unfortunately borrowed from Herbert Spencer.

By 1865, Gregor Mendel, the Russian monk in the then Austrian Czechoslovakia, had discovered and published the laws of genetics that explain how we pass traits from one generation to the next. Even Darwin failed to appreciate the significance of Mendel's pea-breeding experiments—the theory of inheritance. Mendel, the Augustinian monk who worked in the monastery garden, had sent his book, **Experiments with Plant Hybrids** (actually two lectures), to Darwin, but he never read it. Darwin could have used this knowledge of the *dominant* and the *recessive* genes to clarify his theory of natural selection. Darwin concluded, though, that all species might have the same ancestor.

The discovery of the structure of DNA (deoxyribonucleic acid) in the 1950s and the explosive growth of molecular biology bring daily revelations. These revelations explain how changes within cells have allowed humans to evolve, or rise to our present-day status. They explained that genes were a segment of the chromosome. They verify the basic theories of both Mendel and Darwin. We know Mendel, the Abbot of Brno, as the Father of Genetics.

Reading the **Essay** by Malthus triggered Darwin's great insight— how natural selection of favorable characteristics operated among randomly occurring variations in offspring. All species produce far too many offspring for all to survive. Therefore, those offspring with favorable variations—owing to chance—are selected. Malthus called this the principle of the *struggle for existence*.

253

Evil in Mirror Lake

Darwin, with courage, courtesy, and firmness, opposed the older notion of God as benevolent watchmaker. He did not dispose of God, but he did dismantle a singularly deficient notion of God. Although Darwin died as a gentle agnostic or perhaps even an atheist, he nevertheless said in the concluding passage of **The Origin of Species by Means of Natural Selection, or the Preservation of Favored Races in the Struggle for Life**:

> *There is grandeur in this view of life, with its several*
> *powers, having been originally breathed by the Creator*
> *into a few forms or into one; and that, whilst this planet*
> *has gone cycling on according to the fixed law of gravity,*
> *from so simple a beginning endless forms most beautiful*
> *and most wonderful have been and are being evolved.*

Despite the length and weighty content, this book is remarkably easy reading. Unfortunately, through all the tempest and fanfares that have followed it for almost one and some half centuries, few people have actually studied the text itself. I encourage the reader to read all of these basic texts, especially Darwin's book.

Kenneth Miller explains the implications of step-by-step evolutionary change and our cobbled genetic code in his article, "Life's Grand Design" in *Technology Review* (Feb./Mar. 1994). He explains the sloppy way nature developed the genetic code in us—trial and error. He claims that "evolution is not at all inconsistent with a belief in God." However, evolution is inconsistent with a belief in a Hands-On-Creator in whom many believe. The problem is to reach a God who is beyond such lifeless abstractions as "God as primal nudge," "God as a process," "God as in natural selection," "God as a higher organizing principle," or "God as a clever, though sloppy, technician."

Some theologians suggest that I should not think of God as creating individual human beings through a series of interventions. Rather, I should think of God as creating in one Divine Act, all that comprises the whole process. It is this one Divine Act that enables all that is radically new to continually emerge in creation. Above all, it enables the emergence of self-conscious and spiritual human beings. God thus created each of us in radical uniqueness in the image of the Godself.

God invites each of us into a unique interpersonal relationship with the triune God in the gift of grace. Each of us is destined for eternal life that is a participation in the Divine Life of friendship beyond comprehension. The creation of each spiritual being is individual, unique, and personal, and I can think of it as caused through God's one Divine

254

People, Space and Time

Action of continuous creation.

Karl Rahner uses this line of thought. He explains the emergence of the human spirit as *active self-transcendence*. He sees the material universe as *oriented from within by God, in dynamic self-transcendence* toward the human person. Rahner writes in, **Evolution: II. Theological** that in the human being, *the universe finds itself* and is *consciously confronted with its origin and goal*. What Pius XII has spoken of as *immediate creation* of the human soul, Rahner tells us, we can understand as God making possible a *self-transcendence of the material universe in the direction of the spiritual human person.*

Rahner points out that at certain points in evolution substantially *new* elements make their appearance. The emergence of life is such an example. Another is the emergence of self-conscious human creatures. Such evolutionary events spring from inner-worldly cause, and that is the work of science to explain. He rejects the notion of *occasionalism*, the idea that God, at certain points, intervenes as one cause among others to bring about a new direction. Rather, God upholds and empowers the process of evolution from within, claims Rahner, as the power enabling creation itself to cause something new. This means that when something new emerges in evolution, at one level, the change will be the effect of finite causes, such as genetic mutation and natural selection.

Nevertheless, at another level, evolutionary change is the effect of God's creative activity, working through the power of self-transcendence from within creatures. God, then, does not intervene as one cause among others but is always present as the dynamic absolute Being, which enables creatures not only to exist but also to transcend themselves and to become what is new. Rahner discusses this in his **Foundations of Christian Faith**.

The image of a God who works through evolution, not predetermining and commanding, but allowing his children to mature and make free decisions, "corresponds extremely well" with the God of the Bible, said Jesuit Father George V. Coyne, Director of the Vatican Observatory in a Faith vs. Science Seminar at the Vatican in 2000.

Denis Edwards in **The God of Evolution** says that I can understand the human being as the universe coming to self-awareness in a particular time and place. The goal of the world is God's self-communication with it, $E=mc^2$. This experience of God's presence occurs in moments when we encounter transcendence and mystery at the heart of life. When we say "Yes" to this mysterious presence and self-communication from God, we are holy.

Evil in Mirror Lake

Edwards says:

> *We can become aware of the Holy Spirit, as the
> unspeakable closeness of God, in silence before the
> mystery of the universe that opens up before us with the
> aid of the Hubble telescope, in delight in the flashing
> colors of a parrot on the wing, in the exuberant
> experience of sunshine on a day in spring, in the
> experience of mutual friendship, in finding that there is a
> holy presence with us in times of suffering and grief, and
> even in what seems at first like nothing but absence and
> abandonment. It is the Spirit who stirs within us in the
> experience of faith in the Gospel, in our participation in
> the eucharistic communion of the church, in the sense of
> global solidarity with all human beings and with all god's
> creatures, and in our union with Jesus before the One he
> called **Abba** and who can also be called our beloved
> Mother. The Holy Spirit is inexpressible personal
> closeness in these ways and in many others.*

However, the human race must beware for our continual rise is not
inevitable. In the year 2126 August 14, the comet Swift-Tuttle has perhaps a 1-in-10,000 chance of hitting the earth, and thus obliterating
people from this planet. We may yet go the way of the dinosaurs.

Another danger facing modern civilization is knowledge. "We strive
for the forbidden" (Ovid's **Amores**, III, 4,17). We have built education
upon the almost sanctified premise that social progress depends upon
the unfettered pursuit of truth wherever it may lead. But the danger of
knowing too much and the need for prudent restrictions on human inquiry have dominated the ancient stories of Prometheus and Pandora,
Psyche and Cupid, along with Adam and Eve and the tree of forbidden
knowledge. (That was then, and the fears were based on knowledge as
it was then. This is now. Are we still bound by such ancient views? If
not, should we be?)

"Such taboos rooted in the mystery of religion gradually gave
way to the more open-ended investigations of modern science," says
Roger Shattick in **Forbidden Knowledge: From Prometheus to
Pornography**. The author correctly goes on to caution us in the pursuit of DNA research, atomic weapons research, eugenics, the Human Genome Project and even violent pornography. Shattick argues
that limits on individual freedom are necessary for the benefit of society as a whole, and have been so since customs and laws came into

256

People, Space and Time

the social scene. Our society has already made this restriction regarding child pornography.

"Because of the new genetic knowledge, our children may know cancer only as a constellation of stars and not as a disease that kills and maims," announced President William Jefferson Clinton at the White House on Monday, June 26, 2000. "Today… marks an historic point in the 100,000-year record of humanity," J. Craig Venter, chief scientist of Celera Genomics, proclaimed. "We have caught a glimpse of an instruction book previously known only to God," said Dr. Francis Collins, director of the National Human Genome Research Institute. Some 3.12 billion chemical base pairs that make up the human genome have been sequenced and assembled in the correct order.

This is part of what people are all about—learning nature. Yet, we must see to it that our knowledge is put to only good use—making good decisions. Here lies the challenge of both our communal and individual lives as we struggle with our selfishness.

On the other hand, "There is no higher and/or lower nature in human beings. It's all one. Every act of spirit is fleshly and spirit forms every physical act. Dualism is absurd," says David Denby as he reflects on Montaigne in his book, **Great Books**.

People are becoming better because we are on the rise from our lower nature to becoming more like the all-knowing and all-loving, if not always all-powerful, God, into whose image and likeness nature made or evolved us. The great joy in life is to put knowledge into active use.

SPACE

Space is where our new homes will be as we live in harmony with each other and with a loving God after the General Resurrection and after we have eliminated all evil from life. On our part, we will regain our loving, dependent, and meaningful relationship with God—the garden revisited and extended. When I look up at night and see the stars, I wonder at the immensity, even extravagance, of space. We have come a long way since Aristotle taught that space is an immovable vessel containing perfect things. The Hubble telescope now indicates that the universe may be as old as ten to fifteen billion years and is expanding, at least for now. In the region of the universe that we can now see, multiplied millions (one with eighty zeros after it) of particles of matter exist. Let us get our bearing within space.

The universe is composed of perhaps 200 billion galaxies, and these galaxies cluster into groups. For every star that I can see with my na-

257

Evil in Mirror Lake

ked eye on a clear night, sixty-six million galaxies exist. Each galaxy and each group of galaxies have a gravitational tug on each other that always forms a pattern. Our ancestors grouped the stars that they could see into eighty-eight constellations, twelve of which form our zodiac. Years ago, we first thought that our earth was the center of our solar system, and later that our galaxy was the universe. Nicolaus Copernicus, the Polish canon and astronomer, began the process of casting men and women from the center of the universe. It remained for Danish astronomer Tycho Brahe, the Pythagorean Johannes Kepler, the Italian Galileo Galilei and finally the Englishman Isaac Newton to finish this.

Abbot Copernicus, the cloistered monk living a life of solitude, studied astronomy combined with meditation. The third century B.C.E. Greek philosopher Pythagoras, along with his disciple Aristarchus of Samos, and later Hipparchus had correctly stated that the sun was the center of our solar system; nevertheless, the doctrines of Ptolemy, a Helenic Egyptian king, guided by Aristotle's influence, prevailed—a belief that the Earth was the immovable center of the universe with all the planets, stars, and moons revolving around it. In addition to his limited sightings—through slits cut in his observation room— Copernicus was convinced that nature behaves in the simplest and most economical of ways. We still believe this today. As he lie on his deathbed, his friends gave him the first printer's copy of his **Concerning the Revolution of the Celestial Spheres** (1543). This became the launching point of modern astronomy.

Galileo was an experimental scientist and mathematician. Probably, like Kepler, he was a Pythagorean. He wished to explain the universe in terms of numbers. Besides the heliocentric (sun centered) hypothesis, he taught us that objects fall at a constant rate of thirty-two feet per second, per second. His dropping weights from the Leaning Tower of Pisa is, sadly, probably apocryphal. His persecution by the Church remains a mystery about why. In 1600 the heliocentric hypothesis was a dangerous novelty, but by 1700 few educated people believed in a geocentric (earth centered) universe. It was Galileo's development of the refracting telescope into the first complete astronomical telescope in 1609 that opened the universe to our eyes. This resulted in his greatest work, **Dialogue on the Two Chief World Systems, The Ptolemaic and the Copernican** (1629). Galileo's great problem was that his experimental proofs could not outweigh the revered two-thousand-year-old laws of Aristotle—and the Church. He argued as ridiculous the contention that "the same God who has endowed us with senses, reason, and understanding does not permit us to use them." His pleas

People, Space and Time

went unheeded.

Johannes Kepler, the son of a Lutheran pastor, published his 1619 classic, **The Harmony of the World**, in which he clearly explains his three laws that explained the movements in the universe. Not until Newton, father of the Age of Reason, explained gravity as a force did his laws become completely clear. To try to separate Kepler's mysticism from his science is vain. Bureaucrats of both religions, Catholics and Protestants, persecuted and inconvenienced him, but he survived.

Since I was a teenager, we have recognized a smudge in the constellation Andromeda as another galaxy—which Immanuel Kant called an *island universe*. It was in 1923 that the American astronomer Edwin Hubble showed that the Andromeda Galaxy was found outside our own galaxy. Andromeda, our closest spiral galaxy (M-31), is under mutual gravitational influence with of our galaxy. It is also the most-distant object visible to the unaided eye. Andromeda is a heavenly spot of light-mist beyond the lower left hand corner of the Great Square of Pegasus, and it is around 3 million light years away. A single light year is approximately 5.88 trillion miles. This remains the most studied galaxy other than our own.

The closest star in our galaxy is Alpha Centauri, or more correctly, for the time being, its tiny red dwarf companion Proxima Centauri. It is only 4.3 light years away, or 25.7 trillion miles. "Two things fill the mind with ever-increasing wonder and awe…: the starry heavens above me and the moral law within me," said Immanuel Kant.

"If we find the answer to why it is that we and the universe exist," Stephen Hawking says, "then we would know the mind of God." Gottfried Leibniz, in 1714, asked the most basic question of all, "Why is there something rather than nothing?" There is wisdom in the Kabbalah's insight of the *unknowable* nature of the *Ein Sof* (God). By simple meditation upon what we simply cannot know, we learn more than those who seek a certainty.

What we now know only well enough to ask questions of, is the *known unknown*. We cannot even begin to ask questions about the *unknown unknown*. The *known unknown* may someday become known and something of the *unknown unknown* may emerge sufficiently to call forth a question. I am for now limited to the *known unknown*. An example of the *unknown unknown* is what happened before the last Big Bang, the explosion that may have spawned our universe. (Fred Hoyle originally coined this phrase—Big Bang—to make fun of this new theory of his friend, George Gamow.)

A little of this once *unknown*, which today we know something about, is that this Big Bang took place approximately fifteen billion

259

Evil in Mirror Lake

solar years ago, to use a term by which we have decided to measure time. All the matter and energy forming the known universe of today expanded from an extraordinarily hot spot from which precipitated out its energy—in the form of hydrogen atoms and helium atoms and light. Matter and energy in its simplest form had been born. Atoms fused together forming larger atoms. Later, atoms bonded together and formed molecules. Up the stairway of complexity, the universe lunged again, up to the point of intricacy. Gravity and electromagnetic force formed. From this expanding spot, the force of gravity accumulated clumps of matter into increasingly denser areas from which stars started and galaxies started to coalesce.

After the first Big Bang, a second Bang affected us. Supernovas have occurred since a few million years after the first stars were born, right up to the present time. But about five billion years ago, or ten billion years after the first Big Bang, a certain supernova star exploded after having cooked hydrogen and helium, through thermonuclear fusion, to create the new atoms of carbon, nitrogen, iron, gold and all the other elements that make up the periodic table of our present universe.

The 149 million-year reign of the dinosaurs, or thundering lizards, came to an abrupt end. A current hypothesis says that an unnamed and unnumbered iron asteroid collided with the Earth in part of the Gulf of Mexico. The resulting ecological disaster made way for humans. This third Bang—the closest to the human scale—took place about sixty-five million years ago, and it was essential for evolutionary development and diversification of mammals. **Evil came into existence only with the coming of people**, (or with the coming of angels).

Philip M. Dauber and Richard A. Muller described this for us in their recent book, **The Three Big Bangs:**

> *One day without warning (to the dinosaurs?), a comet, or possibly an asteroid, smashed into Earth, forever changing life on our planet. The impact blasted out a giant crater in the present-day Yucatan, in Mexico. The atmosphere, the oceans, forests, and jungles were totally disrupted in ways scientists are now busy unscrambling. Dinosaurs and most other life forms vanished, including most existing mammals. Our ancestors survived and went on to flourish.*

It takes our sun over 200 million years to circle the center of our Milky Way, a spiral galaxy whose diameter is about 100,000 light years. Our Milky Way Galaxy and the Andromeda Galaxy are the largest gal-

People, Space and Time

axies in our Local Group that consists of perhaps thirty galaxies all in motion around each other. Our whole Local Group is moving toward the Virgo Supercluster, which is a much larger group. In 1986 we learned that our Local Group and the Virgo Supercluster are in turn part of a flotilla of many thousands of galaxies that share a bulk motion toward an as-yet-unmapped mass concentration—the Great Attractor.

"We forget that our sun is only a yellow G star destined someday to burn out. The time scale of its transience so far exceeds our human one that our unconditional dependence on its life-giving properties feels oddly like an indiscretion we'd rather forget," said Gretel Ehrlich in **The Solace of Open Spaces**.

Yes, our universe or space has come a long way in less than fifteen billion years. In her book for amateurs, **The Friendly Guide to the Universe**, Nancy Hathaway tells us that our sun is in mid-life. It is a later generation star, formed probably some five billion years ago, perhaps after an earlier supernova exploded. Most of the matter went to form our sun, but a small amount collected to form the planets that now orbit the sun. Only the inner planets have lots of dense matter — the outer planets are gas giants. This is our space to live in. The process of forming our solar system took about 100 million years after the supernova had exploded. The universe was born restless and has never since been still.

Unless humans exist in outer space, no evil exists there—neither moral nor physical. Evil or terrible things happen only to humans or by humans. Great violence exists out there—supernovas exploding—but no evil unless it impinges upon the well-being of people.

It is to bring home this point of evil being associated only with people that I am speaking about our physical beginnings in which there were no people and therefore no evil.

If the asteroid Swift-Tuttle actually strikes our planet on August 14, 2126 A.D., it will be a physical evil—a terrible thing for humankind. Whereas, the unnamed asteroid that struck earth 69 million years ago, destroying the dinosaurs, making way for mamals and eventually people to come onto the scene, was good for us. This was no evil. No terrible things happened to any people. Similarly, another asteroid that struck our planet, later coalesced some of the atmospheric debris circling our Earth, thus creating our pot-holed moon. This in turn made the tides, that, with the help of lightning, were necessary for life to spawn in pools. This was similarly good for us.

Around Christmas 2001 A.D., Comet C/2000 WMI (Linear) will probably be bright enough to be visible to the unaided eye. Some day, one of these cosmic objects may hit the Earth. Such an impact could

Evil in Mirror Lake

destroy our advanced civilization or even eliminate humanity all together. However, with sufficient warning, nudging a near earth object slightly might be possible and so make it miss the Earth instead. As of 1999, the Lincoln Laboratory telescope has also discovered more than 26,800 new asteroids in the main asteroid belt between Mars and Jupiter. It has also discovered many new near earth orbit objects. So far, we have been lucky—none of them are in orbit that pose a danger to the earth. On the other hand, the object with our name on it could be discovered any day.

About 4.5 billion years ago, the accretion of infalling material created this blue-green planet of ours, Lawrence M. Krauss, in his down-to-earth book, **The Physics of Star Trek**, explains: Life on earth evolved from the blue-green algae, aided by the tides caused by the moon, more than 3.5 billion years ago. This took place less than one billion years after the formation of the earth. Next came algae, or bacteria, which exhaled oxygen that can sustain more complex life. (See Richard Fortey's **Life: A Natural History of the First Four Billion Years of Life on Earth.**)

During the last billion of this 3.5 billion span, nature finally developed the much needed atmosphere of oxygen. It has taken almost three billion years to develop the complex multicellular structures that compose intelligent life. People in our space evolved during this last billion years. "Within a few years, 100 million, of the earliest possible time that life could have evolved on Earth, it did," said Krauss. "Scientists studying Australian rocks," the *AP* reported on 8-13-99, "found that they have evidence that primitive forms of life existed 2.7 billion years ago—a billion years earlier than had been previously shown," This is according to researcher Jochen J. Brocks as reported in the journal, *Science*.

If you compress Earth's four and a half billion years into a twenty-four-hour day, human life began on Earth only a few seconds before midnight. Microbes, though, were here before sunrise. Of our sixty to eighty thousand genes, two thousand are identical with the genes of microbes.

Five billion more years from now, nuclear fusion will have consumed the sun's hydrogen. The remaining core of highly condensed helium will then burn to cause the sun to balloon into a red giant. This expanded fire ball will boil away our oceans and scorch the earth. The once mighty sun will then shrink into a lump of carbon and oxygen known as a white dwarf.

The sun-star will still shine, but it will derive its glow from the leftover heat of the contraction, not from nuclear fusion. Over billions

People, Space and Time

of years, our sun will cool until at last it blinks out. It will finally become a black dwarf, a cold, dark globe of crystallized carbon and oxygen—a sort of diamond… a stellar corpse the size of the earth, which some call *the snowball effect*. See *TIME* magazine (6-25-01) "How the Universe Will End"

Meanwhile, our moon is gradually slowing the rotation of the earth due to the friction generated by its tidal interaction with the earth. About 900 million years ago, the day was only about 18.2 hours long. This transfer of energy to the moon speeds up its own orbital motion and moves it farther away from earth approximately at about 1.5 inches a year. Little things add up after a few billion years. As Senator Everett Dirksen of Illinois once said, "A billion here and a billion there, and pretty soon you're talking about real money."

Those of us who have problems with evolution, have problems imagining a billion years and what that adds up to. Ten thousand years is only 400 generations ago.

What is the fate of our space, the universe? Expansion would gradually slow for billions of years. Then in some future era say 50 or 100 billion years from now, it could reverse entirely into a Big Crunch. One popular speculation about this closed universe theory is that it would bounce and explode again in a Big Bounce. Because of left over black body radiation, the past number of bounces would be limited to about a hundred.

On the other hand, an open universe would be unbounded, infinite, and expanding forever. Its future is cold. Since the expansion has no end, all stars will eventually run out of nuclear fuel and die. We'd be alone and slowly freeze to death.

Finally, in a third model, the universe may be right on the border between closed and open. The ultimate fate of this flat universe would be much the same as an open one—a cold sea of radiation at essentially absolute zero that barely stops expanding after an infinite time.

Using any model, the question remains: Where does it leave us at the end of time? Will there be evil out there? No moral evil is out there if there are no people, and no physical evil is out there unless that comet Swift-Tuttle makes its rendezvous with us in 2126 A.D., and we are still here.

So much for the reaches of outer space. Not only is it interesting but it also helps me visualize my place in the universe of beings—a microbe on a speck of dust. Yet I am a child of God and an heir of eternity. Likewise, the realm of the small is just as fascinating and mind boggling.

Let me begin with something that I can recognize—water. A drop

Evil in Mirror Lake

of water is composed of perhaps 10^{21} molecules of water. A molecule is a group of atoms like H_2O—two atoms of hydrogen (H) and one of oxygen (O). These atoms, or elements, essentially contain different numbers of protons and neutrons in their nucleus. To date, scientists have separately identified 112 elements by the number of protons found in their nucleus.

Democritus (460-370 B.C.E.), in the fourth century B.C.E., correctly taught that all matter consists of tiny, indivisible particles called atoms. When later day scientists thought that elements were the smallest particles in the universe, they were incorrectly labeled *atoms*. Later, in 1897, scientists found the atom itself to be composed of a nucleus that was in turn surrounded by a cloud of electrons.

To give perspective to their relative sizes, if the atom were the size of the earth, the nucleus would be a football field at its center; or if the atom were the size of Carnegie Hall, the nucleus would be a grain of sand at its center. The nucleus contains at least one positively charged proton. Each proton is nearly two thousand times as massive as each electron.

In 1932, James Chadwick proved that these positively charged protons had something to hold onto without being electrically repulsed by each other. Scientists call these additional subatomic particles neutrons, as they have a neutral charge. Nucleons are this combination of neutrons and protons in the center of the atom. Scientists then discovered they could sometimes divide this nucleon by the splitting of the atom.

I have two practical examples of elements that helped us win a hot and a cold war. Uranium, which is one of the most massive naturally occurring elements, contains ninety-two protons and over 140 neutrons in each nucleus. If there are 143 neutrons, then we have the isotope uranium-235. If it has 146 neutrons, then we have uranium-238. Hydrogen, on the other hand, has a nucleus containing one proton and one neutron with one electron outside it. It is the lightest of all the elements, followed by Helium.

In the 1940s, scientists, led by Robert Oppenheimer, at the Los Alamos Lab in New Mexico, discovered that if they bombarded heavy nuclei, such as Uranium-235, it would split, forming other nuclei. This process released tremendous energy. This is the basis for our atomic bomb and all of our nuclear plants today. Albert Einstein ended up being against using the atomic bomb, and worked the rest of his life as a pacificist.

Scientists then learned that they could fuse light nuclei together thus forming a more stable element. This process also released a tremendous amount of energy. This fusion process of hydrogen atoms

People, Space and Time

provides the energy for our hydrogen bomb. The problem is that it takes much heat and pressure to make this happen, yet it happens all the time in our sun-star.

In both these processes, fusion and fission, it is the atom that contains all of this power, and yet it is almost impossible to see. It measures 10^{-8} centimeters across. This mathematical short hand means a decimal point followed by eight zeroes and a one. Around 1932 scientists discovered anti-particles. The negative electron has a positron. The neutron couples with a neutral anti-neutron, and the proton with an anti-proton. Photons, or packets of light energy, are composed of wave/particles.

Scientists realized that something bound together the neutron and proton so they looked for and discovered the strong nuclear force. They later discovered a weak nuclear force—causing certain types of nuclear decay. It is necessary to cause the chain reaction for an atomic explosion. Thus, nature now has four known forces including the long known electromagnetic and gravitational forces.

Scientists have dug deeper into the fathomless, fascinating hole of nature. Welcome to the world of quarks. John Gibbin tells us in his moderately understandable book, **The Search for Superstring Symmetry and the Theory of Everything**, "The everyday particle, the proton, neutron, and electron and the pion, which carry the strong force, can all be described simply in terms of two or three quarks, which are given arbitrary labels in order to distinguish them from one another. One (quark) is called 'up' and another is called 'down.' By assigning a definite mass to each quark, it gives the right mass and angular momentum for each of the known particles."

"Just as protons and neutrons are held together by the exchange of pion (during the pion exchange), the carriers of the strong force, so quarks must be held together in some way, by an exchange of particles which were dubbed 'gluon' because they glue the quarks together to make protons, neutrons and so on," says Gibbin. On the other hand, it is not just four particles. "Each quark comes in one of these colors, red, blue and green. A stable nucleon has one quark of each of these colors. Also the electron and its neutrino also have antielectrons (positrons) and antineutrinos," says Don Bless, a teacher of astronomy at John A. Logan College in southern Illinois.

So, in this latest picture of reality, the interactions of ordinary matter all involve "just four particles—the up and down quarks, the electron and its neutrino," explains Gibbin.

"In addition as each particle gains energy, it becomes more massive. For example, strange and top are heavier versions of down quarks,"

265

Evil in Mirror Lake

continues Bless, "There are also virtual particles which spontaneously come into existence. They exist because of the quantum nature of the Universe. Unseen to us, existence moves back and forth between matter and energy. The energy needed to create virtual particles is borrowed from the space around them, and it is returned to space when the particles annihilate each other," says Don Bless, in his unpublished astrophysics lecture notes.

The word *quark*, coined by Murray Gell-Mann, is a meaningless word used in **Finnegan's Wake** by James Joyce. Thus, what Democritus meant to be the **atom** of all existent matter, scientists now call a **quark**. What does all of this have to do with evil? This book is about life and mystery—not just evil. The mystery of nature, which I can vicariously see through the Hubble telescope and the electromagnetic microscope, reveal mystery—not based on faith, but on experience. This is part of the search for the mystery of evil. Evil is basically the absence of good in human life.

TIME

Time is slipping away from us. Time is a way of measuring where we have been, and when to expect things. Steven W. Hawking, in **A Brief History of Time**, describes the beginning of time in our world:

> *The earth was initially very hot and without an atmosphere. In the course of time it cooled and acquired an atmosphere from the emission of gases from the rocks. This early atmosphere was not one in which we could have survived. It contained no oxygen, but a lot of other gases that are poisonous to us, such as hydrogen sulfide (the gas that gives rotten eggs their smell). There are, however, other primitive forms of life that can flourish under such conditions. It is thought that they developed in the oceans, possibly as the result of chance combinations of atoms into large structures, called macromolecules, which were capable of assembling other atoms in the ocean into similar structures. They would thus have reproduced themselves and multiplied. In some cases there would be errors in the reproduction. Mostly these errors would have been such that the new macromolecule could not reproduce itself and eventually would have been destroyed. However, a few of the errors would have produced new macromolecules that were even better at*

266

People, Space and Time

*reproducing themselves. They would therefore have had
an advantage and would have tended to replace the
original macromolecules. In this way a process of
evolution was started that led to the development of more
and more complicated, self-reproducing organisms. The
first primitive forms of life consumed various materials,
including hydrogen sulfide, and released oxygen. This
gradually changed the atmosphere to the composition that
it has today and allowed the development of higher forms
of life such as fish, reptiles, mammals, and ultimately the
human race.*

Yes, we have come a long way in less than fifteen billion years, and we have an eternity to go. Whether our beginning Big Bang will be followed by the Big Crunch, will depend on whether black matter, which we cannot see except for its effects, really does make up 90 percent of the matter in the universe. An English royal astronomer, Martin Rees, remarks, "It's embarrassing that 90 percent of the universe is unaccounted for" (1995). Does the Big Crunch call for another Big Bounce to begin life again? Whether we are in the first or twenty-fifth, Big Bang, are questions beyond our ability even to speculate. Some calculate the Big Crunch of the universe as $10^{(106)}$ years after the Big Bang. This is ten with 106 zeroes behind it. The Big Crunch would reduce matter and radiation to a point of infinite density (God?). Time and space would cease to exist.

One way that astronomers measure time is to link the sunrise at the vernal equinox to the early morning backdrop of stars in a particular constellation. In the year 2500 A.D. this constellation will be Aquarius, thus at this time we are in the dawning of the Age of Aquarius. Presently we are in the Age of Pisces, the season of the fishes that began in 334 A.D. The Age of Aries preceded it, having begun in 1832 B.C.E. Aquarius is the season of the winter rains. The wobble of the earth's rotation on its axis causes this changing of constellations, which takes place about every 2,166 years. Today, the wobble is 72 feet off the center like a cockeyed top spinning on its axis. I just thought you would like to know.

Twelve constellations exist in the zodiac, a belt in the sky extending 8 degrees on each side of the path of the sun, through which the moon and most planets pass. Since the ancients, we have discovered other planets with different orbits. This division into twelve parts was the result of giving each part roughly a 30-degree arc of the sky, thus 360 degrees for the full circle. It was the Sumerians as early as 3500

267

Evil in Mirror Lake

B.C.E. and especially the Chaldians by 1600 B.C.E. who were studying a zodiac very similar to our own. They had firmly established the Zodiac as we know it today by 400 B.C.E., along with much of the mythology associated with it. Their zodiac, however, had only 11 constellations, the 12th was added by the Roman, Augustus. One constellation is Leo. Mine, though, is Sagittarius for whatever that may mean, if anything.

An important and mystical day in our ancestor's time has been the vernal (green) spring equinox (night and day are equal), representative of new life. In the Julian (Julius Caesar) calendar this equinox was March 25. Taking its clue from nature's new life, the Catholic Church assigned this date to the Annunciation of the Angel Gabriel to the Virgin Mary. Thus Christmas was nine months later, or December 25. When the Gregorian calendar, promulgated by Pope Gregory XIII, was adopted in 1582, the world lost ten days—October 5 became October 15. It took Protestant England almost three hundred years to abandon the inaccurate old Julian calendar. Now, the average Gregorian year is about 26.3 seconds longer than the solar year. By the year 4316, our Gregorian calendar will have gained one day on the sun. Years marking the century would not be leap years unless divisible by 400, as is the leap year 2000. The year 1900 was not a leap year. The winter solstice (sun stands at its greatest distance from the equator) now comes on December 22, plus or minus a few hours. Nevertheless, the Church and the world retained March 25 (Annunciation) and December 25 (Christmas) as its respective Holy Days. The winter solstice is the day that the growing of the nights ceases, and the sun begins its comeback. Ancients celebrated this event believing that the Sun would bring a new cycle for growing crops. Christians celebrate the birth of the Son of God and the Light of the World using nature with its sun as its backdrop.

Early Christians, especially in Rome, did not know the date of Jesus' birth. They were too busy celebrating his resurrection. But in due time they also wanted to celebrate his birth so they looked for a symbolic date somewhat distant from his death. They looked to the sun or its solstice, when the lengthening of the nights reversed itself, and light began to conquer darkness again.

As the pre-Christians took the holiday to worship the sun of nature, the Christians worshiped the birth of the Son of God. To the early Christians this was December 25 according to the old Julian calendar. The solstice, was actually December 21. The Julian calendar, at the time of its conception, was three days too fast. In the year 4909, our Gregorian calendar will need a double Leap Year to keep in regular

People, Space and Time

time with the solstice of the sun—December 21.

Don Bless recommends making the year 3300, which should not be a Leap Year, into a Leap Year. "It is just about the time when the calendar drift has reached 12 hours, and so making it a Leap Year would mean that for many years afterwards our calendar would grow more accurate every year," How is that for planning ahead?

Since the early Christians had already canonized December 25 as the date of the birth of Jesus, everyone decided to keep celebrating this date on the new calendar instead of the actual solstice. After all, the Christians were not worshiping the sun of nature but rather the Son of God's birth as the Christ—Merry Christmas.

Whenever two full moons appear in the same month, astrologers call only the second a *blue moon*. Once in a *blue moon* happens on average once every 2.7 years. The lunar cycle takes 29.2 to 29.9 days to complete all four phases of the moon. About every thirty-three years, two blue moons appear in the same calendar year. This happened last in 1999, a nonleap year, when the full blue moon came on January 31 and again on March 31. February had no full moon that year.

The **Old Farmer's Almanac** is probably the origin of the name *blue moon*. It is said that when printing calendars, they printed the first full moon of the month with red ink. When a second full moon occurred in the same month, they printed it in blue. The next blue moons are December 30, 2001, July 31, 2004, June 30, 2007, and December 31, 2009. Remember only the second full moon in a month is a blue moon. The first full moons in these months are December 1, 2001, July 2, 2004, June 1, 2007 and December 2, 2009. What does all of this mean? I find it simply interesting. Part of our job, especially in this information age, is to be able to distinguish between the simply amazing and the incredibly significant facts in life.

In a few thousand years, we will be trekking through space and time, seeking ever newer frontiers. We will all be making good decisions, and our understanding of nature will be so thorough that we can probably understand and adapt to the changes in nature, and so not be caught off guard by one of nature's violent acts—yes, even those black holes.

Chaos science is the study of things that are still becoming, rather than of what already is. No end to our chaotic problems is in sight—no end to our physical evils—but that is precisely why we are here—to solve problems in a compassionate godlike way.

In solving the problems of nature, physical evils will begin to cease. The elimination of moral evil is much more difficult to imagine. Notice how all the futuristic movies (Blade Runner) still have bad people

Evil in Mirror Lake

in them. George Lucas, the maker of Star Wars, says that evil will always be with us, although he always makes good triumph in his future.

The closer we come to eliminating both moral and physical evils, that will be fairly close to the general resurrection. "Nothing is too wonderful to be true," said Michael Faraday (1791-1867). The poet Walt Whitman once said, "Every cubic inch of space is a miracle." Yet, Edward Tyron said, "It may be that the universe is just one of those things that happen from time to time."

THE GENERAL RESURRECTION

Day has gone and my thoughts zoom to the distant future. My imagination progresses to the general resurrection. Joseph and I continue to lie in the now damp grass, perusing the sky, lost in space. How do I know that a general resurrection is coming? I am dependent upon faith in this regard. Witnesses have passed down to us the tale that after Jesus' death and burial they saw him again, first by the women, and then by the 120 people gathered in the upper room. This the Bible tells us.

Each time Jesus appeared, he was unrecognized at first. This leads me to believe that his resurrected body is partly the same and partly different from what it had been. "Although this Second Coming (Rev. 21:1-5) is a crucial event in salvation history and an essential part of our faith," says Richard P. McBrien of Notre Dame University, "the event itself has no analogy in ordinary human experience. We have nothing with which to compare it. While we believe it, we don't really know quite what to make of it."

After having presented logical hypotheses and having explored my argument using a methodology that an empiricist can accept, now I go off on a theory that is supported only by faith. If Jesus spoke in metaphor at times, why do I take the resurrection (Jesus' and ours) so literally? Answer: The resurrections are the basis of our faith in Jesus.

After death, I know that my soul is not the total me. I am composed of a body and a soul, and so for me to be complete, I should have my body back. A body requires space. If I accept the findings of the anthropologists who tell me that knowing and caring humans have been here on earth for at least thirty-five thousand years, then we must account for many bodies. If the human race lasts another 144 million years, as I predict it will, I will have even more bodies to accommodate. Our sun will not yet have burned out even by then. That will be at least another four billion years.

Where are all these resurrected human bodies going to exist? I

People, Space and Time

think that is why such vast space exists. Many stars are suns which (probably?) have planets revolving around them, as does our own solar system. We have only recently sighted or discovered the first of these planets. In fact, by 1995, researchers have found seventeen planets outside our solar system with the help of new telescopes and better technology. Using a technique called radial velocity measurements, scientists watch for a telltale wobble in a star's orbit being caused by the gravitational tug of an orbiting body. In 1999, for the first time, scientists have found three planets orbiting a single distant star. "Rocky planets like Earth may orbit most of the 100 billion stars in the Milky Way galaxy," a new study by astronomer Norman Murray suggests.

I contend that this vast universe exists to have nature provide many planets for us—much like our own—on which we will all live in our glorified bodies. These bodies will be partly the same and partly different from our present bodies. One similarity will be our need for space. A difference will be our means of travel. Like Jesus, we can probably think ourselves to different places "despite the doors being locked, he stood in their midst." We will become planet gypsies or nomads or hoppers.

After the end of the Earth, as we know it, and after the general resurrection, evil which comes to us through nature, our own bad decisions and the bad decisions of others, will be history, except for the devils and fallen humans who will continue in their bad decisions. Between then and now, heaven is simply being with God who is pure spirit. We also will be pure spirits after death and before the general resurrection.

To make the four forces—gravity, electromagnetism, strong nuclear force and weak nuclear force—of the universe work together in a unified whole, we will need more than the usual four dimensions of life. A *flat lander* is a person who experiences only length and width—two dimensions of life. Such a person may intuitively know that there also had to be height and time—two more dimensions of life—if the first two dimensions were to make sense.

So it is with us. We experience all these four dimensions of life, but they make sense only if we presume that more dimensions exist which take into account the result of the good and evil of our life's experiences.

I have this idea that has served me well in life—I always strive to remember that two plus two never equals five. If I do think it, I am psychotic. If I cannot stand that they equal four, I am neurotic. For example, Susie Johnson wanting to kiss me after not so much as a glance before—it just did not add up for me. If I need everything else

271

Evil in Mirror Lake

in life to make sense, why should I not expect life itself to make sense. It only makes sense if I take into account a future life. When I look up at the stars, I feel grateful. If I feel grateful, there ought to be someone to feel grateful to.

A higher dimension could very well be where immortal souls exist along with the glorified bodies of Jesus and Mary—the forerunners of the General Resurrection. Glorified people will fill all of our inhabitable planets throughout the universe if given enough time and eternity. This is why the universe is so immense.

Meanwhile, back at the Lake, I have been talking to myself for some time now, Joseph having slipped back into my subconscious. Lying in the damp evening grass, looking up into the twinkling sky, I fall into a deep sleep. I dream about running out of a valley forest with my clothes on fire. Instead of dropping and rolling, I jump into a placid, mirrorlike lake. After my lungs inhale water for the second time, I begin to go limp thinking that this is not too bad after all. My final thought is a phrase I learned in Latin class, "Noscitur a socio," or "No man is wise at all hours." I awake all alone and emerge to see—once more—the stars.

Leo Joseph Hayes

Chapter XII

THE REST OF MY LIFE

Symbolically, biblically, the book should have 12 chapters—the fullness of life and evil. My life lived is to be the twelfth chapter. Read this book again, all for the same price. Hopefully the eleventh chapter will make a difference in the twelfth.

EPILOGUE

Let my tombstone read: **He solved the mystery of evil**. It came to me when I realized that the all-powerful God has freely given up absolute power over both nature and people's free choices. God, though, is guiding my life by the power of influence, while the devil and/or my lower nature are similarly making its influence felt. I am being tried for a lifetime which will determine my eternity.

I beg forgiveness for my lack of literary ability. I would gladly have written better if I had had the skill. I get by with a little help from my friends, as John Lennon sang. Did you figure out who Joseph is? He who knows me, also knows Joseph. I too was at the drowning of Tom. It was I who once raised up his fist in God's face.

The End

Discussions to:
Father Leo Joseph Hayes

Oakland Publishing Press, Incorporated
Suite 145
St. Charles (Chicago), Illinois 60174

(630) 377-2734

www.evilinmirrorlake.com

ACKNOWLEDGMENTS

After ten years or so, I find it hard to remember everyone who has had input into this book. The process probably began with the encouragement of Jim and Margaret Genesio. They had seen my notes for the classes I taught at Menard Correctional Center. These classes were a result of my open-ended dialogue homilies with the inmates. They soon dubbed the query, "Why do bad things happen to good people?" as the eternal question.

I would be remiss if I did not acknowledge the invaluable assistance of my fabulous typist. Susan DeMonge heroically transcribed my nearly illegible handwritten text into the typewritten version. I must also acknowledge all she did for me in the past. She typed me through two master degrees, three not-for-profit books and other things.

Readers included Teresa Marotta, a parish Coordinator of Religious Education, Msgr. Carl Scherrer, who said he still saw mystery there, Fr. Henry Ray Engelhart, who analyzed the book—and me, and William Allen, a Notre Dame man, who on August 15, 1954 had walked across the Grand Canyon with me; he instructed me on the Oriental insights. Ray and Rose Marie Nowacki offered the conservative/traditional approach to life and evil. Helen Sustechek, a great proofreader, persevered through all the revisions and helped give the book its spiritual depth through her comments and suggestions. Bill Eyer, a published author, gave the book some class. Don Bless, a professor of astronomy at Shawnee Community College, gave me helpful corrections for my last chapter concerning nature in outer space. Gary Marx, the news editor for the Southern Illinoisan, chased commas for me, and helped me to develop this book so it can be read on two levels. Canice Timothy Rice, Jr. of St. Louis, gave the book a legal going over, and he offered many valuable theological insights.

On a different level, I acknowledge three great authors who responded to my requests: Andrew Greeley, Richard McBrien and John Powell, S.J.

On the most basic level I wish to thank my deceased parents, Leo and Angela. I was most blessed at home along with all the schools to which they sent me—the best education I could profit from—Holy Angels Grade School, St. Louis University High, St. Henry's Preparatory, St. Meinrad School of Theology and Southern Illinois University at Carbondale. My sister Virginia Desmond has always been very supportive. Lastly, I thank Bob and Judith Griffin for their encouragement and support throughout the years.

MY EVENING PRAYER

The fiery sun is already going down
Blessed Godhead, three in one,
Bring light to my mind and heart
So I may know my evils of today.

I made humble prayer to you this morn
When I sang your great praises.
What good today have I left undone?
What disorders did I begin today?

May my evening prayer ascend to you,
And may your mercy descend upon me.
From my unknown, unthinking sins
Deliver me to a better life tomorrow.

May no ill dreams or nighttime fantasies
Come near me or defile me in sleep.
Now you may dismiss your servant.
Into your hands I commend my will.

Not only do I fear the loss of heaven
And dread the pains of hell,
But most of all, I have offended you,
You who have been so good to me.

I firmly resolve with the help of your
grace,
To confess my sins, do penance,
And mirror my life into your likeness
So I can live forever with your saints.

This day is soon coming to an end.
This night is fast approaching.
May God grant me a peaceful night
And a perfect end to an unique day.

I must be sober and watchful
My adversary the devil or my nature
Is ever seeking to devour me
As a roaring lion or a churning lake.

I must resist him, steadfast in the faith,
The spirit is willing enough,
But the flesh is weak indeed.
Now, on me, Lord, have mercy.

Let my guardian angel dwell here
To guard me until morning rising.
If I should not rise from this bed,
Let it be because I am with you, my God.

Amen, Alleluia!

COLOPHON

This book was typeset in Adobe's Times at a setting of 11/13 and Woodtype Ornaments 2 in association with *Street Poetry Productions, Incorporated.*

Cover Design: LonGraphics
Photography: Westrich Photography
Design: Bob Long

ABOUT THE AUTHOR

Fr. Leo Joseph Hayes is a country pastor of three small Catholic parishes located at Ava, Raddle and Willisville in southern Illinois. He has served there for thirty-three years while at the same time working as the Catholic Chaplain for twenty-five years at Menard Correctional Center—the largest maximum security penitentiary in the State of Illinois. There he served all inmates, including those in the Condemned Unit (Death Row).

For his services at Menard, DePaul University's, College of Law in Chicago awarded him The John Courtney Murray Award—For Distinguished Service To The Center For Church/State Studies, on April 5, 2000.

Previously, he earned two master degrees, one Master of Divinity from St. Meinrad School of Theology and a Master of Arts from Southern Illinois University at Carbondale in Rehabilitation Counseling.

He spent about a year and a half as a missionary in El Progreso, Guatemala, C.A.

His hobbies are reading the classics, tennis and skiing.

QUICK ORDER FORM

Oakland Publishing Press, Incorporated takes orders for copies of this book, "Evil in Mirror Lake," by mail, phone, or e-mail. **Please add $3.95 for Shipping and Handling for EACH copy desired and send order to:**

Oakland Publishing Press, Incorporated, 2774 East Main St., Suite 145, St. Charles (Chicago), IL 60174.

E-mail: evilinmirrorlake.com, or phone: (800) 639-2161.

Name _____

Address _____

City/State/Zip _____

Visa/MasterCard #_____Exp._____

❑ Hardcover: Quantity ___ x ❑ $24.95 .... = $_____

❑ Softcover: Quantity ___ x ❑ $14.95 .... = $_____

Discounts for Quantity Purchasing Available